LIBRARY
North Dakota State University
GIFT OF

Dr. Catherine Cater

Miss Delsie Holmquist

Copyright 1951 by Cornell University

Cornell University Press

London: Geoffrey Cumberlege

Oxford University Press

✤

FIRST PUBLISHED 1951

DC
123.9
L25
B5

PRINTED IN THE UNITED STATES OF AMERICA BY THE
VAIL-BALLOU PRESS, INC., BINGHAMTON, NEW YORK

The Life and Adventures
of La Rochefoucauld

MORRIS BISHOP

Cornell University Press

ITHACA, NEW YORK

François VI, Duc de La Rochefoucauld

The Life and Adventures of La Rochefoucauld

Contents

	The Principal Characters	vii
I	The Accent of the Homeland	1
II	The Perilous Trade	14
III	Reason's Fever	23
IV	Who Lives without Folly . . .	39
V	The Heart's Dupe	55
VI	The Queen's Martyr	66
VII	La Bonne Régence	78
VIII	The Disgust with Things	94
IX	Men's Valor, Women's Virtue	114
X	Ambition, the Soul's Activity and Ardor	130
XI	The Land of Egotism	159
XII	Love of Glory, Fear of Shame . . .	176
XIII	Stratagems and Treasons	190
XIV	Glorious Crimes	207
XV	The Wounds of the Soul	229
XVI	A World of Grimaces	246
XVII	Few Know How to Be Old	258
	Bibliographical Note	274
	Index	275

The Principal Characters

ANNE OF AUSTRIA (1601–1666). Daughter of Philip III of Spain. Married Louis XIII, 1615. Queen Regent from 1643 till Louis XIV's majority, 1651.

BEAUFORT, FRANÇOIS DE VENDÔME, DUC DE (1616–1669). Younger son of Duc de Vendôme and grandson of Henri IV. Popular leader of Fronde.

BOUILLON, FRÉDÉRIC-MAURICE, DUC DE (1605–1652). Elder brother of Turenne. Enemy of Richelieu, leader of Fronde.

CHÂTEAUNEUF, CHARLES DE L'AUBESPINE, MARQUIS DE (1586–1653). Keeper of the Seals, Chancellor, lover of the Duchesse de Chevreuse.

CHÂTILLON, ISABELLE-ANGÉLIQUE DE MONTMORENCY BOUTEVILLE, DUCHESSE DE (1627–1695). A Montmorency by birth, a Coligny by marriage. Mistress of Nemours and Condé.

CHEVREUSE, MARIE DE ROHAN-MONTBAZON, DUCHESSE DE (1600–1679). A Rohan by birth, married first to Duc de Luynes, then to Duc de Chevreuse, of Lorraine family.

COLIGNY, MAURICE DE (c.1616–1644). Son of Maréchal de Châtillon. Killed in duel with Guise.

CONDÉ, HENRI II, PRINCE DE (1588–1646). Of Bourbon family, related to Louis XIII.

CONDÉ, LOUIS II, PRINCE DE (1621–1686). The Grand Condé. Famous general. Known as Duc d'Enghien until his father's death, 1646.

THE PRINCIPAL CHARACTERS

CONTI, ARMAND, PRINCE DE (1629–1666). Son of Henri II de Condé, brother of Louis II de Condé and Madame de Longueville.

GOURVILLE, JEAN DE (1625–1703). La Rochefoucauld's valet de chambre and friend. Later important financier.

HAUTEFORT, MARIE DE (1616–1691). Maid of honor of Queen Anne, favorite of Louis XIII. Later Duchesse de Schomberg.

LA FAYETTE, MARIE-MADELEINE PIOCHE DE LA VERGNE, COMTESSE DE (1634–1693). Author of *La Princesse de Clèves*, intimate friend of La Rochefoucauld during his last years.

LAPORTE, PIERRE DE (1603–1680). Gentleman servant of Queen Anne, imprisoned for her sake.

LA ROCHEFOUCAULD, FRANÇOIS V, DUC DE (1588–1650). Father of

LA ROCHEFOUCAULD, FRANÇOIS VI, DUC DE (1613–1680). Our hero.

LONGUEVILLE, HENRI II D'ORLÉANS, DUC DE (1595–1663). Married, first, daughter of Comte de Soissons, by whom he had Mademoiselle de Longueville, who married Duc de Nemours; second, Anne-Geneviève, sister of Grand Condé.

LOUIS XIII (1601–1643). Son of Henri IV and Marie de Médicis. Became King in 1610, married Anne of Austria in 1615.

LOUIS XIV (1638–1715). Son of Louis XIII and Anne of Austria.

MARCILLAC, PRINCE DE. Name given to eldest son of Duc de La Rochefoucauld until his accession to dukedom.

MAZARIN, JULES (1602–1661). Cardinal, Prime Minister during Anne of Austria's regency and under Louis XIV.

MONTBAZON, MARIE DE BRETAGNE, DUCHESSE DE (1612–1657). Stepmother of Duchesse de Chevreuse, rival of Duchesse de Longueville.

MONTMORENCY, HENRI II, DUC DE (1595–1632). Marshal of France, leader of revolt against Richelieu.

MONTPENSIER, ANNE-MARIE-LOUISE D'ORLÉANS, DUCHESSE DE (1627–1693). La Grande Mademoiselle, daughter of Gaston d'Orléans.

THE PRINCIPAL CHARACTERS

MOTTEVILLE, MADAME FRANÇOISE BERTAUT DE (1621–1689). Lady in waiting to Anne of Austria, author of invaluable Memoirs.

NEMOURS, CHARLES-AMÉDÉE, DUC DE (1624–1652). Lover of Duchesse de Châtillon and Duchesse de Longueville. Killed in duel by brother-in-law Duc de Beaufort.

ORLÉANS, GASTON, DUC D' (1608–1660). Younger brother of Louis XIII. Commonly called Monsieur.

RAMBOUILLET, CATHERINE DE VIVONNE, MARQUISE DE (1588–1665). Directress of précieux salon.

RETZ, JEAN-FRANÇOIS-PAUL DE GONDI, CARDINAL DE (1613–1679). Bishop Coadjutor of Paris, leader of Fronde, writer of Memoirs.

RICHELIEU, ARMAND-JEAN DU PLESSIS, CARDINAL DE (1585–1642). Prime Minister from 1624, effective ruler of France.

SABLÉ, MAGDELEINE DE SOUVRÉ, MARQUISE DE (1599–1678). Patron of letters, mistress of select salon.

TURENNE, HENRI DE LA TOUR D'AUVERGNE, VICOMTE DE (1611–1675). Younger brother of Duc de Bouillon, famous general.

VENDÔME, CÉSAR DE BOURBON, DUC DE (1594–1665). Natural son of Henri IV and Gabrielle d'Estrées. Father of Duc de Mercoeur and Duc de Beaufort.

Note

The author has interpolated in his text 242 of the Maximes of La Rochefoucauld, usually without quotation marks or other acknowledgment.

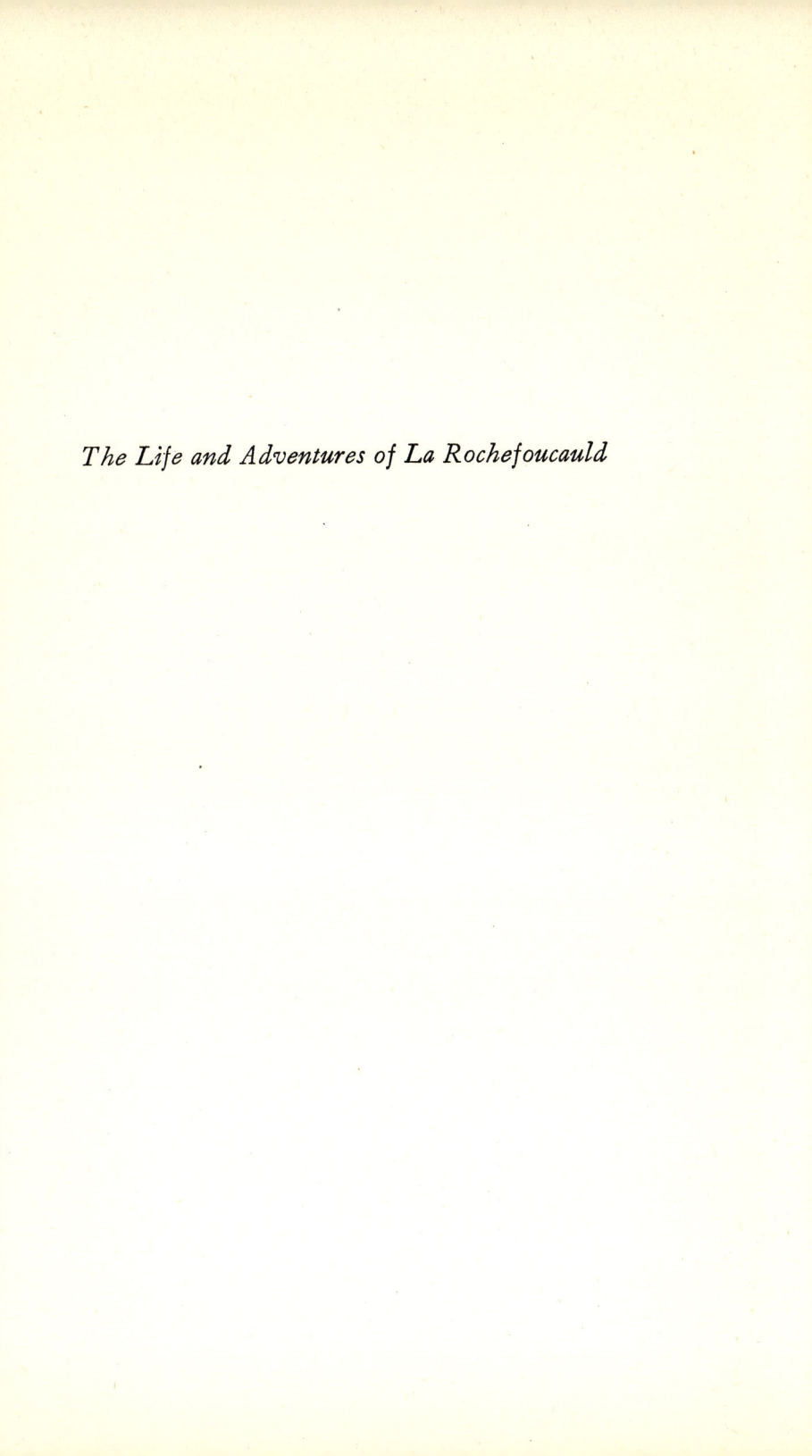

The Life and Adventures of La Rochefoucauld

CHAPTER I

The Accent of the Homeland

1613–1628

I SEE Verteuil on a summer day, in the early years of the seventeenth century. The castle stands on a little hill above the bland Charente, twining and coiling on its way to Angoulême, Cognac, and the western sea. The castle is already old, with the look of pride and strength, not of conscious beauty. Its three round machicolated towers rise defiant against catapult and arquebus; the black artillerymen of the new day measure them with a contemptuous eye. All is stone within and without, rough stone under foot and under hand, to betoken the hard might of noble hearts. But, to keep the figure, grass has come to diaper the cobbled courtyard, flowers grow in the oozing crannies of the walls. In the dark narrow-windowed halls and chambers little of the new elegance lightens the gray medieval stone. The furnishings are sparse and gross, save for an occasional fine tapestry, a gigantic bed, an oaken wardrobe as large as a room. The noble family is content to dine off pewter ware, to dress in the coarse country linen of the yeoman.

This was the home of François de La Rochefoucauld, Prince de Marcillac. This was his countryside, the Angoumois of western France, a rich land of broad valleys and swelling hills, each topped with a little village clustering around a church tower. Everything grows well here, wheat, vines, trees, men. Everything takes instinctively the shapes of beauty; the painter finds his subject at any halt in the road. But the beauty contains within it a hint of violence, of fury. Much blood has stained this earth and reddened these streams. Men have fought here for gain, for honor, for religion. The symbol of this land is its brandy, sweet with all the savors of its soil, and always ready to destroy a man or arm him to destroy his fellows.

The accent of one's homeland remains in the mind and heart, as it does in one's speech.

François VI de La Rochefoucauld was born, to be sure, in Paris, on 15 September 1613. He was the first-born of the fifth Count François of the ancient line of the La Rochefoucaulds. His father was a vain, petulant gallant of twenty-five, Grand Master of the Wardrobe to Queen Marie de Médicis, who was widow of Henri IV and Regent for her twelve-year-old son, Louis XIII. The mother, Gabrielle du Plessis-Liancourt, came of a no less noble line. The boy's baptism was a notable social event. He had for godfather the Cardinal de La Rochefoucauld, for godmother his grandmother, the Marquise de Guercheville, dame d'honneur of the ex-Queen Marguerite de Valois. (Henri IV had courted her in vain; a good and pious woman, she had underwritten the tragic expedition of the Jesuits to colonize our state of Maine in 1611.)

Soon after François' birth, his mother retired to the estates of the family in the west country, the noble château in the village of La Rochefoucauld, where the descendants still reside, the ancient castle of Marcillac, west of Angoulême, the town house in Fontenay-le-Comte, and the favored residence of Verteuil, a league from Ruffec.

ACCENT OF THE HOMELAND

The father remained much in Paris, "making his court," as the phrase went. He was properly obsequious to his young master, Louis XIII. When off duty, he drank and brawled with his friends and fought with them for the favors of the accessible ladies of the Court. He was a "clumsy mocker," said an acquaintance. One of his jests sat so ill upon its butt that he nearly had his ears cut off. Richelieu himself reproached him for declining an important embassy in order to figure in a ballet. It was notorious that he dyed his beard.

He made his court, however. In 1614, the year after his son's birth, he received from his royal master the post of Lieutenant-général of the province of Poitou, with a present of 45,000 livres. In 1620 he led an expedition against the insurgent Protestants of his region, and capably defeated them. In the same year he had his great reward. Louis XIII raised the domain of La Rochefoucauld to the rank of a dukedom, and François V became a Duke and Peer. He was outranked only by Royal Princes, Royal Bastards, and Princes of the Blood. The King called him "Cousin," as he did Princes and Cardinals.

There was only one difficulty. To make the ducal appointment legally binding, it was necessary that it be registered by the Parlement de Paris. The Parlement, like all deliberative bodies, was endlessly deliberate. A few years' delay was normal, but as time went by without the registration of his dukedom, the new Duke began to suspect that mysterious influences were at work against him. He was quite right; the King had given secret orders to the Parlement to pigeonhole the matter. The King knew well the usefulness of keeping his courtiers in a state of constant thwarted anticipation.

In the meantime, François V was a *duc à brevet*, a Temporary Duke, with all the social advantages of his rank. He had the disadvantages too, for ducal magnificence comes high. He was perpetually embroiled in lawsuits over land and property. He laid hands on his wife's dowry, so much so that she was obliged to sue, only eight years after her marriage, for a separation of property and independent control. Thus the son grew up in the family habit of splendid expenditure, with constant outcry of the need for economy, to the sound of mutual parental reproaches, for prodigality, for meanness.

He learned his letters from tutors. When he was of an age for the Latin rudiments, his mother took him to Fontenay-le-Comte, a town which made a specialty of learning, as it did of potted pork rillettes and *mojettes de haricots*. The mother opened the family house, which is still known as the *maison du Gouverneur*. She engaged as the boy's preceptor the King's Attorney, Julien Collardeau, author of a number of wearisome works, including a satiric novel in Latin against balls and masquerades.[1] Young François learned from him little Latin, but something of life and character. Hearkening to his glum teacher, he began to suspect that gravity is a mystery of the body invented to hide the defects of the mind. Other untoward thoughts came to him, to be later fined and formulated. The master prated much of philosophy, the guide of life. When he fell into some inconsequential rage, the pupil was vaguely aware that philosophy triumphs easily over past evils and evils to come, but present evils triumph over her. And when the master alleged the merits of sobriety, the pupil noted that sobriety is respect for health, or it is the inability to eat much.

François studied, as was normal for a princeling, a little music, less mathematics, some heraldry, and a deal of dancing

[1] Possibly the tutor was the father of Julien Collardeau, who bore the same name. He resigned the charge of *procureur du roi* in 1621, in favor of his son, in order to give his time to study and to defend himself from his friends, whom he called "the honest thieves of time" (*Revue du Bas-Poitou*, I, 48).

and fencing, for good grace is to the body what good sense is to the mind. He was trained in courtly manners, in etiquette, the least of all laws, the most obeyed. He learned the depth of the bow to be made to every rank. (To a person of highest quality, one louted low, ungloved the right hand, touched the floor.) Blowing his nose in company, he placed the handkerchief over the face, the hat over the handkerchief. He learned that if your valet commit a fault before your guests, you should not beat him until after their departure.

(The books of etiquette picture an elegant society, but the gossip writers reveal that the elegance was often a mere furbelow, *point de Venise* on dirty flesh. There was a parlor buffoon, says Tallemant des Réaux, whose game was to make a funny speech on fifty-two methods of spitting, with demonstrations on the carpet of his noble hostess.)

The education prescribed for the first-born was chiefly one of pride, gallantry, and self-interest, to prepare him to enhance the greatness of his ancient house.

Young François learned that he was of the twenty-first generation, in the direct line, from Foucauld I, seigneur de La Roche. It was the family habit to die sword in hand, fighting for the faith, though the faith might change from time to time. His great-grandfather, François III, a Protestant, was killed in the Saint Bartholomew massacre. His grandfather, François IV, was slain by the Catholic Leaguers. But his father shifted to the Catholic side and fought the Protestants with a constancy which, as we have seen, was well rewarded. He was aware that gallantry might as well be turned to profitable ends.

The father, down from Paris or back from the campaigns, busied himself with his lawsuits, with the begetting of noble offspring—François had six brothers and seven sisters—and with the formation of his son's mind.

He taught the boy the necessity of noble honor, the feudal duty of fidelity to one's liege lord. But one must always bear in mind the interest and advantage of one's House, and one must advance it by every means, fair or foul. (Or at least one might dispute as to what means were actually foul.) The titled noble must strive forever to bring new luster to his name and increase his family holdings of land and goods, for consideration in the world is inevitably tied to property.

François V inculcated in his son the social values of his caste. One shows all respect to one's wife, for she is the vessel of the family honor. But when one has once begotten male heirs, one need not be bound by niggling fidelity. A few illustrious conquests in the lists of love bring a man the world's regard.

He praised the valor of the courtly duelists, who were thinning the ranks of the nobility about as fast as Nature could supply replacements. He revealed the savagery seething under a crust of civility. He told, perhaps, how Monsieur d'Atis killed a porter, in order not to pay a charge which he thought excessive, and how Monsieur de Vaubecourt toughened his ten-year-old son by making him pierce with his little sword the prisoners taken in war.

He told his son the news of the Court and introduced him to its chief figures. The sovereign was young Louis XIII, born in 1601, a sorry creature, futile and capricious, more interested in hawking, tennis, and music than in ruling his realm. He had a low taste for vulgar employments, forging, printing, cabinetmaking; he grew green peas and sent them to market, he larded meat and made jams in his kitchen, he even shaved his gentlemen for amusement. People said: "He has a hundred valet's virtues, not one master's virtue." The lustiness of his father, Henri IV, was drained away; it took him years even to consummate his marriage with Anne of Austria, and he was as yet childless. The business of his government he had turned over to his minister, the Cardinal de Richelieu. "His grandfather was a mere lawyer before the Parlement de Paris!" sneered the Duc de La Rochefoucauld.

The Cardinal's purpose and policy were becoming all too cruelly clear. Now that the nobles had their great opportunity to gain power and prestige from a young, weak king, the Cardinal was stepping in to foil them. This upstart hated the nobility, obviously. By his influence over the King he was blocking the legitimate claims of the great, filling the government with baseborn creatures of his own, putting his agents in controlling posts throughout the country. If this went on, it would mean the ruin of the nobles. Of course, one's duty toward one's King did not imply that one had any duty toward his minister, who was usurping the King's rights. In the old days, when a noble rebelled against the government, he either won land and privileges, or he was worsted; and if he was worsted, he signed a treaty with the Court, recognizing his loss of land and privileges. But Richelieu did not seem to know the rules. He was likely to execute a noble rebel, or at best he would grant a pardon, thus implicitly denying the noble his right to rebel. The situation was really intolerable.

The Duc de La Rochefoucauld, home from the Court, had many a tale to tell of the resentful nobles and their deeds. In 1626, when his son was thirteen, he brought a fine story of conspiracy and dark adventure. In the midst of the conspiracy was the King's brother, Gaston d'Orléans, commonly called briefly Monsieur.

Monsieur was eighteen years old, a queer, inconsequential, lightheaded youth, intelligent enough in his way, but volatile, devious, and a most arrant coward. No fools are so troublesome as the clever ones.

It was time for Monsieur to be married. Cardinal de Richelieu proposed, reasonably enough, that he should espouse Mademoiselle de Montpensier, the richest heiress in France. But the Queen, Anne of Austria, was opposed, for she was childless, and she had no wish that the King's younger brother should produce a presumptive heir to France. The Prince de Condé, first Prince of the Blood, joined the opposition. He was only two steps from the throne himself, and a male heir to Monsieur would set him a step lower. The Comte de Soissons, also of the Blood, joined too, for he wanted Mademoiselle de Montpensier for himself. The Duc de Vendôme and the Grand Prieur de Vendôme, natural brothers of the King, came in out of policy or whim. The fascinating Duchesse de Chevreuse, the Queen's dearest friend, who loved conspiracy and love equally well, was in the thick of the plot.

Madame de Chevreuse had a splendid idea. King Louis was a sickly fellow; he would probably die soon, and no one would mourn him much. Let Monsieur refrain from marriage, and if the King should die, God forbid, Monsieur would marry Anne of Austria, with all the prestige of Spain and the Empire upon her.

The splendid idea was broached to Monsieur. The ringleaders talked him down, persuaded him to join the conspiracy against his own wealthy marriage to Mademoiselle de Montpensier. He made known his refusal of the proposed match. Richelieu soon learned his real reason, and countered by putting some minor members of the cabal in prison. The plotters met, made vague plans to assassinate Richelieu and to set on foot a rebellion. Spain, England, Holland, and Savoy were sounded out, and were found to approve heartily of civil war in France.

Henri de Talleyrand, Comte de Chalais, joined the conspiracy because he loved the Duchesse de Chevreuse. He was a handsome young man, a ranging lover, not credited with amorous or intellectual constancy. And he talked too much. Richelieu soon knew everything. With the King's approbation, he arrested the Vendômes, the King's own half brothers, and forced the timid Monsieur to sign a humble protestation of complete submission to the King's will. Monsieur revealed the whole extent of the plot, named all his accomplices, the Queen herself. Richelieu summoned the Queen, sat her on a folding chair instead of the armchair required by etiquette, and interrogated her brutally. He banished the Duchesse de Chevreuse. The Comte de Soissons fled. Monsieur's only punishment was to marry, with pomp and circumstance, Mademoiselle de Montpensier and her great properties.

Two weeks after the marriage, Chalais, the victim of Monsieur's revelations, was condemned to death. Chalais' friends spirited away the headsman, hoping that delay might somehow save him. But Richelieu promised pardon to a malefactor in the death chamber if he would perform a decapitation. The clumsy executioner hacked in vain at Chalais' neck. At the twentieth stroke, the sufferer was still crying: "Jesus Maria et Regina Coeli!" It was necessary to turn him on his back to finish the operation, which was completed with the thirty-fourth stroke.

When the boy François de La Rochefoucauld heard this story he was charged with righteous fury, with hatred of the cruel Cardinal, with young ardor for the lovely, unfortunate Duchesse de Chevreuse. Flexing his thin sword arm, he let his mind run on fine imaginations of gallant adventure in the service of his Queen and of his caste against their base enemies. In his dreams there dwelt always a beautiful lady, distant but suddenly kind, to whom he might vow his fidelity, his love. This dear object was cloudily assimilated to the figure of the Duchesse de Chevreuse.

His dreams were woven in the pattern of the Book.

The Book was *Astrée,* a pastoral novel by Honoré d'Urfé. It is the story of the shepherd Céladon. The shepherdess Astrée doubts the sincerity of his woeful love, and banishes him from her presence. He immediately flings himself headlong into the little river Lignon, but he is rescued by a band of nymphs, who sigh for him as he sighs for Astrée. He is faithful for five thousand pages, until Astrée lifts her decree of banishment. Innumerable subplots coil and twine through the meandering tale; innumerable lovers flute their pain, as they battle, suffer, and despair, only to hope once more. It is a dreamworld, ruled by Love in its highest and holiest form. Constancy, devotion, the worship of purity, the horror of fleshly grossness rule here. Everyone is handsome and young; illness is unknown. External nature is purified, as is the heart of man. The story is set in the actual region of the Forez, in the mountains west of Lyon, but in this country the golden streams forever murmur under perpetual sunlight. The landscape is sweetly ordered, with tidy gardens, grottoes, aviaries of enchanted birds. Hydraulic organs play amid barbered groves and flowery parterres arranged to imitate embroidery. "Love is the soul's all, for souls are made in the image of God, whose essence is love. Love is then the principle of all activity, all knowledge, all virtue. Religion is only love, since it relates to God, and even when love is directed toward a creature of flesh and blood, it is still a religion, so much does it bring the soul close to its perfection. In fact, he who knows how to love perfectly knows all that is beautiful and good, dares all that is beautiful and good, and turns away from the contrary by the very virtue of his love. Love is the foundation of states, as it is of families, for the contrary of love, which is hatred, is the ruin of mankind. Love is the principle and the end of everything, it engenders justice, which engenders peace, which engenders order, whence is born happiness, which resolves itself in love. Thus, by constancy to its own principle, the soul becomes constant to the principle of love." [2]

In this dreamland the imaginative boy could live for endless hours. And all his life he would escape to it, out of the world of ugly fact. The pure aspirations of the romance would somehow mix with the meanness of court intrigue. In the midst of a calculated triumph of court gallantry the lovesick shepherd with his beribboned bagpipe would incongruously appear.

Subtly, *Astrée* colored the minds and determined the acts of a whole generation. The Book showed a world dominated by women. They represented force and decision; the obedient swains were their subjects. The great ladies and gentlemen of the court of Louis XIII accepted this social code in at least a part of their behavior. We shall see how the women ruled there, and how the Fronde was a Woman's War.

The flowery land of *Astrée* beckoned to the boy François, for he was ill at ease in the real world about him. With all the gifts of nature and fortune, a handsome face, a straight body, fine curling black hair and alluring black eyes, a quick mind, the assurance of wealth, rank, and power, he was still troubled in spirit. He could not accept his responsibilities without questioning his own worthiness. He was an introspective; he would withdraw from himself to examine that self and usually to condemn it for its insufficiencies. A wave of self-abasement would engulf him, and he would appear timid and shy. His father, not knowing that timidity is a fault it is dangerous to reprove, would shower him with angry abuse. That his eldest son, with his great destiny, should be embarrassed, *honteux!* In later years François consoled himself with the thought that young men entering society should properly be either embarrassed or blundering; a composed,

[2] E. Montégut, *En Bourbonnais et en Forez*, 268–9.

capable air is likely to turn into impertinence. But this thought was not yet formed; he knew only that he was sometimes overcome by an unreasoning shame, and he was ashamed of his shame. And then he would try to justify himself, to regard his timidity as sensitive understanding. For we try to commend ourselves for the faults which we don't want to correct.

The father certainly was baffled and troubled by his son's absent, brooding fits. By God's wounds, the boy was queer! Probably what he needed was a woman. Very well, he should have a woman; better still, he should have a wife. What! You object that the boy is barely fourteen? Ha! I remember when I was fourteen . . .

The father had his eye on the right girl for him. Andrée de Vivonne, her name was, and she was the only daughter and heir of André de Vivonne, formerly Grand Falconer of France, and now dead. The girl's mother had married again, and she would be glad to establish her inconvenient daughter with a most handsome dowry. It was a very good match, an ideal arrangement.

The contract was signed on 20 January 1628 and the ceremony took place soon after. François, Prince de Marcillac, was aged fourteen years and four months. His wife's age we do not know, but she could hardly have been much older or much younger.

We know little of Andrée, indeed, for her husband accepted the social rule that one should not speak of one's wife, and none of the gossip writers has anything to say of her. She was apparently not beautiful; she was unquestionably a worthy and faithful wife, devoted to her husband and his interests, much concerned with guarding the family's prestige and property.

But to her young, timid, dreamy husband, she was not

Astrée, nor Galatée, nor any of the shining nymphs of the Book. She was a frightened stranger, thrust into his room to live with him and interrupt his dreams. No one mentioned the word *amour* in connection with his marriage. His parents and the swarm of notaries talked forever of land and rents; his companions made the traditional lewd jests; but who would counsel him about the love of the spirit, the long agonized search for the ideal?

Probably he found her body terrifying. Surely the marital business embarrassed, or shocked, both the partners. It was an uncomfortable matter, best dismissed from the mind.

Ah well, he later reflected, there are good marriages, there are none delicious.

CHAPTER II

The Perilous Trade

1628–1631

THE boy husband and the girl wife were established in Paris, that they might begin in good time to make their court. They lodged in the rue du Bouloi, just north of the Louvre, in fashion's center.

Young François, Prince de Marcillac, surely found the life of the swarming streets a constant delight. The hawkers, pushing their barrows and crying to ancient tunes; the blowsy women, brawling with shameless words; the black-robed, round-toqued doctor on his soft-footed mule; the apothecary with his clyster, hurrying to the bedside of an overfed lady; the gallant in his wide plumed hat, with his laces and ribbons, his clanking sword, yielding place to no one—the show was a splendid one.

His only business was to be present at the King's levee. He stood for dreary hours in the chill halls of the Louvre, waiting for a glimpse of his royal master or his beautiful Spanish Queen, exchanging quips and gossip with young gentlemen of his own rank. Immobility, futility, bore heavy on the boy, accustomed to an active country life.

There were, to be sure, diversions: promenades, fencing

practice, tennis, occasional staghunts in the King's train. From time to time he and his little wife had the pleasure of a ball at court.

The preparations were a great affair. First the long ordeal of dressing, all in rosy red or light blue or gold. The fitting of the starched neck ruff, which held the head erect as with a checkrein; and the adornment with innumerable loops of ribbon, with puffing laces at wrist and knee. The adjusting of the curly peruke, for bald Louis XIII had in 1624 set a fashion which was to afflict the gentry of two continents for two centuries. Meanwhile Andrée was very busy, ordering her three petticoats of different colors, the Secret, the Modest, and the Rogue. She fitted her grim steel corsets, and above her small hips the farthingale, or bolster, from which hung her ponderous brocade gown in the form of a bell. Then the couple set forth in their gilded carriage, bouncing over the cobbled pavement. Linkboys with torches ran before, for there were no street lights. The coachman whipped out of the way any commoners who sprang too slow. Beggars, heedless of the spurting mud, ran by the coach doors, showing their sores, true or false.

François and Andrée dismounted at the Louvre gate, for only a few Dukes and Peers might roll into the courtyard in their carriage. They ascended to the Salle des Fêtes, where, in an intolerable press, they watched the bowing and nodding dancers. They applauded the ballet, wherein the King performed, singing, dancing, playing instruments, to music of his own composition. François felt too young and timid to join the rout or the courtly badinage. Silence is the best course for one who mistrusts himself. He envied certain sprigs of the nobility with an air of social ease. But most young people think they are natural when they are merely coarse and unpolished. At least he was presented to Their Majesties, he had a smile from the beautiful Queen and an abstracted look from the King. And he could pick out and observe the great: Monsieur, the Princes of the Blood, such warrior nobles as were not busy with the siege of La Rochelle. And the Cardinal, the real ruler of France, smiling and laughing like an ordinary mortal, knowing all the while that half of his interlocutors would gladly plunge a dagger through his sacred robes to reach his heart.

Then home in the last of the dark or the first of the milky dawn. At a street corner stood a cowled monk of the Penitent order, lantern in hand, ringing a bell and intoning: "Awake, sleepers! Think of the dead!" The great ball was a sodden memory. The angelus rang from a hundred churches. Green-piled carts lumbered past, bound for the markets in the quarter of Saint-Eustache. Herdsmen guided steers, pigs, and sheep to their doom. The brandy sellers were out, with their small barrels in slings, ready to soothe the quaking stomachs of the workmen confronted with a new day.

François shared in the Court's excitements, learned to know the leading actors. He vowed a boyish cult to Anne of Austria. She was now twenty-seven, tall, very white and blond, full-breasted, full-figured. The beauty of her hands was famous, and she was proud of their delicate whiteness, and was forever pulling off her gloves in public. "They were hands made to carry a scepter," says her adoring waiting woman, Madame de Motteville. Her voice was thin, high, and shrill.

Her look was kindly and sad. It was notorious that she loved her royal spouse dearly, and that the King, who loved only the hunt and mechanic diversions, never came to her room by night. Eager scandal had only one poor tale to tell of her: that she had been a little moved by the adoration of Buckingham, the English envoy, and that the Duchesse de Chevreuse had arranged a private meeting in a garden. But when the two were left alone, the Queen immediately began to cry and shout for the ladies of her train.

She loved her husband, and most unreasonably, in the opinion of the courtiers. He was a poor thing, unkingly, always sick, stuttering his words in a high, squeaky voice. There was something horrible in his character. He liked to imitate the facial convulsions of dying men. When, in this year 1628, the Comte de La Rocheguyon was on his deathbed, the King sent a gentleman to inquire how he was doing. The Count spoke bitterly to his visitor. "Tell the King," he said, "that he will have some amusement soon. You haven't long to wait, I shall begin my death-grimaces shortly. I have helped him many times to imitate others, I shall have my turn now."

The King's great virtue was the chasing and killing of beasts, if this is to be counted a virtue. He hunted several times a week, and his toll of dead animals and birds was enormous. He was a master falconer, and even kept a covey of small hawks in his bedroom, to hunt sparrows and mice down the great corridors of the Louvre.

But he was a sorry husband, getting no heir for France, bringing shame and sorrow to his full-blooded wife. And, in the furtive whispered opinion of the nobles, he was bringing shame and sorrow to France. Out of sloth and weakness he left his duty undone and turned over all the control of his realm to his creature, Richelieu.

(It must be said that later times have recognized the extent of Richelieu's service to France and have applauded his purposes and methods. He brought the ambitious nobles low, and we think he did well. But we need not now be concerned with the judgments of history.)

The King and the Cardinal, with their paid agents and beneficiaries, stood alone against the Court. The nobles hated Richelieu for his deeds, and no less for his pride. He yielded only to Kings, stepped before the Prince of Piedmont and the Princes of the Blood. Condé stood aside for him, raised the tapestry for him to pass. When the greatest showed him such deference, what could the lesser nobles do but sweep their plumed hats on the ground before him, muttering mockeries between their teeth?

"Can no one do anything?" inquired the young Prince de Marcillac of his companions. They shrugged their shoulders. The last plot had failed miserably. Monsieur had capitulated; anyway, he was a weak reed to lean on. The King's half brothers, the Vendômes, were in prison. And that great woman, the Duchesse de Chevreuse—

Yes, the Duchesse de Chevreuse?

She was out of France, having taken refuge at the border Court of Charles, Duke of Lorraine, and neither she nor the Duke concealed that they spent their nights as well as their days together. She had helped to rouse an international attack on France. But the assault had failed; the Cardinal had repulsed the English fleet under Buckingham. Now the report ran that she was ready to renounce her plotting. She was said to be suing for a pardon, for the right to return to France.

There is no immediate chance for an uprising, said the wise ones. The only course is to make the best of things, to pray that the constant illnesses of the King and Cardinal may prove fatal, and to get what advancement one can under the present system.

And how does one do that?

Why, by going to the wars, my codling.

The Prince de Marcillac, or his father for him, determined that he should go to the wars.

"The wars" were the normal background of life. They had lasted as long as the Prince de Marcillac could remember; they were to last through all his young manhood. We call them today the Thirty Years' War, but to their times they were the permanent war. The enemy changed from time to time, as Richelieu played prince against prince, nation against nation, Protestant against Catholic. The Cardinal's constant purpose was to create a balance of power in Europe, with France holding the balance. Against his purpose loomed the Empire: Austria, the Low Countries, Spain, under Emperor Ferdinand II. The strategy of the wars bewilders the modern reader, and it bewildered the participants almost as much.

François, Prince de Marcillac, took no thought for the wars' purposes. To him they meant adventure and escape from the boredom of a courtier's life. Perhaps also escape from the boredom of marriage. At fourteen one looks forward eagerly to life, one must be galled by finding it settled and arranged by one's elders. At fourteen one may fall in love, one revolts at love provided by others' prudence. François longed to be away in the army, among men, and Andrée probably longed to have him go.

By May of 1628, when he was four months married, he was given command of a unit of light horse.[1] In March of the following year he received the colonelcy of the Auvergne Regiment. Not for his military merits, certainly; according to the accepted system, the King issued the commission, the new colonel paid the old, brought his regiment up to a thousand men by cajoling volunteers or impressing the unwary. He equipped his men, fed them, paid them four sous a day each, and led them into battle, in the hope that victory would bring him glory, advancement, gifts from the King, and plentiful loot.

The boy officer's first sight of his men was terrifying. They were a motley band, for the uniform was not yet thought of. They had the look of bandits, of every nation and tongue,

[1] Bassompierre, *Mémoires*, III, 378.

mercenaries risking their lives for plunder and the soldier's violent joys. Their blasphemies were frightful; Cardinal Richelieu himself grieved that these agents of his policy greased their boots with holy oil, set up the crucified Christ for target practice. Slatternly women idled about the camps, sutlers and soldiers' doxies, nursing their anonymous babes.

François learned ere long that these ruffian soldiers could march, fight, suffer, and die, as ruffians so often do. Valor, for the common soldier, is simply a perilous trade that he has undertaken to earn a living.

In the late winter of 1628-1629 the armies of France were set in order. They converged on the Alpine barrier between France and Italy. With the King and Cardinal at their head, they climbed the narrowing defiles, hauling the artillery up through melting drifts, sleeping in the snow, eating rarely. The King led the way over the pass of Mont-Genèvre, and down through the territory of Savoy toward Italy. At the Pass of Susa the Duke of Savoy, furious at the violation of his principality, awaited the invaders. The pass of Susa is a narrow, twisting gorge between high walls; it was triply barricaded and commanded by two forts. The King and Cardinal marched by night, reached the Pass at three in the morning, attacked furiously. The assault was spearheaded by the Duc de Longueville and a commando of two hundred gentlemen. The gentlemen took the barricade by surprise and storm, and the common soldiers followed close. The Duke of Savoy fled; when he came to a French unit in his own service, he cried: "Gentlemen, let me pass; your people are angry!"

The Prince de Marcillac was at the Pass of Susa. Very probably he was in the commando band, for by youth and rank he could claim the post of greatest danger.

(François, look well at your commander, the Duc de Longueville. You will cuckold him one day.)

The way to the Lombard plains lay open. Five thousand French marched into the Montferrat, between Turin and Milan. The King and Cardinal returned to France, to deal with the rebellious Protestants of the south. The Prince de Marcillac evidently remained in Italy with his new regiment. The Austrians sent large forces to oust the French. In France, the Cardinal assembled an army of forty thousand men, and in March 1630 he again crossed the Alps. He took by storm the fortress of Pignerol at the foot of an Alpine pass. The Prince de Marcillac was there. He admired the martial Cardinal, in a dead-leaf costume, gold-embroidered, with a cuirass of water-blue steel and a wide hat with a fine waving feather. His Eminence was splendidly mounted, and had a sword at his side and two pistols at his saddlebow. Two pages rode beside him and two before, one carrying his gauntlets, another his battle headgear.

Marcillac fought at Carignan, on 6 August 1630.[2] In October his regiment formed part of a garrison beleaguered in the city of Casale. The French chose to attack the Austrian and Spanish besiegers. They emerged from the city and advanced to musket range, a matter of a mere seventy yards. Here they halted for prayer. The musketeers planted their forks in the ground, lit the fuses with flint and steel, loaded their pieces with a ramrod, wound the fuse around the serpentine, took careful aim. The Spanish cannon fired some great bouncing iron balls, dangerous only to the unwary.

At this moment a horseman appeared between the lines, spurring his mount to a gallop, waving a crucifix and shouting: "Peace! Peace!" The two battle lines held their fire in amazement.

Thus dramatically Giulio Mazzarini made his entrance on the stage of history.

[2] Hardy de Périni, *Batailles Françaises*, III, 155.

He was a servant of the Pope, who had been endeavoring to make peace between the French and the Empire. He had been to France to interview Richelieu, and the Cardinal was much impressed by the young man's ability. He had made the rounds of the Italian princelings, the Austrian commanders. He had obtained the last signature to his peace proposal on the very morning of the battle.

The Prince de Marcillac, standing ready for the attack at the head of his regiment, was furious to find himself balked of glory by this Italian mountebank.

(And look well at him too, François. He will be forever the enemy of your glory, the frustrater of all your designs.)

After the peace of Casale, there was nothing more to be done in Italy. The army returned to France. In the following year, 1631, the Prince de Marcillac sold his title to the regiment and resigned from the service.

He had learned much about himself and about men's behavior. The poetic gallantry of *Astrée*, he found, did not accord well with the actual gallantry of men in battle. Wounds, suffering, and death are horrible things to watch, horrible to envisage for one's self. Most men expose themselves in war enough to save their honor; few are willing to expose themselves enough to bring to success the political design for which they are exposing themselves. Valor itself is a reality; had he not seen the two hundred gentlemen march against the barricades in the Pass of Susa? But perfect valor is much rarer, for that is to do without witnesses what one would be capable of doing in the eyes of the world.

CHAPTER III

Reason's Fever

1631–1635

BACK in Paris in 1631, the Prince de Marcillac informed himself of the happenings at Court during his absence.

The King, totally occupied with his small accomplishments, left more and more the conduct of his Kingdom to the Cardinal de Richelieu. In general, those who busy themselves too much with little things become incapable of great things.

The Cardinal had had, to be sure, a scare, a difficult moment.

The Queen Mother, Marie de Médicis, had been his first patron. She had picked him out of a poor and filthy bishopric to be the effective ruler of France, nay, of Europe. But she was jealous of his rise and had turned against him. She recited his misdeeds to her son, King Louis; she dwelt on his presumption, avarice, duplicity; she asserted that he was in love with Queen Anne.

Indeed, perhaps she was telling the truth. The Cardinal seems to have aspired to the Queen's favors, as the crown of his overweening pride. Perhaps he was actually in love with her. But if one judges love by most of its effects, it more resembles hatred than friendship.

On 10 November 1630, in a private room of the Luxembourg Palace, the Queen Mother put to her son the peremptory choice: either he goes or I go; choose between us. The King was borne down by his imperious mother. He yielded; the warrant for the Cardinal's downfall would be signed on the morrow.

The door opened, and the Cardinal stood before them. He had gained entry to the palace by a secret postern. His power filled the room. He said calmly: "I will wager that Their Majesties are speaking of me." The Queen Mother broke into an Italian fury, railing and cursing. The Cardinal bowed; humility would serve him better than impertinent argument. He withdrew. The Queen Mother, panting with spent rage, celebrated her victory while the King stood uncomfortably by. As soon as he could escape he rode off to his hunting lodge at Versailles, to be quit of his mother's rejoicing. She did not accompany him, for the lodge at Versailles lacked all *confort moderne*. This was her great mistake.

In a matter of minutes the news spread to the Court that the Cardinal had fallen. The great roused to pay their service to Queen Marie, to toast with her the favorite's destruction. There was much high talk. All Richelieu's villainies, falsities, and arrogances were rehearsed with glee.

The names of the celebrants were carefully noted.

In the lucid morning that followed, certain friends of Richelieu waited on the King at Versailles. The King had spent the night reflecting on the state of his monarchy, on the Government's policy. He could see no one to replace Richelieu as Minister, no one who would not deliver the King over to the nobles . . . He sent a messenger to Richelieu, bidding him appear instantly in the presence.

The Cardinal kissed the messenger on both cheeks and set off for Versailles at a gallop.

Within a few hours the report was published that the Cardinal continued in favor, that he had never fallen out of favor.

This was the Day of the Dupes. The Dupes, who had shown their hand too soon, were picked off one by one. Some were jailed, some exiled, some made prudent voyages abroad. A Marshal of France was executed.

Richelieu enjoyed himself thoroughly. He called in the Maréchal Bassompierre and told him, laughing, that he was going to arrest him and the Queen Mother herself. Bassompierre roared at the excellent joke. Shortly after, he was indeed arrested and lodged in the Bastille, where he remained until Richelieu's death, twelve years later. The Queen Mother was sent into retirement, far from the Court. In fear of worse to come, she fled France, and spent the rest of her life in tearful poverty in the Low Countries.

François V, Duc de La Rochefoucauld, was one of the Queen Mother's party and shared in her disgrace. He was removed from his governorship of Poitou and bidden to retire to a house of his near Blois. There he had plenty of leisure to abuse the tyranny at Court, to review the happy days past, to plot for happier days to come.

But his son, our François, was permitted to remain at Court, to pay the duties required of his rank. He was now turning eighteen, a handsome, well-made youth with a fine aristocratic face and naturally curling black hair. There was a contained ardor in his black eyes, and a reserved and brooding look, hinting of mystery. He spoke with sense and wit, but he was easily taken aback, easily embarrassed by roguish ladies who found his shamefacedness amusing. He had, in short, all that was needed to succeed in the game of court life.

With the more serious-minded courtiers, he attended the

intellectual feasts at the Hôtel de Rambouillet.[1] This was the home of the *précieux*, who were not yet ridiculous. Here reigned a delicate gallantry, the praise of pure love in the manner of *Astrée*. Here ruled high thought and a pretty, if too laborious, wit. All coarseness of speech and action were rigorously banished.

In Madame de Rambouillet's famous Blue Room young Marcillac met many of those who were to play a great part in his life: Condé, Conti, Retz, Madame de Longueville, Madame de Sablé. He found companions who believed, as he did, in honorable love, fidelity, heroism. He learned respect for literary style, for the manner of speech as well as its substance. He learned that conversation can be an art, and a means of education as well. He later confessed: "The conversation of well-bred people is one of the pleasures I enjoy the most. I like this conversation to be serious, and to deal chiefly with moral questions."

At the Hôtel de Rambouillet he found at the same time an excess of strain and effort among the rival wits. He was a little young to toss conceits to and fro with the champions at the game. He recognized the distraught look in the eyes of drolls, pretending to listen while they prepared a riposte. No doubt he was frequently bored. At any rate, he did not become one of the faithful habitués of the salon.

It is more necessary to study men than books. Life drew him more than literature. For the noble, the source and origin of all life was the Court. And at Court, the loadstone of his eyes, of his heart, was beautiful Queen Anne.

To her he paid his homage, availing himself of the rights of his rank. He honored her Spanish piety, her queenly vir-

---

[1] P. L. Roederer, *Histoire de la société polie*, in his *Oeuvres*, II, 422, says that La Rochefoucauld was presented at the Hôtel de Rambouillet in 1631. I can find no source for this, but the date is a reasonable one.

tues. He respected her kind heart, knowing that she even visited the prisons in disguise to bring comfort to tortured felons. He adored her gaiety, for she was no foe to jests and laughter, and liked to attend the comedy, hiding behind a maid of honor. Mostly he loved her suffering. He was indignant at her shame as a wife, her subjection as a Queen. She was a persecuted heroine out of *Astrée* and he was a young knight sworn to her service.

The Queen was touched by the boy's adoration. She spoke to him freely, dropping her royal reserve. She seemed to have no need of caution with him, and he was excited and tremulous to be so honored. Nothing flatters our pride more than the confidence of the great, he later reflected, because we look upon it as the result of our merit, without thinking that it usually proceeds from vanity or from an inability to keep secrets.

By the Queen's side was her oldest and dearest friend, the Duchesse de Chevreuse. Richelieu had lifted the decree of her exile, for she had done more harm by her plotting at the court of Charles of Lorraine than she could do under his watchful eye. For the privilege of life in Paris she readily consented to work with the Cardinal against her lover Charles, whose affairs and purposes she knew so well. Her blond beauty, the aura of many loves which followed her like a perfume, captivated Richelieu. She put off his advances, roused his desire. She was skilled in handling love's potencies in aid of her ambition. Serving the Cardinal, she made him serve her.

She had "a powerful beauty," says Richelieu himself in his Memoirs. She was now in her early thirties, in the full ripeness of her charms. She was bound to Queen Anne by many shared memories. As Duchesse de Luynes by her first marriage, a bride of seventeen, she had been assigned to the Queen's service. Though the senior of her sovereign by only a few months, she had instructed her in life, bringing her the obscenest of books, telling her all the lewd tales from which Spanish Infantas are protected. (And how had she amassed such a store?) Unfortunate Chalais testified at his trial: "All the said lady's conversation turned on licentious acts, giggling tales, gallantries, and taking God's name in vain." And there was a grim passage in her story. In 1619 Queen Anne had promised an heir to France.[2] The Duchesse, in high spirits, had raced the Queen across the great hall of the Louvre, now the Salle Lacaze. The Queen stumbled on the steps of the throne and fell on a sharp corner. The result was a miscarriage, the end of France's hopes, the end of Anne's happiness. Yet the Queen bore no ill will toward her companion; rather, she felt bound to her in a common misfortune.

Now, in 1631 and 1632, the old intimacy of the two was

---

[2] The consummation of the royal marriage makes a somewhat scabrous story, which it would seem wise to inter in a footnote, since I am told that no one ever reads footnotes. The courtiers, including the clergy, did their best to rob the King of his chaste innocence by lauding love's delights. The King stopped his ears. Finally in January 1619 the Duc d'Elbeuf married Mademoiselle de Vendôme, the King's illegitimate half sister. Evidently the new-married couple invited the King to join them in the nuptial chamber. The Venetian Ambassador (quoted by A. Baschet, *Le Roi chez la Reine*, 323) wrote to his masters: "On Wednesday the Duc d'Elbeuf was united to Mademoiselle de Vendôme, and it was the King's will to be present for a good part of the night on the very bed of the couple, in order to see the marriage consummated. The act was reiterated more than once, to the great applause and particular pleasure of His Majesty. Thus it is thought that this example has actively concurred to excite the King to do the same thing. It is also affirmed that his sister, Mademoiselle de Vendôme, encouraged him thereto, saying to him: 'Sire, you do the same thing with the Queen, and you will be the better for it.'" The King returned, however, to his own chamber. A few nights later the Duc de Luynes entered the King's bedroom by night, reproached him with his failure to do his duty to France, and carried him struggling into the Queen's apartment. Luynes deposited his monarch on the Queen's bed. All went well, and the Court was filled with thanksgiving.

deepened and strengthened. The Duchesse's vivacity and gaiety were welcome to the indolent Queen. The Duchesse sincerely loved her mistress; she was at the same time fully aware of the promise of power implicit in their friendship.

François, Prince de Marcillac, adored the Duchesse de Chevreuse with all the chivalrous respect of eighteen for thirty-two. With him she wore a frank, comradely air; they were merely fellow servants of their beloved Queen. With her dear François she could be entirely herself, abjure all formality and coquetry. But the abjuring of coquetry is itself a coquetry.

This was not love, in the narrower sense. Madame de Chevreuse had her lover, Monsieur de Châteauneuf, Keeper of the Seals, a vigorous gallant of fifty. François was merely her pretty darling, and no doubt she went no farther with him than to ruffle his black curls. Such sweet trifling was all he dared ask, perhaps all he wanted.

Ah, youth—he said to himself in later years—youth, it is a perpetual drunkenness, it is reason's fever.

In this happy harmony there sounded a discord. The King, it was reported, was in love!

In his own peculiar way, to be sure. When ill in Lyon in 1630 he had been strangely drawn by a girl of fourteen. She was Mademoiselle de Hautefort, beautiful with that golden loveliness which those times most admired. Her constant adorable laughter displayed a set of adorable dimples. Her air was innocent; she was a good girl, and her goodness radiated from her. The King arranged that she should be brought to Court by the appointment of her grandmother to be Mistress of the Bedchamber to Queen Anne. Soon he expressed his desire that Mademoiselle de Hautefort be added to the band of maids of honor.

Queen Anne at first rebelled. "I'll have her nose cut off!"

she cried. Disregarded as she was, why should she give aid to a rival? But she summoned the dimpling child and questioned her long. Like everyone else at Court, she was captured by Mademoiselle de Hautefort's joyous purity of spirit. Probably by the advice of Madame de Chevreuse, she determined to accept the situation and turn it to her advantage. She knew her husband, that his loves did not go beyond sighs and mooning looks.

The courtiers watched the royal courtship with furtive delight. Its first outward manifestation occurred during a sermon for the Queen's household. The maids of honor were seated on the floor. His Majesty whispered to an aide, who rose, took the King's own hassock, and solemnly laid it before Mademoiselle de Hautefort. Every eye was upon her, and none upon the preacher, faltering in his harangue. The girl blushed to a flame, looked to the Queen for help, and met her gracious smile. Reassured, she bobbed her head to His Majesty, but she dared not touch his hassock. All the onlookers approved; she had acted with admirable tact.

(But the preacher, the poor preacher, who had labored over his court sermon for long weeks! Oh, his despair!)

The King, fearing to distinguish further his beloved among her fellows, invited all the maids of honor to his hunts. Mademoiselle de Montpensier, only daughter and heir of Gaston d'Orléans, Monsieur, tells the story prettily. "We were all dressed in bright colors, on fine hackneys richly caparisoned, and to keep off the sun each had a large hat adorned with many feathers. The hunt was always situated near one of the great houses, where fine collations were prepared; and returning from the chase the King would sit in my carriage between Mademoiselle de Hautefort and myself. When the King was in good humor he would talk to us very agreeably about everything.

"As soon as we got back we would go to the Queen's quarters. I enjoyed serving her at her supper, and her maids carried her dishes. Three times a week regularly we had the divertissement of music given by the chamber-music of the King, and most of the airs sung were of his own composition. He would even write the words, and the subject was always Mademoiselle de Hautefort. The King was of such a gallant humor that at the country collations he would not sit down, and he would serve nearly all of us, although his civility had only a single object. He would eat after us, and he seemed to show no more complaisance toward Mademoiselle de Hautefort than for the others, so fearful was he that his gallantry would be noticed. If there was some quarrel between them all diversions were abolished, and if at such a time the King came to the Queen's apartments he would speak to no one and no one dared to speak to him. He would sit in a corner, and usually he would yawn and doze. His melancholy would chill everyone, and during this sulky mood he would spend his day writing down what he had said to Mademoiselle de Hautefort and what she had answered him; and this is perfectly true, because after his death they found in his strong-box long records of all the squabbles he had had with his ladies, in praise of whom, as in praise of him, one may say that he loved only the most virtuous."

Indeed, the King's immaculacy amazed the Court. "No naughty thoughts!" he would caution his courtiers. He had a poet write words for a tune he had composed for Mademoiselle de Hautefort. The poet included the word "desires." "It's all right," said His Majesty, "but you must take out 'desires,' for I desire nothing." He was shocked and angered by any brazenness. Once a lady in a deep décolleté, such as fashion permitted, stood close to him at dinner. The King pulled his hat down over his eyes. As she would not take the hint, he filled his mouth with wine and spurted it on the bare breast of the demoiselle. *Elle en fut bien honteuse.*

How the Duchesse de Chevreuse giggled at the royal virtue! And the Queen herself, and dimpling Mademoiselle de Hautefort! Once when a letter was handed to Mademoiselle de Hautefort in the presence of the King and Queen, His Majesty, suddenly jealous, asked to see it. Since it contained some pleasantry about her new favor she thrust it into her bodice. The Queen, in high humor, seized her maid's hands and told the King to take the letter from its hiding place. Louis advanced his hand and drew back. He took a pair of tongs from the hearth side and with them tried to explore her bosom. But the letter had gone too deep; he could not reach it. The Queen screamed with her shrill laughter.

The Prince de Marcillac was an amused spectator at such quaint scenes. "I was a very close friend of Mademoiselle de Hautefort," he says. "She would often talk to me of all her interests and her feelings with utter confidence, although I was very young; and she obliged the Queen to tell me everything without reserve."

It was an honorable friendship, for Mademoiselle de Hautefort's virtue was unassailable. But the intimacy was very sweet, very heady. Her frank camaraderie was charming enough in itself; more, it made François in some sort the rival, the triumphant rival, of the King himself. Louis loved with sighs, self-torture, jealousy. Where fidelity consists only in thought, a warm, kindly thought for another constitutes infidelity. When Mademoiselle de Hautefort told François some funny secret about the King's wooing, François felt that he was spiritually cuckolding the monarch of France.

Did he try to push his advantage farther? True, women don't know all their own coquetry, and often their virtue is the love of their reputation and their ease. True, the code of the courtier commanded him to seek by whatever means the Gift of Mercy, as it was prettily called, and then to publish his success abroad. (The Duc de Guise, having gained the Gift of Mercy, seemed very restless to his companion. "What's the matter?" she said. "Why, I wish I were already up, in order to tell people." That reminds me for some reason of the Maréchal d'Estrées, who was left alone with a young lady of the Court. He began to fumble at her skirts. At her outcries, the courtiers ran up and took him to task. "Well, after all," he protested, "I hardly know her. I couldn't think of anything to say.")

But François was still living in the dream of *Astrée*. If pure love exists, free of the admixture of other passions, it is the love hidden in the depths of our hearts, unknown to us. So he loved, purely, honorably, as Mademoiselle de Hautefort wished to be loved. So, hardly aware of his own heart, he could delight himself with the nobility of his thoughts and dreams.

And what of his wife Andrée, sulking at home while he pursued his lofty fate? Was she jealous, when he reported the little sayings and girlish jests of Mademoiselle de Hautefort? Naturally he does not tell us. He remarks only that it is sometimes agreeable for a husband to have a jealous wife; he is forever hearing about the one he loves.

Meanwhile high policy was writing day by day its entries for History, with incomprehensible wars on the border, with insurrections at home.

Gaston d'Orléans, the King's brother, was making trouble again; troublemaking was his one excellence. Few find any kind word for him. He had wide, blank, staring eyes; he whistled most of the time, and when he ceased he let fall his pendulous lower lip and gaped. He was forever making faces. His hands were always in his pockets. He was volatile and fidgety; his valet had to dress him on the run. He was inordinately vain, never allowed a woman to sit in his presence nor a man to speak with his hat on. In his youth he had had some gentlemen thrown into a Fontainebleau canal for lack of respect. Yet he was intelligent in his way, with a pretty taste in pictures, books, medals, and botanical rarities. There are some bad people who would be less dangerous if they had no good qualities.

During the Chalais conspiracy, Monsieur had abandoned his fellow plotters and had married the rich Mademoiselle de Montpensier. His wife died in childbirth, leaving him her vast estates and a daughter, la Grande Mademoiselle, who took her mother's maiden name.

After the Day of the Dupes Gaston presented himself before Richelieu and in a great gust of bravado insulted him grievously. Then, overcome by terror, he fled to the Court of Lorraine, where he was received with jubilation by Duke Charles, the former lover of Madame de Chevreuse. He married clandestinely the Duke's sister, Marguerite de Lorraine. In June 1632 he entered France at the head of a tiny army, announcing that he was about to free France from her domination by an unworthy Minister.

Richelieu allowed the invaders (eighteen hundred men with ten Field Marshals) to traverse France unopposed. His policy displayed his usual cunning. The French nobles, remembering the Chalais affair, distrusted Gaston's sincerity. Weak men cannot be sincere. The nobles paid their respects to Gaston on his passage, inspected his sorry cavalcade, and made vague offers of good will. Gaston thrust his hands in his pockets and whistled.

He made his way to southern France, and there he gained an important recruit. Henri de Montmorency, brother-in-law of the Prince de Condé, the darling of the court ladies and of his subjects, was Governor of Languedoc.[3] Seduced by ambition, he joined his levies to Gaston's army. The royal troops, under Marshal Schomberg, met the rebels in the field. Gaston's hirelings immediately ran away; only Montmorency and a small band of faithful gentlemen fought. Montmorency was brought down with ten wounds. The King's army reported eight men killed and two wounded.

Gaston philosophically surrendered and signed a shameful treaty, abandoning in return for favor all his unfortunate allies. He promised "to love particularly the Cardinal de Richelieu."

One commits treacheries more often through weakness than from a fixed purpose to betray.

The Cardinal now prepared to demonstrate to the nobles the consequences of insurrection. He established a special tribunal in Toulouse, and put at its head Châteauneuf, Keeper of the Seals and Madame de Chevreuse's lover. He had been educated as a page in the Montmorency household. The tribunal duly reached its foregone conclusion, and the former page condemned his master to be shamefully decapitated.

The Court was in Toulouse. Madame de Chevreuse, with others of the great, besought the King for his pardon, but he was in one of his obstinate moods. All night he heard, unrelenting, the people of Toulouse crying "Mercy!" under his window. On the morrow Montmorency was beheaded in the court of the Hôtel de Ville by a primitive guillotine, a great broadax fitted in a pair of slides. (No doubt Richelieu remembered the public's horror at the fumbled chopping at the head of Chalais.) The guillotine severed the head cleanly. The people were admitted, to dip their handkerchiefs in the martyr's blood.

[3] He was Viceroy of New France from 1618 to 1625. The Falls of Montmorency near Quebec are named after him.

Did the Queen watch the grisly decapitation? I find no text in proof. In any case she was in Toulouse with her spouse, and in any case she remembered that the victim had once dared to aspire to her favors. She had of course rejected him with scorn, but now she could feel only horror and pity at his dismal end.

In Paris and throughout France the nobles were filled with indignation. Montmorency, the handsome, the beloved, had the tribute of every heart. His rebellion seemed not a disservice to France, but a splendid protest against tyranny. The Prince de Marcillac burned with high and holy admiration, as he added his voice to the general honor of Montmorency. In a way we share in fine deeds by praising them heartily.

From Toulouse the King returned to Paris, while the Cardinal, Queen Anne, her dear Madame de Chevreuse, and Châteauneuf proceeded to Bordeaux. The Duchesse bore no ill will toward Châteauneuf for his part in the death of Montmorency. The faint smell of blood on his hands was perhaps stimulating.

In Bordeaux the Cardinal fell ill, and came near to death with a retention of the urine. The Queen, Madame de Chevreuse, and Châteauneuf would not pause for his troubles. They went on gaily, dancing at the halts, to La Rochelle. There the Queen presided at jolly festivals, and no one missed the Cardinal. When he rose from his bed he was outraged, and so was the King his master. The doings of Madame de Chevreuse were passed in review. It was discovered that Châteauneuf had let fall some secrets to his darling, and that she had promptly forwarded them to Charles of Lorraine, the enemy of France. How can we expect another to keep our secrets, if we cannot keep them ourselves?

In February 1633 Châteauneuf was arrested and jailed. He was not to emerge from prison for ten years, till the King and Cardinal should die.

Fifty-two letters from Madame de Chevreuse, mingling love and subversive politics, were found in Châteauneuf's effects. Her game was evident. Both the King and the Cardinal had one foot in the grave. The death of one would bring the downfall of the other. The future lay in the hands of Gaston d'Orléans; the farseeing would follow his star.

The punishment of Madame de Chevreuse was strangely light. She was merely exiled to her château of Dampierre, twenty miles from Paris. Evidently the Cardinal wished to use his hold over her, to turn to account her influence over Charles of Lorraine. But it was very hard to control Madame de Chevreuse. Disobeying Richelieu's orders, she would slip into Paris by night and meet the Queen at the convent of Val-de-Grâce.

We may suppose that the Prince de Marcillac, the Queen's faithful knight, was Her Majesty's guard and companion at these romantic secret meetings.

The Cardinal, whose spies were everywhere, soon learned what was going on. The Duchesse de Chevreuse was banished to the château of Couzières, in Touraine, with orders not to leave the grounds.

There she consoled herself as best she might, with what intrigues of love and sedition she could contrive. An adoring Englishman, Count William Craft, paid her a winter-long visit. Another Englishman, Baron Walter Montagu, was equally well received. There are women who have never had any gallant affairs, but those are rare who have had only one.

In these years, from 1633 to 1635, the Prince de Marcillac served his Queen by bearing secret letters to and from Madame de Chevreuse. He was looked upon askance by the Cardinal because of his exclusive devotion to the Queen, but he was not yet formally banished from the Court. He found frequent pretexts to visit his estates in Poitou, and the château of Couzières lay directly on his path.

And did the charming Duchesse grant the messenger the fullest of her favors? The smallest fault of women who have given themselves up to love is making love. In the loneliness and boredom of her country exile, no doubt she gave the bearer of the Queen's letters a proper welcome. She did not accord an unreasonable importance to *la bagatelle*. And François was a young man of singular charm. Surely this great woman, this great lover, advanced the sentimental education of the Prince de Marcillac.

She did not, however, have his heart. He loved, with all respect, the ever laughing, ever virtuous Mademoiselle de Hautefort. The absence of Madame de Chevreuse from Court brought him still closer to her and to the Queen, in delightful intimacy and confidence.

In the spring of 1635 François volunteered for the campaign in Flanders. At Avein, in Belgium, the Spanish army barred the way. On the eve of the battle, he sought out the Marquis de Hautefort, brother of his beloved. François put in his hands a letter, requesting that if he should die in battle the Marquis would deliver the letter to his sister and tell her that the writer had died with true love for her in his heart; but if he should not die the letter should be returned to him, and the Marquis should forever keep silence.

So Céladon would have acted, in *Astrée*.

François did not in fact die in battle. He finished the campaign and returned to Paris, only to find that he was banished to his country estates. The grounds given were that he had talked too freely about the operations during the campaign; "but," he says, "the principal reason was the pleasure the King felt in spiting the Queen and Mademoiselle de Hautefort by exiling me from the Court."

CHAPTER IV

Who Lives without Folly . . .

1635–1637

THE Prince de Marcillac spent the winter of 1635–1636 in his western homeland. He busied himself with country duties, country sports. He played with his baby sons, François and Charles. In the winter evenings he told his stories of palace life, of his adored, unhappy Queen. His father countered with tales of an earlier day, when gusty Henri IV ruled a gay Court, when Queen Marie de Médicis was young. The Princesse de Marcillac listened over her embroidering frame and held her peace. Her thoughts have not been preserved.

In 1636 François saw an uprising of the peasantry, desperate at the cruel wartime taxes. The government agents, recruited among the most heartless men of the kingdom, took even the women's dresses, the men's shirts, so that in certain regions the people could not, from shame, attend Mass. Some eight thousand motley rebels roamed the realm, tearing to pieces anyone they took to be a tax collector. They were called, in derision, the "croquants," clodhoppers, chawbacons.

The savagery of the people was more than equaled by the savagery of the repression. François did his best to watch the executions unmoved. Pity was womanish weakness, and stoic hauteur his noble ideal. Yet he did not attain the insensibility he approved. A little later, in an unguarded moment, he confesses that the misery of the commoners made him regard their rebellions with pity.

From his country doldrums he was roused by ominous news from Paris. A Spanish army was invading France from the Belgian border, heading toward Paris as all invaders do, and brushing aside the feeble opposition of French garrisons. The Spanish commander was the Cardinal Infante of Spain, brother of Queen Anne of France.

The call went out for volunteers. Royal disfavor and decrees of exile were forgotten for the moment. Gaston d'Orléans, Monsieur, led one army, the Comte de Soissons, Prince of the Blood, another. The Prince de Marcillac happily seized his opportunity, rode to Paris and thence to the defense of his country.

The Cardinal Infante came to a pause near Amiens, ninety miles from Paris. On seeing an army of 45,000 men arrayed against him, he prudently retired. The French lost their chance for a decisive victory, for the King forbade his brother to risk his life in an attack, and Monsieur, in a jealous fury, forbade the Comte de Soissons to join any battle from which he was excluded.

The French laid siege to the town of Corbie, strongly held by the Spanish. In the idle days the nobles amused themselves with a little treasonous plotting. They persuaded Monsieur and the Comte de Soissons that this was the proper time to kill Cardinal de Richelieu. Marcillac was not asked to join the plot. No doubt he was felt to be not quite reliable. He thought too much; he would have ideas of his own, sudden scruples. He would be jumpy in an assassination.

The perfect occasion presented itself. The King, Richelieu,

Monsieur, and the Comte de Soissons were holding council in the château they used for headquarters. The King departed for Amiens and the other three remained in conversation. The conspirators plucked at Monsieur's sleeve; the moment had come. But Monsieur hesitated, whistled uncertainly. His manner revealed all to the astute Cardinal, who called his guards and quickly made his way to his carriage.

"I was present," says the Prince de Marcillac, "and although I knew nothing of their designs, I was amazed that the Cardinal, cautious and timid as he was, had so exposed himself to his enemies, and amazed that they, who had so much interest in his destruction, let slip an opportunity so sure and so difficult to find again."

François found no reproach on his conscience. When the campaign came to a close, toward the end of 1636, he expected that he would be allowed to remain at Court in the service of his Queen, in the companionship of Mademoiselle de Hautefort. But no; he was peremptorily bidden to retire again to his western homeland.

He paid a dutiful call on the Queen in Paris. Slyly, she despatched her attendants on specious errands, and received him in the presence only of Mademoiselle de Hautefort and her faithful serving gentleman, Laporte. She was spied upon, she said. She had caught one of her maids of honor in pretended prayer, holding her Book of Hours upside down, while she tried to read a letter over the Queen's shoulder.

Was the letter important?

Well, yes. It was a business letter. The Queen had had enough of Richelieu's highhandedness. She would settle his affairs for him. Spain and France were both trying to win over the Duke of Lorraine; she was helping her brother, the King of Spain, sending him some useful information about France's proposals. She was also sending her other brother, the Cardinal Infante in Belgium, some interesting tips on French affairs, for instance, news that England was secretly negotiating with France against the interests of Spain . . .

François was neither surprised nor shocked. To him, as to most of the great, family stood above country, and family frontiers were wider than political frontiers. France was the King's person, and surely a misused wife had the right to deceive her husband. "Patriotism" was an idea that as yet had not taken form; indeed, the word itself hardly existed. To Queen Anne, as to many women of other times, politics was a matter of personalities, not of defined aims and policies. Since Richelieu was a wicked man, his policies were wicked too. By circumventing his wicked policies she would destroy him, and then all would be well. Such reasoning is not the appanage of women alone.

Now here was a letter, said the Queen, which the dear Prince de Marcillac would carry to her dear Madame de Chevreuse in Touraine. It was a long letter, but perfectly innocent; just news about the intimate doings of her friends. The Queen smiled, and François smiled too. He had seen Madame de Chevreuse wash the Queen's letters with a mysterious fluid, and had seen another letter appear between the lines of the ostensible one. He hid the letter in his doublet and knelt to kiss his lady's hand.

How delightful to ride westward in a cloud of mystery and danger on the Queen's errand! He made sure he was not followed; he watched for the Cardinal's spies in the roadside inns. The Queen's letter must never leave its hiding place above his heart. When he drew near the château of the Duchesse de Chevreuse, he journeyed by night, entered unnoticed and unannounced, to surprise her in her warm bed. She roused to decipher the secret writing of the Queen's letter with passionate attention. Then the two talked long and freely, and she told of her great plot to rouse Spain, Germany, Savoy against France.

How could he think that this rich, golden woman was an ominous person? Later he wrote in his Memoirs: "She was gallant, sprightly, bold, enterprising; she used all her charms to succeed in her designs, and she nearly always brought misfortune to the people she engaged in them." The Court compared her to the horse of Sejanus, which carried all its riders to an unhappy end. Already Chalais was dead on the scaffold, Buckingham assassinated, Châteauneuf jailed, and Duke Charles of Lorraine was proceeding toward disaster. Lord Montagu had conjured his fate by becoming a monk.

Marie de Chevreuse, in sweet colloquy with François, recalled her dead lovers with proper sighs and tears. A thought was implanted in his mind: most women weep the death of their lovers not so much because they loved them as to appear more worthy of being loved. He was dimly aware that in women's first passions they love the lover, but in the others they love love.

He wanted something from her that he did not receive. Certainly it was amusing to hear her recollections of the great, their intimate follies and perversities, the imbecile comic moments of their loves. Certainly the frankness with which she drew on her large experience was fascinating. Thirteen years his senior, she gave him a love that was richly maternal and wise, but a little condescending. And despite all her ardors and protestations, she had her negligences, inattentions. Her plots and ambitions would recur most inopportunely. He was jealous of her passion to rule the world. Of all violent passions, he thought, the one which is least unsuitable to women is love.

The time came for parting. François rode on to his home,

full of sensuous recollections. Madame de Chevreuse returned to her letter writing.

During the long winter and the spring of 1637 the image of Madame de Chevreuse faded in his mind, while that of Mademoiselle de Hautefort grew brighter. Absence diminishes mediocre passions and augments great ones, as the wind extinguishes candles and swells a fire. He concluded that he did not quite like being overmastered by the mature, imperious Duchesse de Chevreuse. A resentment against her gathered in his spirit. Observing himself, he reflected that if we resist our passions, it is rather through their weakness than through our strength.

In the summer the best of news was brought to Verteuil.

Long years before, in 1622, François V de La Rochefoucauld had been named Duke and Peer by King Louis, but the Parlement de Paris forever delayed the registration of the King's decree. At last François V appealed to Condé, and that powerful prince slipped the decree through the Parlement during a moment's distraction on the part of Richelieu. And still the decree was not published. To the fury of the La Rochefoucaulds, Retz was formally proclaimed Duke and Peer in 1634, and Saint-Simon in 1635. (Saint-Simon, indeed, that toady, who reached his eminence because he companioned the King on his hunts and never slobbered into the royal hunting horn!)

Now, in July 1637, the Duc de La Rochefoucauld and the Prince de Marcillac were summoned to Paris for the completion of the formalities and to take their oaths of fidelity. At the same time the decree of rustication was lifted; they might reside at Court.

Why was this favor shown them? We do not actually know, but we have an excellent hint. Gaston d'Orléans made overtures to the father in that year, and was rebuffed. "Rather through weakness than on the principle of honor," says one of Gaston's men,[1] "La Rochefoucauld avoided engaging in a party which would have been strong enough to destroy the tyranny." Having resisted temptation, François V would naturally expect a reward for his merit. No doubt he informed the Cardinal, with protestations of his loyalty, and with whatever facts concerning Gaston's plans he had been able to pick up from emissaries. And no doubt the Cardinal agreed that permission for François V to return to Court as a full-fledged Duke was proper pay.

The La Rochefoucaulds arrived in Paris in time to witness a royal drama, threatening to turn to tragedy.

In mid-August the Cardinal arrested the Queen's gentleman cloak bearer, Laporte, and found on him a letter from Her Majesty destined for Madame de Chevreuse. The letter was happily no more than an innocent little note. Laporte was lodged in the Bastille, questioned, threatened with torture. He stoutly professed complete ignorance about everything.

The Chancellor Séguier made a search at the convent of Val-de-Grâce, Queen Anne's hide-out, her letter drop. The Mother Superior was ordered by her Archbishop to tell all, under penalty of excommunication. She told too much; the hounds were hot on the trail of a traitor Queen.

The Chancellor interrogated the Queen as if she were a common criminal. He had her searched; his own hand violated the royal bosom. With his long experience in extorting confessions, in trapping foolish witnesses, he found out something, but he did not find out all. The Queen had her own slyness. She confessed enough to allay Séguier's suspicions, not those misdeeds of high treason which would be beyond forgiveness.

[1] Montrésor, *Mémoires*, 314.

But her disgrace was deep. The rumor ran that the King would repudiate his childless wife, that she would be jailed in the fortress of Le Havre.

She sat in the drear apartments of the Louvre, in tears and terror. Nearly all her friends abandoned her; they had, after all, their own careers to think of. But still faithful was Mademoiselle de Hautefort, laughing no more, revealing, even to herself, an unsuspected integrity of spirit. Her fidelity to the Queen cost her the favor of the King. No matter; she followed her heart, and the heart knows nothing of worldly advantage.

The Prince de Marcillac learned these horrors shortly after he set foot in Paris. His one thought was to rush to the Queen's side, to offer her his loyal service. Fortunately he had a kinswoman, Madame de Senecé, in the Queen's suite. She slipped him through the guardroom, up to the *grand cabinet*, where the Queen sat beneath her own portrait, with its fixed, ironic smile.

Queen Anne received him with hysterical delight. She was no longer a Queen, she was a desperate, harried woman. "Everyone has deserted me!" she cried. "I am surrounded by spies! I dare trust no one, save my dear Mademoiselle de Hautefort."

"And me. You can trust me," said François, swelling with his own nobility.

"Take me away!" cried the Queen. "Arrange for me and Mademoiselle de Hautefort to escape! Carry us across the border to Brussels, where I will be safe in the hands of my brother!"

François' heart sang with high purpose. The abduction of a Queen was an exploit out of *Astrée*, a noble adventure to be celebrated in song and romance, if it should succeed. If it should not, his head would of course roll free of his body.

(Abductions were, indeed, common in these years, for romantic literature makes for romantic life.)

He writes in his Memoirs: "Whatever difficulty and peril appeared in such a purpose, I can say that it gave me more joy than I had ever had in my life. I was at an age when one loves to do extraordinary and sensational things, and I thought that nothing would be more so than at the same time to rescue the Queen from her husband and from the Cardinal de Richelieu, who was jealous of her, and to carry off Mademoiselle de Hautefort from the King, who was in love with her."

He made whirling plans for the overpowering or the corruption of the guards. He measured the height of the Queen's windows; a ladder or a rope? He meditated on disguises, on the means of passing the city's gates. He pictured himself galloping over the northern roads, with Mademoiselle de Hautefort, in page's clothes, galloping by his side. But the indolent Queen, unused to the saddle—would she have the fortitude to outride pursuers?

He seemed unable to make tight and workable plans. Prudence kept shouting objections in his ear. Well, despite all the praise one gives to prudence, it cannot assure us of the smallest success. There are some hazards in life from which only a little madness provides a happy exit.

Afterwards he looked back tenderly on his own romantic folly. Who lives without folly is not so wise as he thinks.

His courage was not, in fact, put to the test. The Queen had first one more trick to play in her game with the Cardinal.

When interrogated by Chancellor Séguier, she had reserved certain damning facts. Now she thought of her faithful Laporte in a Bastille cell. Séguier would certainly examine Laporte, and he would certainly tell Laporte that the Queen had broken down and revealed all, and he would stay his statements by quotations from the Queen's testimony, and he would call on Laporte for corroboration, lead him on to further, and fatal, revelations. However faithful Laporte might be, he might yield to torture. And one could hardly expect that he would go dumb to the scaffold if he were convinced that the Queen had already made a full confession.

It was very important that Laporte should be informed exactly how much the Queen had told Séguier. He could then confess so much and no more, save his own life, and give credence to the Queen's words.

The Queen turned, in her desperate need, not to Marcillac but to Mademoiselle de Hautefort. Perhaps the Queen felt that Mademoiselle de Hautefort was better equipped by nature to deliver a message to a Bastille dungeon.

Mademoiselle de Hautefort hesitated not a moment. This laughing girl of twenty-one had already revealed the iron in her character. She had lost a King's favor out of fidelity to her abandoned mistress. Now she was ready to risk the loss of her honorable name and even death to serve her Queen.

First she persuaded a relative of hers to carry to Madame de Chevreuse in Touraine a message detailing the state of affairs. Madame de Chevreuse must burn her papers, be ready to flee. But not yet, for her flight might arouse suspicions in the Cardinal's mind. She would be warned in time. If the Queen succeeded in allaying suspicion, she would send Madame de Chevreuse a Book of Hours bound in green. But if all was lost, she would send a Book of Hours bound in red, and Madame de Chevreuse must escape, flee the kingdom without a moment's delay.

Then the Queen wrote a letter to Laporte, reporting everything she had told Chancellor Séguier. Mademoiselle de Hautefort pocketed the letter, disguised herself as a shopgirl, painted her rosy face dark, hid her golden hair under a coif.

She put a faithful maid on guard at her door, with orders to tell the King, if he should pass, that she was ill in bed. She slipped out of the Louvre before dawn and made her way to the Bastille.

She said to the guard, in a broad Paris accent: "I want to see the Commandeur de Jars."

"What for? And what are you doing up so early in the morning, ma mignonne?" said the guard, rallying her with heavy soldier's humor. She smiled and played her part to perfection. "I'm the sister of his valet de chambre. I came to tell him that my poor brother is dead."

The guard composed his face and sighed with her.

"And there are all the Commandeur de Jars' possessions we don't know what to do with. He must appoint someone to take care of them. And there are lots of other things."

The guard saw no great harm in admitting the girl to the visitors' room. The Commandeur de Jars had been condemned to death for political reasons, had even mounted the scaffold, when the King's commutation of sentence had been handed him. The timing of this good news was a kind of joke. The Commandeur had taken some time to recover from the joke. Now he was held under light arrest, and was permitted a good deal of liberty.

The guard waved Mademoiselle de Hautefort across the drawbridge. Within the clammy stone walls, quaking with terror but outwardly composed, she told her story to the warder. With her innocent blue eyes, her lovely air of grief, she disarmed his suspicion. The Commandeur de Jars was brought to the grilled wicket, and was self-possessed enough to play up to the story of his valet's death. Mademoiselle de Hautefort distracted the warder's attention for a moment, and thrust the letter sealed with the Queen's arms through the grille. She explained quickly what it contained, that it must, by some means, be delivered immediately to Laporte. De Jars hesitated. "Well, I must do what the Queen asks," he said. "I have just come down from the scaffold; I will mount it again."

Mademoiselle de Hautefort bade him farewell and hurried back to the Louvre. It was still early. Her little maid reported that no one had asked for her. Safe in her room, she fell on her knees to thank God for having preserved her. She hastily removed her disguise and appeared in her court costume, ready for her day's innocuous employments.

The Commandeur de Jars was aghast to think of what he had done. If the Queen's letter should be found on him his shameful death was a certainty. Yet how could he waft it through a series of stone walls to Laporte? For Laporte was closely confined, and according to the prison grapevine he had a guard in his cell night and day.

The story, as Laporte tells it in his Memoirs, is too good to abbreviate or revise.

"De Jars took into his confidence the valet of a prisoner named l'abbé de Trois, an intelligent fellow named Bois-d'Arcy. This valet pondered on what had to be done, and he found no method which appeared shorter than to win over the prisoners who were in the tower room above me, and those who were at the top of the tower. By good luck Bois-d'Arcy found that under a cannon-mounting directly on the summit of the tower where I was kept, one of the large stones which pave the platform was broken at a corner.

"He took advantage of the time when the sentinel who continually patrols this platform was at the other end. He lifted the piece of stone, and he heard below the voices of some *croquants* of Bordeaux, who were there for some sedition. Keeping his eye on the sentinel, he talked to them, and they promised to help him, for all prisoners have charities for each other which are not imaginable, and I would never have believed them if I hadn't experienced and practised them myself. These *croquants* made a hole at the top of their vaulted roof, which Bois-d'Arcy covered with his piece of stone. They made another hole in their floor and they talked to the prisoners who were underneath them, one of whom was the Baron de Tenance, and the other was named Réveillon, and he had been an adherent of the Maréchal de Marillac. These offered willingly to do whatever was wanted. They also made a hole in their floor, under which was my cell, and they covered it with the foot of their table-leg. And when they heard my guard open my door to empty the slop-bucket on the landing and they knew I was alone, they lowered on a string the letters which the *croquants* received from Bois-d'Arcy, who received them from the Commandeur de Jars.

"The first letter which I received by these means from the unknown writer stated that a friend of mine had come to speak to him, inquiring what had been asked of me in my interrogations, and also my friend had something further to tell which the intermediary would send me as soon as he would know that his letters would be returned to him. He also said that I should have confidence in him, as he was a prisoner, a good friend of mine, and a servant of my mistress; and he advised me not to trust anyone, and that I should hold everyone in the place suspect.

"Therein I obeyed him perfectly well, for he himself was thoroughly suspect to me. I did not recognize his handwriting and I did not know who was writing to me, for he had not dared to set down his name, fearing that his letter would not reach me. I had to reply to him, but I had no paper nor ink, and besides I feared that it was all a trick to undo me, and so I did nothing.

"Two days later, as soon as breakfast had come and my

guard had gone out for his ordinary function, I saw another letter descend. This urged me strongly to write, and gave me some indications which assured me that the letters came from a friendly source, and so I took some confidence in them. And when night came and my guard had gone to sleep I got up and putting myself between the candle-flame and his face, I crumbled some coal and a little ash of burned straw and I soaked them in a bit of salad-oil remaining from supper, and I made a kind of ink from them. Then with a stalk of straw trimmed to a point I wrote on a letter-top which had been left in my pocket, and I said that my interrogators had asked me so many things that I couldn't write them down in my present situation, but that I had not said anything which could harm anyone, because I didn't know anything.

"The prisoners who were above me spoke to me when they heard my guard go out, and they let down a string with a small stone on it, and I took this off and tied my fine letter to it, and they pulled it up. This gave much assurance to the Commandeur, who saw by this means that I was receiving his letters, and so he was emboldened to write me others, much clearer, and to reveal his identity to me. He sent me paper, pens, and ink by a prisoner who, choosing his time to see the *croquants* when my door was open and my guard was doing his housemaid's duty, adroitly sent me this ink and paper, which I hid in my bed. After that I wrote at my ease, and our commerce continued. Mademoiselle de Hautefort sometimes came to see the Commandeur to get my news and to give him information; so that I was fully informed of what the Queen had confessed, and of what it was needful for me to confess."

The Queen was saved. When Laporte was examined anew he corroborated her own confessions word for word. The interrogators tried in vain to trick and trap him into new revelations. They were not entirely satisfied, but they had to yield in the face of the complete concordance of evidence. Laporte was returned to his cell, and nine months later was set free, with a caution.

Meanwhile the Queen's agony continued. She submitted to a final inquisition from the Cardinal, and succeeded in concealing the worst of her treasons. He showed some signs of relenting, indicating that she would not be publicly repudiated. She descended to the depths of humiliation, cried out her gratitude, her praise of him in his moment of triumph. "How kind you must be, Monsieur le Cardinal!" Again, "Give me your hand!" she sobbed. The Cardinal drew back his hand, out of respect, he says, but any reader must perceive his satisfaction in thus humbling, thus fouling with contempt, the great Queen herself. She had scorned him once; it was his turn to scorn her now.

We have the record of this abasement of the Queen, written in the Cardinal's own hand, with diabolic delight. He says: "The Queen having said all that she wanted to say, the Cardinal went to tell the King, who found it good that she should write it all down, and he promised that he would forget the whole matter. Afterwards His Majesty ascended to the Queen's quarters and she besought his pardon, which the King willingly granted, both of them embracing at the supplication of the Cardinal."

It is for us to read the play of emotions in this wonderful scene. The King, still hostile, reluctant, shuddering even to touch the flesh of his traitor wife; the Queen, in a tumult of relief and fear, kissing her husband for the first time in years; the Cardinal, playing the kindly father, relishing this forced embrace. He had aspired to her love—if the court gossip is true—and she had denied him, offended his superb pride. Now, by forcing her to kiss in his presence he was perversely more the master than if he had obtained a free surrender of her will.

The King, in fact, never forgave his wife, but treated her always with suspicion and submitted her to every indignity. And yet—so inconstant is human behavior—he gave an heir to France on a certain fateful night in December of this year 1637. He had been to call on the saintly Mademoiselle de La Fayette in her convent; she had taken the place of Mademoiselle de Hautefort in the King's peculiar affections. Converse with a beautiful young woman promised and sanctified to God stirred the King's sluggish blood. His thoughts were full of her as he rode back to Versailles. Night fell; a heavy, blinding snow beat in his eyes, made his horse slip and stumble. Annoyed, he turned into the Louvre. Now in those days the King's bed was transported to the King's current lodging; it was far away in Versailles. In his pompous state chamber in the Louvre he found no place to sleep. He went fretfully to the Queen's quarters . . . Nine months later Louis XIV was born.

CHAPTER V

The Heart's Dupe

1637

"It was necessary to keep Madame de Chevreuse informed of all these matters," says the Prince de Marcillac in his Memoirs, "to prevent her from taking alarm and trying to flee to safety. The Queen had been obliged to swear to have no dealings with her, and I was the only one who could inform her of all that had taken place. The Queen left this task to me. I proposed the pretext of returning to my father's estate, where my wife was sick, and I promised the Queen I would reassure Madame de Chevreuse and give her the news. While I was talking to the Queen, Madame de Senecé, her lady of honor, a relative and a good friend of mine, stood at the door to keep us from being surprised. Before the Queen had finished what she had to tell me, Monsieur des Noyers entered with a paper which the Queen was to sign, in which the rules for her conduct toward the King were exactly laid down. On seeing Monsieur des Noyers I had only time to take my leave of the Queen.

"I then went to take leave of the King. The Court was then at Chantilly and the Cardinal at Royaumont. My father was with the King. He urged me to leave, through his fear that my attachment for the Queen would bring new trouble upon us. He and Monsieur de Chavigny escorted me to Royaumont; neither omitted anything in representing to me the perils into which my conduct, which had long been disagreeable to the King and suspect to the Cardinal, might bring my whole house; and they told me positively that I would never return to Court if I passed through Tours, where Madame de Chevreuse was, and if I did not break off all relations with her.

"This order, precise as it was, cast me into extreme distress. They warned me that I was watched and that everything I did would be exactly reported. Nevertheless I was so expressly charged by the Queen to inform Madame de Chevreuse of what had happened in her deposition to the Chancellor that I could not fail to give her this report. I promised my father and Monsieur de Chavigny that I would not see Madame de Chevreuse. In fact I did not see her. But I asked Craft, an English gentleman who was a friend of hers and mine, to give her a warning from me that I had been forbidden to see her, but it was necessary that she send me a trustworthy man by whom I could convey to her all that I dared not tell her in person in Tours. She did what I asked, and she was informed of all that the Queen had told the Chancellor, and of the word he had given the Queen, that she and Madame de Chevreuse would be left in peace provided they had no further relations."

Now this is all very well and very sensible; but it marks a turning point in François' life. Only a few days before he had been ready to dare all, risk all, to be the Queen's knight-errant, to abduct her and bear her away to the enemies of France. He had just promised her that he would carry her messages to the Duchesse de Chevreuse. Surely a true paladin, surely Céladon, would have been true to the word plighted his lady, would have rejected with scorn any appeal to prudence and advantage. But there is another man in our paladin. He is a La Rochefoucauld after all, deeply conscious of the ancient fame of his house. Unlike Céladon, he has two sons. He has a duty to the great line of La Rochefoucaulds to come, century after century. He must preserve the luster of his name and pass it on enhanced, untarnished.

We have more strength than will, and it is often to excuse ourselves to ourselves that we imagine that things are impossible. The father's words, on the ride through the wide forest of Chantilly, seemed to François entirely reasonable. The counsels of duty and good sense were hardly to be denied. Yes, he agreed, it was impossible that he should see Madame de Chevreuse in person. But all the time he was excusing himself to himself.

He was aware of a vague dislike of Madame de Chevreuse, who was the cause, though innocent, of his dilemma. Without her he could have remained the spotless servant of the Queen. Without her he need not have been forced to choose expedience in place of pure devotion. Most of all, he would not have been conscious of the stain on his own image of himself.

In the course of a week he had suffered a great change. Well, one is sometimes as different from oneself as one is from other people. We don't really know who we are until some necessity shows us to ourselves. Circumstance makes our virtues and vices appear, as light makes objects appear.

So François rode to Verteuil, making a resentful circuit around Tours. He sent his reassurances to Madame de Chevreuse, with relief that the whole matter was settled.

Unfortunately it was not settled at all. In Paris, Mademoiselle de Hautefort, evidently unaware of Sir William Craft's trip to Touraine, bethought herself of her promised message to Madame de Chevreuse. If all was going well with the

Queen, Mademoiselle de Hautefort was to send her a Book of Hours bound in green, as a signal that she should sit tight. If all was lost she would send one bound in red, to counsel immediate flight. Well, the Queen had outwitted her persecutors and Madame de Chevreuse must receive her instructions. Green, stay quiet; red, flee. But wait a bit; was it perhaps the other way round: green, flee; red, stay quiet?

Either Mademoiselle de Hautefort was confused and sent a red-bound book, or Madame de Chevreuse was mixed up, and took the green-bound book to mean "flee." Anyway, someone made a tremendous mistake.

The book (red or green?) was delivered to Madame de Chevreuse. For two hours she lay prostrate. Then she assembled her great vigor in service of her terror.

She must flee. Whither? Southwest to Spain, in the hope of outdistancing any agents setting forth from Paris with orders for her arrest.

She rubbed her face with a mixture of soot and brickdust, till it was dark as a gypsy's. She donned a curled blond wig, and bound it with a strip of black silk across her forehead, suggesting that she had been wounded in a duel. She dressed in a casaque, a musketeer's black field jacket, breeches, and jack boots. In her pocket she put some rolls of gold pieces, her finest jewels, a small enamel watch; no change of linen, no baggage of any sort. She ordered her two faithful servants, Hilaire and Renault, to prepare her three best horses. She mounted her own favorite, a piebald mare.

At nine o'clock on Saturday night the three set out on the great southern highway. Thirty-three miles to Châtellerault, which they passed in the dawn. Twenty miles further to Poitiers. They traversed the city sedately, on the watch for the King's men. Twenty miles more to Couhé. The horses and their riders could do no more, so there they spent the night.

On Monday they were off at dawn, and by eight in the morning they had done the nineteen miles to Ruffec.

The gallant young rider dismounted painfully at the Chêne Vert, called for a room, a fire, and three napkins. She threw herself on the bed and slept for two hours. After a hasty lunch she attempted to mount her horse. A stableman helped her into the saddle. She cried out in pain. On the saddle appeared a spot of blood.

Ninety-two miles at a stretch is hard enough, God knows, for a seasoned horseman. What must it have been for the tender flesh of a lady trained to the sidesaddle, unused to the harsh chafe of breeches against leather!

She could ride no farther. But she was by no means at her wits' end. She quitted the highway and went at an easy amble toward Verteuil, only three miles distant. When near the village she turned aside into a little wood and dismounted. One of the servants had an inkhorn and paper. She wrote this letter to the Prince de Marcillac:

"Sir, I am a French gentleman and I ask your service, for the sake of my liberty, perhaps for my life. I have had an unfortunate duel and have killed a man of high station. This forces me to leave France speedily, for I am hunted. I believe that you are a generous enough person to serve me without knowing me. I need a carriage and a lackey or two to serve me."

Hilaire carried the letter to the château of Verteuil and was brought before the Prince de Marcillac. Naturally Marcillac recognized him, and naturally Hilaire told the Prince everything. The letter's only use was to appease the Duchesse's romantic spirit.

"Madame de Chevreuse is near by? I shall go to see her!" cried Marcillac.

"Pray do not," said Hilaire. "She bids you not to come, as she fears discovery above all things."

"Indeed," said Marcillac doubtfully, "if my gentlemen see me depart with you, they will think a duel is afoot. They will insist on accompanying me; it will be hard to throw them off." Easily persuaded to bide at home, too easily persuaded, he ordered out his four-horse coach and had four escort horses saddled. He sent his own body servant, ordering him to obey whatever orders Hilaire's master would give.

The party found Madame de Chevreuse waiting in the roadside wood. She asked Marcillac's man if there was some place near by where she might rest for a few hours. Yes, he replied, only two leagues away was a house of Monsieur de La Rochefoucauld's. She crawled into the coach and lay down.

After a brief rest, she journeyed south in the coach for a night and a day. Again able to mount a horse, she returned the coach and servants to the Prince de Marcillac, with all her thanks. At Cahuzac, south of Bergerac, she descended at the house of one Malbâti, an agent of the La Rochefoucaulds. At her urging, Malbâti consented to accompany her south to the Pyrenean watering place of Bagnères-de-Bigorre.

Malbâti soon suspected that he was escorting a lady in disguise. He put it to her: "Who are you, really?" She hung her head. "I must confess. I will tell you the truth. I am the Duc d'Enghien, son of the Prince de Condé! There was a duel, of which I may in honor say nothing." Then, to put off further questioning, she burst into praise of Corneille's new play, *Le Cid,* and declaimed long passages from it.

There were many incidents. At one stop a peasant woman who saw her asleep exclaimed: "That's the prettiest boy I ever saw in my life!" She brought four eggs as a tribute, and the pretty boy ate them with gratitude and grace.

There were other incidents which seem to have been engendered in the prurient imaginations of the wits of the Court. These are not to be recorded by a chaste pen.

At Bagnères, at the foot of the Pyrenees, she was going to the baths (of all things) when she was accosted by a gentleman. "I would take you for the Duchesse de Chevreuse," he said, "were you otherwise dressed." "Indeed, I am one of her near relatives," she replied. At her request he arranged that a guide should lead her over the mountain paths to Spain.

The Duchesse, Malbâti, and one companion arrived at a shepherd's hut on the high pass at three in the morning. They threw themselves on the straw and slept.

At dawn the promised guide, a Spanish peasant, appeared. Madame de Chevreuse had the pleasure of revealing all to faithful Malbâti. She was bound for Spain, to escape ruin. She would rather throw herself into the fire than be shut up in prison. She would stay in Spain only a few days, and then the King of England would send a great warship to fetch her to his country. Would kind Malbâti carry a letter to the Archbishop of Tours? And return Monsieur de Marcillac's horse? And also—she fumbled deep in her casaque—a precious packet, the best of her jewels, which Monsieur de Marcillac would kindly keep for her. And—here—for good Malbâti this roll of gold pistoles.

Malbâti accepted her commissions but refused the money. He finally took seven pistoles to cover his actual expenses. The Duchesse flung her arms around him and kissed him warmly. The lips that had kissed Buckingham and Chalais brought a certain amount of bad luck to Malbâti.

The Duchesse, on foot, followed the guide up the sheep path over the high mountain pass.

She got safely into Spain and was cordially received by the King in Madrid. Rumor said that she returned his cordiality with the gifts of which she was so lavish. After all, a King! (Even though a solemn King who laughed only three times in his life.) Then she tired of Spain and Spain of her, and in April 1638 she was courteously escorted to England, where she embarked on an active career of international intrigue and amour.

Malbâti, parting from his heady Duchesse on the mountain pass, retraced his steps most thoughtfully. His first act was to confess and go to Mass. He returned to his home and faithfully performed his commissions.

The hue and cry was already up. The King and Cardinal, extremely annoyed, sent out an investigator, who found the scent very difficult to follow. He called at Verteuil, and recognized Madame de Chevreuse's piebald hackney in the stables. The Prince de Marcillac, under questioning, showed the Duchesse's letter. He was amazed to learn that the distraught young gentleman was the Duchesse de Chevreuse. He had no idea what had happened to her. The investigator, baffled, returned to Paris.

To avert the storm, Marcillac's father and mother wrote letters to Paris, testifying to his complete innocence. They asserted that his relations with Madame de Chevreuse were sentimental, certainly not political. A full-dress inquiry was set on foot. The eminent judge in charge threatened and reprimanded Malbâti, but he could find no clear evidence of wrongdoing on Marcillac's part. However, the Cardinal was not satisfied, and he summoned the young man to Paris, in October 1637.

"I saw the Cardinal," says Marcillac, "and he talked to me with much civility, exaggerating however the seriousness of my fault and the possible consequences if I should not make amends by admitting all I knew. I answered him in the tenor of my deposition, and as I seemed to him more reserved and terse than people commonly were with him, he became annoyed and told me rather sharply that in that case I had only to go to the Bastille. I was taken there on the following

THE HEART'S DUPE

day by the Maréchal de La Meilleraie, who treated me with much warmth in the whole course of this affair, and who obtained the Cardinal's promise that I would be there only a week.

"The short time that I remained there presented to me more vividly than anything I had yet seen the frightful picture of the Cardinal's domination. I saw there the Maréchal de Bassompierre, whose merit and agreeable qualities were so well known; I saw the Maréchal de Vitry, the Comte de Cramail, the Commandeur de Jars, Le Fargis, Le Coudray-Montpensier, Vautier, and an infinite number of people of both sexes and of every rank, unfortunate and persecuted by long and cruel imprisonment. The sight of so many pitiable creatures augmented the more the natural hatred I had for the administration of the Cardinal de Richelieu.

"The Maréchal de La Meilleraie came to release me from the Bastille a week after he had brought me there, and I went with him to Rueil to thank the Cardinal for the liberty he had granted me. I found him cold and serious. I did not enter upon any justification of my conduct, and it seemed to me that he was irritated. I thought myself very fortunate to have emerged from prison at a time when almost no one was being released, and to return to Verteuil without its becoming known that I was keeping Madame de Chevreuse's jewels."

The story of the Duchesse's adventures made a great stir in France. It was in the mood of the times, which loved disguises, abductions, galloping flights. The Prince de Marcillac was held to have meritoriously served his lady. His neighbor Guez de Balzac, scholar and précieux, wrote to a Paris friend that Madame de Chevreuse's escape was really a state affair. But "cavaliers will always obey the fair sex and will not deliberate on safety or peril when their service is in question. They talk so much of the empire and sovereignty of the ladies and their heads are so full of novels and strange adventures that they think they can do everything that was done under the rule of Amadis de Gaule. They think they must espouse the cause of honorable behavior against all the remonstrances of policy."

Opinion, then, in Marcillac's circle approved his conduct. He had risked severe punishment by favoring the Duchesse's escape. He had defied the Cardinal, had spent a week in the Bastille, and had been released only to be sent back in disgrace to his country home. Certainly he had done his duty as a loyal servant of the Queen and as a captive of the Duchesse's imperious orbs.

But Marcillac knew that he had done less than his knightly duty. When word had come to him in Verteuil that the lady was at hand, suffering and in danger, he had sent her only servants, horses, a coach. Prudence had won, or at least a half prudence. Men's merit has its seasons, as do fruits. A year or two before he would have rushed to the Duchesse's side, and would have ridden with her across France to the mountains, and beyond the mountains, if she had bidden him. He would have had his rewards from her. He would have had, besides, the reward of his own esteem. He could have preserved entire the image of himself as the faithful squire, daring all, losing all, for love.

Now he had to confess that the Duchesse's demands irritated him. The whole ridiculous affair was needless folly. Her flight was nothing but a mistake in the first place. Most women's wit serves more to fortify their folly than their reason. She was ready to jeopardize all the well-being of the house of La Rochefoucauld for the sake of her romantic adventure. And then she had calmly put her jewels in his keeping! If the fact should be discovered—and she was so indiscreet—he would again see the inside of the Bastille, and probably he would never see the outside again. All this just when his father had at last obtained, after fifteen years of delay, the final ratification of his title of Duke and Peer!

She thought, forsooth, that a smile, a kiss, a night of love were sufficient pay for any calamity to her lover. Well, her lovers had had more than their share of calamity. Her favors were too dear at that price, though God knew she held them cheap enough. She was up to her old tricks in Spain, and now that she was there she had better stay there.

Many men conceive a kind of hatred for their own young selves. They remember their youthful grotesquerie with reluctance and shame. To suppress importunate memories they prove their adulthood by attacking those young people who resemble themselves when young. No one is so bitter against the devout boy, dreaming of saintliness, as the faithless elder who was once such a boy himself; and conversely, the mature convert is the worst enemy of the prating adolescent atheist. There is an impulse toward spiritual suicide within us.

Defending himself by argument, hating himself by instinct, François jogged homeward on the great western road. He had aged in the past few months. He was a grown man now, aware of his responsibilities and duties in the world. Good sense, reason, should be his guide. The time had come to make an end of folly. The heart, with its silly commands, had ruled him long enough.

But the mind is always the heart's dupe.

CHAPTER VI

The Queen's Martyr

1637–1642

THE Prince de Marcillac, returning to Verteuil in December 1637, was treated to a well-meditated lecture by his father. His shortcomings, his follies, his lack of thought for his parents and his house, were passed in review. The young man listened with due humility. "I pray God," writes the father at this season, "that he will behave better in the future than he has for the last two or three years, and that he will have a better and happier conduct."

François had his secret consolations. Among the courtiers he was dubbed "the Queen's martyr." Martyrdom is well known to be a source of keenest joy to the martyr. He was aware that he had left his name in high honor among all true lovers of sighing fidelity, all haters of ogreish tyranny.

And he found plenty of compensations for exile in the familiar life of Verteuil. He had his wife and his baby sons, who were now joined by a baby daughter. A second daughter was to follow in 1638. "I was happy in my family," he says. "I had all the country pleasures I could wish; the nearby countryside was full of exiles, and the common state of our fortunes and our hopes made our commerce agreeable." It was delightful to return tired from a day's hunting to an ample dinner with fine wines to be solemnly tested, and then to spend a long evening in mildly seditious conversation.

The exiles dealt rather with dreams than plots. The King and the Cardinal were both sick men, constantly balancing on the edge of death. It would not be long now. The birth of a male heir to the Queen in September 1638 showed the mold of the future. The Queen would be Regent for her baby son. She would have to choose her Ministers; who could they be but her faithful, suffering for her sake in their far provinces? François saw himself vaguely in some post of power at the Queen's right hand. He did not know exactly what he would choose. *How can we be sure of what we will want in the future, since we do not know exactly what we want in the present?*

Meanwhile life in the country was not idle. François helped his father in the management of the family's far-scattered estates. He also initiated a little business in wines with England, taking the name of Monsieur Graf, to avoid sullying the ducal honor with trade. We find him, somewhat later, taking some of his payment in English horses and dogs.

He had also to deal with the Duchesse de Chevreuse, that dreadful nuisance. In the spring of 1638 an agent of hers appeared, showed his credentials, and asked for her jewels which Marcillac was hiding. Marcillac turned them over with a great sigh of relief.

Our excessive eagerness to acquit ourselves of an obligation is a kind of ingratitude.

The agent brought a request that Marcillac should again bear the Duchesse's clandestine letters to the Queen. He refused outright. Enough was enough. It was vain for her to appeal to his old love for her. *The duration of our passions is no more within our control than is the duration of our life.* His infatuation had come to its destined end.

Poor woman, she was having a hard time in England. She was short of money; the English Court gave her a cold welcome; her conquering charms seemed to have lost some of their magic. After all, she was thirty-eight in a society that worshiped youth.

François found that he put on a self-righteous air in commiserating her woes. We all have strength enough to bear the troubles of others. In fact, in the adversity of our best friends we always find something which does not altogether displease us.

During the dark hours of country winters he discovered, perhaps for the first time, the consolations of good literature. He read history, the milder philosophies, Descartes' *Discours de la Méthode,* just out, the works of courtly poets. He had as his guide an eminent citizen of Parnassus, his father's secretary, Jacques de Sérizay.

Though Sérizay's own poetic gift was small, he had a considerable talent for correcting the poems of others. He had also a notable capacity for being present when men of letters met. He was one of a group which gathered regularly in Paris to talk at ease of literature. Richelieu, who saw everything, proposed that the informal club should receive his official blessing and that it should put its new prestige to the service of governmental policy. The justification of literature, he might have said in modern terms, is that it serves the state. The clubmen unwillingly yielded, forewent their pleasant evenings of unsupervised talk. They accepted the grandiose name of the Académie Française.

Jacques de Sérizay was a charter member and the first Director of the august institution which has dominated French intellectual life for three hundred years. He was chosen for his ability to improvise public harangues, to soothe the great by delicately turned compliments. He was famous for the refinement of his language. He would have turned every noun into the feminine, says a hostile grammarian.

Though Sérizay spent most of his time in Paris as the La Rochefoucaulds' agent in the capital, he made occasional trips to Verteuil. He brought to the Prince de Marcillac the literary gossip and the new books. He told how he and four other Academicians had sharply condemned *Le Cid,* the new play of young Corneille. He called on his fellow Academician, Guez de Balzac, who lived in retirement near Verteuil. Marcillac came to know this vain and pedantic gentleman, who was forever sucking odoriferant pastilles. He profited much by conversation with Balzac and his scholarly friends. He learned from them to prize exactness and elegance of expression. He learned also the tricks of abstraction, of generalization—how to put a special observation to the account of humanity.

His friends did not, however, entirely capture and convince him. He remained detached, outside. It is easier, he thought, to know man in general than one man in particular. These philosophers, pretending a supermundane serenity, were constantly revealing their human weakness, their vanity, self-interest, greed. Did they boast loftily of their scorn of riches? Well, he had observed their pursuit of rewards and well-paid sinecures. He concluded that the scorn of riches among the philosophers was a hidden desire to avenge their merit upon the injustice of fate, by the scorn of the very goods of which fate deprived them. It was a secret to protect themselves from the debasement of poverty. It was a byway to reach that consideration which they could not gain by wealth.

Thus the Prince de Marcillac turned his quiet years to profit. Thus he progressed in the knowledge of man's behavior and in the knowledge of himself.

In 1639 his peace was broken. The perpetual war had come

to one of its recurrent crises. A call went out for volunteers. "The only thing the nobility is good for is to get itself killed," remarks Saint-Simon. The Prince de Marcillac gladly answered the call. In August he saw some hot action in the Flanders plains, and aided in the slaughter of six hundred Croatian mercenaries in the service of Spain. He observed the functioning of the laws of war, which strangely associate the courtly and the savage. The French called on a small country castle to surrender; its commander felt that for his honor's sake the French should at least discharge a volley of artillery at him. The French general objected to such a waste of ammunition and as a correction to the defender's presumption ordered him to be hung. A French officer interceded for the defender's life, and galloped off to obtain a pardon from the Commander in Chief, Maréchal de La Meilleraie. By the time the emissary returned with the pardon in hand the hanging had already taken place, "to content the spectators who were bored with waiting."

"Toward the end of this campaign," says Marcillac, "whereof a good report was made of me to Cardinal de Richelieu, his hatred of me began to slacken. He even tried to attach me to his interests. On his behalf the Maréchal de La Meilleraie offered me the post of maréchal du camp, and he held great hopes before me. But the Queen prevented me from accepting this advantage, and she earnestly desired that I should not receive any grace from the Cardinal which might deprive me of my freedom to act against him when she would find herself in a position to appear openly his enemy. This mark of the Queen's confidence made me renounce with pleasure everything that fortune was presenting to me. I thanked the Maréchal de La Meilleraie with all the gratitude which I owed to his good offices, and I returned to Verteuil without seeing the Court. I remained there for a considerable time in a sort of useless life, which I would have found all too dreary, had not the Queen whose servant I was herself ordered this conduct, and had she not ordered me to continue it, in the hope of a change which she foresaw."

Though he did not see the Court, he must have seen the Queen, whose martyr he was. He tells us elsewhere that she was all grace and condescension toward him; she told him that she had ceased reading the war news when he was out of danger.

There is something a little mysterious in his report of the Queen's dealings with him. The "change" that Anne of Austria foresaw was the death of the Cardinal, by God's hand alone or with the helping hand of man. Why did she send her knight to languish in Poitou? Her explanation seems hardly sufficient. Perhaps she was alarmed that he should seriously propose to take the Cardinal's livery, and so conceived a distrust of his fidelity and judgment. Perhaps she thought that in the affair of Madame de Chevreuse he had displayed something less than complete devotion. Perhaps she had other martyrs, ready to dare all without making bargains.

At any rate, Marcillac, thinking the matter over, began to suspect the purity of the Queen's affection for him. There was a share of self-interest in her beautiful friendship. He was learning to weigh and measure human behavior, to reckon the significance of men's actions. He was forced to more and more sardonic conclusions. He had emerged from the enchanted forest of his youth to a land of wintry plains under gray skies. Here knavish men lay in wait for the wanderer, always ready to beguile him for gain, to lead him unsuspecting into cutthroat inns.

During the summer of 1639, while Marcillac was at the wars, his father was otherwise occupied in Paris. He was paying court to the charming Madame de Sablé, whom Marcillac had certainly known in the précieux salon of Madame de Rambouillet.[1] Madame de Sablé was now forty, a celebrated bluestocking, blond, pink, plump, and soft. She was an intelligent woman, a writer in a small, elegant way, a gourmet and creative cook, and a patron of young intellectuals. We shall meet her again in twenty years.

The Duke retired to the country in the autumn of 1639, to await the happy death, forever postponed, of King and Cardinal. He and his son returned to their country occupations. Embittered by the fact that the Dukes of Retz and Saint-Simon had taken precedence over the Duc de La Rochefocauld, they drew up a long factum, pointing out that the King had proclaimed the La Rochefoucauld dukedom first, and that the date of the King's proclamation, not the date of the Parlement's registration, should establish seniority. The writing of the factum coddled the ducal pride. Pride has its dangers, as Marcillac well recognized. Indeed, it seems that Nature, which has so wisely disposed the organs of our body to make us happy, has also given us pride to spare us the pain of recognizing our imperfections. But pride is not in itself an evil thing. It is as proper to be vainglorious with ourselves as it is ridiculous to be so with others.

Marcillac certainly found his first effort to write persuasively an interesting task. A factum is not literature, but it may engage its writer in many thoughts on the organization of ideas, on the value and power of words.

Meanwhile, at Court, the great became impatient at the Cardinal's perpetual recoveries from illness. The Duc de Bouillon, a prince who had the look of a very intelligent bull, and the Comte de Soissons, who had already been implicated in one plot, mounted a widespread conspiracy. It came to open rebellion and a full-scale battle, in July 1641. The Comte de

---

[1] Chapelain, *Lettres*, I, 487.

Soissons was killed; in fact, it seems that in despair of the issue he pried open his visor with his pistol and shot himself. The Duc de Bouillon was let off with a warning. Richelieu made short work of the underlings.

The La Rochefoucaulds were not implicated. One wonders why not. Where was the Prince de Marcillac, the Queen's martyr? Why did he not seize this opportunity to strike a blow for his lady's freedom? Perhaps because he was not asked, because the conspirators did not entirely trust his purpose and discretion. But more probably because his father, who followed the pacific policy of his patron, the Prince de Condé, forbade his son to take part in the revolt, and the son accepted, with some relief, his father's orders.

In the following year another and greater plot was set on foot. This is known to history as the Conspiracy of Cinq-Mars.

Cinq-Mars was an engaging, turbulent youth of the minor nobility. Richelieu himself had picked him to be the King's companion, and from companion he became the King's dearest friend. For his sake Louis dismissed Mademoiselle de Hautefort from Court, telling her "that she should no longer pretend to his affection, as he had given it entirely to Monsieur de Cinq-Mars." But the royal affection was traversed by suspicions, jealousies, and quarrels. The King, frugal and economical, was shocked by Cinq-Mars's elegance, his fifty pairs of boots. The young man was bored by his master's diversions, the laborious capture of blackbirds with falcons, the smoking out of foxes from their holes. From the château of Saint-Germain he would gallop to Paris for a night with Marion de l'Orme, whose gallantries history has somehow sanctified, or with a drinking club known as *Messieurs du Marais*. On the following morning he would appear late and pale at the King's levee, and the King would go into a sulky rage. The Cardinal himself would be called in to make a reconciliation. At one such moment the King and Cinq-Mars drew up this remarkable certificate of mutual trust: "We the undersigned certify to whom it may concern that we are very content and satisfied with each other and that we have never been in such perfect intelligence as we are at present. In testimony of which we have signed this present certificate."

Now Cinq-Mars, barely twenty, dreamed of playing a high role in the state, of commanding an army and marrying a princess. The Cardinal, furious, dressed him down like a schoolboy, reminding him that he owed everything to the Cardinal himself and that his obligation was to be the Cardinal's spy.

It is notorious that one may not count on a spy's fidelity. Cinq-Mars opened negotiations with Gaston d'Orléans, surely a foolhardy thing to do in view of Monsieur's record of betrayals, and with the Duc de Bouillon, commanding the King's army in Italy. The three sent an agent, Fontrailles, to Spain, with a treasonable proposal for an alliance against the Cardinal de Richelieu, against France. Fontrailles returned to the Court, which was in southern France, with a treaty ready for signature. It stipulated that Spain would send 12,000 men to aid Gaston d'Orléans.

Richelieu's efficient intelligence service secured a copy of the treaty. The Cardinal summoned his chief advisers to a conference. Cinq-Mars remarked innocently on the council meeting to Fontrailles. And Fontrailles, a man of much penetration, replied: "Sir, you are a great tall man. If they should reduce your stature by a head, you would still be very great and tall. But as for me, I am a little fellow. One could not remove anything from me without inconveniencing me greatly and leaving me of most inadequate height. You will therefore, if you please, permit me to dodge those ugly blades." He scraped a bow, leaped to horse, and galloped off for Spain. But Cinq-Mars refused to take fright.

The council referred the conspiratorial treaty to the King, who was grievously ill. When he had read it, he had his bed transported to the room where the Cardinal lay in pain. Side by side in their beds, the two rulers of France wept with emotion, not with weakness. The Cardinal besought the King to arrest Gaston d'Orléans, but Louis could not bring himself so to shame his shameful brother. Cinq-Mars should die, and with him his excellent and worthy friend, François de Thou, who had been informed of the treaty and who was guilty of concealing his knowledge.

This picturesque interview took place at Tarascon, on the lower Rhône. The two young men were arrested. Richelieu had his bed transferred to a river boat, which was to carry him upstream to Lyon. The prisoners were placed on a barge towed behind his boat. On the journey up the river the Cardinal, a dying man, consoled his weakening hours by watching his victims, who should, by God's mercy, precede him to the other world.

On arriving at Lyon, Richelieu constituted a special tribunal, which condemned Cinq-Mars and de Thou with the utmost haste. The two made an edifying end on 12 September 1642. On the scaffold they kissed each other; then Cinq-Mars kissed the headsman, who was to open to him the gates of Heaven.

But those who are condemned to the last extremity sometimes affect a constancy and a scorn of death which are only the effects of the fear of envisaging their fate; so that one may say that this constancy, this scorn of death, are to their minds what the bandage is to their eyes.

Gaston d'Orléans went to bed with a diplomatic colic, blamed everything on Cinq-Mars, and escaped with the usual reprimand.

The Queen herself was implicated. She was unquestionably

aware of the conspiracy, she approved of it, though she was in no position to aid it actively. But she received no punishment; her disgrace was already complete. The Cardinal showed his contempt for her by failing, in her presence, even to rise from his chair.

And the Prince de Marcillac? His good friend de Thou had visited him in Verteuil, with proposals from the Queen that he should join the plot. He had hung back, surely because his father's policy was to follow the star of Condé, who was faithful to King and Cardinal. The leaders of the conspiracy, Cinq-Mars, Monsieur, Bouillon, inspired no confidence in Marcillac. Why rebel against a dying Minister? Much the best course was to wait for his death, then to step in and take control legitimately. Marcillac contented himself with writing a letter of condolence to de Thou's brother after the execution, and with providing a ship and crew to carry one of the minor conspirators to England.

From Lyon the Cardinal, riddled with ulcers, was carried to Paris in a gigantic litter, shrouded in violet cloth, containing his bed, a chair, and a table, whereon a secretary wrote steadily to the dying man's dictation. Twenty-four men, each with his hat in his hand, bore this huge swaying burden over the roads. At nightfall they would tear down the wall of a house, build an inclined plane, and transport the giant litter to shelter. From within came the weak voice of the Cardinal, dictating between his groans.

There are heroes in evil as in good.

On 4 December 1642 the great Cardinal died of his accumulated ills. There was joy in every château of France. Everywhere the nobles assembled their gentlemen, laid out their court clothes, prepared to rush to Paris to seize what they could of the Cardinal's succession.

The Prince de Marcillac had been his enemy through all his

adult life. He had suffered much at Richelieu's hands. Yet the mark of an extraordinary merit is the fact that those who envy it the most are constrained to praise it. Marcillac writes in his Memoirs a sober judgment of his foe, which has in every point been confirmed by history. "Whatever joy his enemies felt on their liberation from so many persecutions, the progress of events made clear that the Cardinal's death was most prejudicial to the state, and that since he had dared to change its structure in so many ways, he alone could have maintained it usefully if his administration and his life had lasted longer. Before his time no one but he had well understood the full power of the kingdom, nor had been able to place it entire in his sovereign's hands. The severity of his ministry had caused much blood to flow, the great ones of the realm had been abased, the people had been loaded with burdens. But the capture of La Rochelle, the destruction of the Protestant party, the reduction of the House of Austria, so much greatness in his designs, so much skill in executing them, should stifle private resentments and give to his memory the praise which it justly deserved."

CHAPTER VII

La Bonne Régence

1642–1643

AT NEWS of Richelieu's death the Prince de Marcillac immediately took horse for Paris. He did not distrust the Queen's constancy to her promises, but he thought it well to be on the spot, a living reminder. On his way he met other disfavored nobles, making the same journey with the same fixed idea.

In Paris he found the Court full of those whom the Cardinal had banished, including the Vendômes and Gaston d'Orléans. He saw also a pallid group just released from the Bastille, among them the Commandeur de Jars and the Queen's faithful Laporte.

But the shadow of the Cardinal still hung over the Court. His appointees continued in office. His testament had stipulated in detail the organization of France. The King, weakening daily, showed no desire to upset his Minister's dispositions.

The King was dying, apparently of a general tuberculosis complicated by chronic enteritis. The physicians were doing their misguided best to hurry his death. In one year his doctor had prescribed 47 bleedings, 212 purges, and 215 enemas. Hardly more than a skeleton now, the King lay in bed, looking into his future, which was not the future of France. Though he did not love God, he feared the devil and hell. (Someone spoke to him of a cleric who had the faculty of recognizing holy relics underground, who would stop and sniff and say: "Dig here." A facetious courtier remarked aside: "If I had him, I would take him with me to Burgundy, he would find me a lot of truffles." The King overheard and screamed: "Scoundrel, out of here!")

As the King's life ebbed, the Queen roused from her usual lethargy to parley endlessly with her old friends. She was now forty-two, a handsome woman, but undeniably plump. No wonder, indeed; it was her habit to rise at ten or eleven in the morning (in days when even the great were astir at dawn), and to breakfast on bouillon, chops, sausages, and *pain bouilli*. Her midafternoon dinner did not suffer. At eleven in the evening she would sup well, and her waiting women would devour her leavings, without plates, knives, or forks.

The Queen found her popularity lessening, even among those who had been most faithful during her trials. One needs greater virtue to sustain good fortune than ill fortune. The Cardinal de Retz says with his usual penetration: "The Queen was adored much more for her distresses than for her merit. She had been seen always persecuted, and in persons of her rank suffering takes the place of a great virtue. People liked to imagine that she had displayed much patience, which is very often manifested by indolence." Marcillac, finding her strangely chill, reflected that no one deserves to be praised for goodness if he hasn't the strength to be evil. Any other goodness is usually only sloth or impotence of will.

She kept putting him off, urging him to wait a time before claiming any state favor. This was reasonable enough. She would soon be Regent, with all the high posts of the kingdom in her hand. And yet Marcillac felt that he deserved something more, at least some intimate confidence, in return for all his sacrifices for her sake. He expected more show of gratitude in her. But gratitude looks forever forward; most men's gratitude is only a secret desire to receive greater benefits.

The Queen's chief concern was the tending of her two sons, Louis, a fine sturdy boy of four, and Philippe, only three. These, the heirs of France, she guarded with a mother's natural solicitude, and also with the knowledge that they guaranteed her own eminence.

In the care of her children, as in the transaction of her royal business, she had found a most sympathetic aide. This was Giulio Mazzarini, henceforth known as Jules Mazarin.

Mazarin was an Italian nobody who had made his way by his wits, by his charm. "He had a fine figure," say the memoirs of Brienne, "a little taller than the average. He had a handsome high complexion, fiery eyes, a large nose, a wide, noble brow, curly chestnut hair, beard and moustache somewhat darker, always primped with a hot iron, very good-looking. He took great care of his beautiful hands." He had studied in Spain, and there had become celebrated for his gains and losses at the games of cards and love. He was always a gambler; he loved to do card tricks with his deft and gentle hands; he loved gigantic stakes. Rather whimsically, he liked to play *boccie*, the Italian peasant bowling game, in the courtyard of the Palais-Royal.

We have seen him at Casale, when he brought dramatic news of the truce to the armies at grips. He was then the Pope's agent, but Richelieu engaged him secretly to work for France's interest. He came to Paris in 1634 as Papal nuncio. Richelieu brought him to be presented to the Queen. "You will like him, Madame; he resembles Monsieur de Buckingham," said Richelieu, with a venomous reference to the past and with an uncanny vision of the future. She did like him, for he used every art of ingratiation to gain her favor. Such were the high stakes he liked to play for. He spoke to her in voluble Spanish; he established with her a sense of common fate. Were not both of them foreigners in a suspicious, unwelcoming Court?

Soon he transferred all his allegiance from the Pope to Richelieu, and the Cardinal came to prize highly his abilities, his faithfulness. But he remained more or less effaced until 1641, when Richelieu obtained for his protégé the Cardinal's hat. At the end of 1642 he suddenly imposed himself on the awareness of every courtier, for Richelieu had named him in his testament Chief of the Council and Premier Ministre of France.

Mazarin accepted the situation with admirable tact. He was very deprecating, almost apologetic. "We saw on the steps of the throne," says Retz, "whence the fierce, redoubtable Richelieu had blasted, rather than governed, humanity, a successor who was gentle, benign, who wanted nothing, who was in despair because his Cardinal's dignity did not permit him to humiliate himself as much he would have liked before the world, who walked the streets behind his own carriage with two little lackeys." This was a fine way of suggesting that he was uncomfortable and out of place on cushioned seats. He let people believe that the appointment as First Minister was only temporary; in a few months, when the tangled affairs of the government should be put in order, he would retire thankfully to Italy.

The nobles despised such a humble master, and he seemed to invite their scorn. The utmost cleverness is to hide one's cleverness.

Mazarin's first task was to prepare for the government of the realm in the event of the King's death. The King would not consent to naming his Queen sole Regent. He distrusted, he hated her too much. When he was told that she repented of her treasonable acts, he said: "In my present state I am obliged to pardon her, I am not obliged to believe her." Mazarin visited the King's sickroom with a reasonable proposal. He persuaded his master to name the Queen Regent but to subject her to a council to be composed of himself, Gaston d'Orléans, the Prince de Condé, and three others. Mazarin justified this action to the Queen on the ground that only so would the King give her the title of Regent.

The statement of his proposal was read aloud to the King. His Majesty accepted it, with the insertion of a clause that the Duchesse de Chevreuse should never be permitted to return to France. When the clause was read back to him he roused from his pillows. "There's the devil in person!" he exclaimed.

The members of the new council were informed of their appointment, and immediately began intriguing for their own ends.

The Prince de Marcillac, in the Queen's train, watched the courtiers play their roles of submission, of devotion to her. He saw them no longer as gallant knights, the Queen's defenders, and wicked giants, her foes. They were simply the strong and the weak, struggling to make their way in the society to which they were born. Each had his ambition, his desire of a post, money, prestige. Marcillac knew how high a value to put on their protestations of esteem and friendship. Most friends disgust one with friendship, and most of the devout disgust one with devotion. Yet the nobles at Court were ordinary inhabitants of our world, honorable in their way, courageous, sympathetic. They had virtues enough. But the virtues lose themselves in self-interest, as the rivers lose themselves in the sea.

The hopeful courtiers paid their proper calls on the King

in his hushed room. "They are coming to see how soon I'll die," he said, with complete justice.

He lay in the high castle of Saint-Germain, which stands on a bluff above the Seine, looking across the river's triple loops a dozen miles to Paris. From his bedroom window he could see the spires of Saint Denis, where his body would lie beside all the Kings of France. "That's where I shall go soon, where I shall bide a long time," he said. He warned of a bad bit of road; one must take care that the cumbersome hearse should not become mired there. He spent his better moments composing a setting for the *De profundis* to be sung at his bedside when he should be no more.

His state worsened. The priests administered the last sacraments. At this solemn moment a burst of laughter was heard in the adjoining room. The kneeling attendants stirred, scandalized. "It can be no one but my Queen and my brother," murmured the King, and he was quite right.

In his mind was a dreadful sense of failure. He had been a poor ruler of his great country. Only the strength of Richelieu had sustained him. Now Richelieu was dead, and he was about to die, and he would leave his country to a traitor Queen and two infant sons. *Pauvre France!*

He died on 14 May 1643. It was at the very hour of the same day of May that his father Henri IV had died, thirty-three years before.

Four days later a solemn ceremony was enacted before the Parlement de Paris. François V, Duc de La Rochefoucauld, stood among his fellow Dukes.

The four-year-old King Louis XIV sat on his ample throne. He said a few well-memorized words, and his mother spoke briefly. Then the Parlement dealt with its important business. It examined the royal testament setting up a Council of the Regency, and decided that the will was unconstitutional.

The Parlement's grounds were sound enough. According to the doctrine of the divine right of kings, the sacred authority passes entire from a dead king to his male heir. The new king has no obligation toward his predecessor, and cannot be bound by any act of his. If the new king should be a minor, ancient usage decrees that his mother shall be Regent, with the co-operation of the Princes of the Blood. The Blood, the sacred Blood of kings, gives these princes the right of succession to the throne and therefore the right to guard the Blood that flows in the veins of the tiny King.

With such argument the Parlement ruled that the dead King had no right to impose conditions on the living King. Louis XIII's testament was void. The Queen should be sole Regent, with full right to choose her advisers, but with no obligation to accept their advice.

It is true that the Parlement obtained a great legal advantage by assuming the right to judge a King's actions, to quash a King's testament. There were whispers that the Parlement was getting too big for its boots, that it was emulating the insolence of the rebellious Parliament of England.

In effect, the Queen was Regent as a result of an accord between herself, the Parlement, and the high princes. The powerful nobles thought that they had taken an important step toward their end, the control of government action.

The heavy funereal trappings of the Court could not damp the spirits of the courtiers. The dreadful Cardinal was dead, the King a child, the Queen Regent kindly, indolent, not very sharp-witted. The happy time had come. It would be hard if the nobles could not regain their old power and privilege.

But how saith the Preacher: Woe to thee, O land, when thy King is a child and the princes eat in the morning!

The situation was briefly this. Next in succession to the

crown was the King's brother Philippe. But at the age of three one can hardly form a party.

Next in line stood Gaston d'Orléans, Monsieur. He had his party, composed mostly of his dependents and vassals, with their lingering sense of feudal obligation. His second wife, sister of the Duke of Lorraine, brought in the support of that powerful house. However, Monsieur gained adherents with difficulty. His unstable character and his bloody record of betrayal were frightening to ambitious nobles in search of a master.

Third in line for the crown was the Prince de Condé, Monsieur le Prince. He had a powerful party, to which the La Rochefoucaulds formally belonged. The Prince de Condé was a mean, rapacious old scoundrel, famous for his filthy hands and hair. His wife, the Princesse, remembered the fantastic courtship of Henri IV, when the elderly monarch had jousted with the younglings of the Court for her favor, had disguised himself as a postillion and worn a false beard to reach her presence. The eldest son of Condé, the Duc d'Enghien, was now twenty-two, a man of power and promise. Ugly, but of an aquiline magnificence, he bore down all opposition by his imperious manner. He had earnestly studied the art of war, and was already proving himself one of the great generals of France's history. His ambition was rather for material rewards, lands and revenues, than for political dominance. His younger brother, the Prince de Conti, now only thirteen, was a poor sickly hunchback, destined for the Church.

The brilliant star of the family was the eldest child and only daughter of the Condés, the twenty-three-year-old Duchesse de Longueville. By all testimony, she was the loveliest in a Court filled with beauty. She was tall and well proportioned, with eyes of tender blue and delicate ash-blond hair that framed her oval face in rippling curls. The poets strained the resources of botany to find likenesses to her complexion. Her voice was soft and musical. Her usual air was one of aristocratic indolence, even of disdain, but this was often broken by flashing bursts of vivacity and passion. She was well aware of her incomparable charms and enjoyed testing their power upon impressionable young gentlemen of the Court. In June 1642 she was married to the Duc de Longueville. He was forty-seven, twice her age, weak-spirited, irresolute, suspicious. He was, however, immensely wealthy, and held most of Normandy by feudal rights. He had had a long career of gallantry, and at the time of his marriage he was notoriously the lover of the notorious Madame de Montbazon. If he had the intention of giving her up, she purposed merely to allow him a short honeymoon vacation.

Here, whispered the young gallants, is a great opportunity. Who can capture the enchanting Madame de Longueville, that noble heart? Who can gain the honor of subduing the great Condé's daughter, the cousin of Kings?

The Prince de Marcillac heard the whisper, and wondered if such glory was beyond even the reach of his dreams.

After the Condés came the Vendômes. The Duc de Vendôme was the son of Henri IV and the fair Gabrielle d'Estrées. As a royal bastard he stood high, but he could not enter the King's Council nor attend his person by birthright alone. The hopes of the house were placed on the Duc de Vendôme's eldest son, the Duc de Beaufort. He was brave and handsome, with flowing golden hair. He affected a loud, gross, and common air. The Queen was amused by his hearty sportsman's manner, his specious frankness, his picturesque street language. The commoners of Paris, especially the women, adored him, and he cultivated their adoration.

The nobles played for position, made alliances, bid for

recruits. They looked hungrily to the Queen's bounty, weighed each of her favors, calculating its political effect. For a time their bright expectations were fulfilled. The Queen distributed the vacant government posts as largesse, but with a capricious feminine liberality. Marcillac, covertly watching her impulsive lavishness, reflected that liberality is usually only the vanity of giving, which we prefer to the thing we give.

These happy days came later to be known as *la bonne Régence*. The poetic St. Evremond recalls:

> J'ai vu le temps de la bonne Régence,
> Temps où régnait une heureuse abondance,
> Temps où la ville aussi bien que la cour
> Ne respiraient que les jeux et l'amour.

("I have seen the good days of the Regency, when happy abundance reigned, when Paris as well as the Court breathed only diversion and love.")

The Court saw the return of figures long absent. "All those who had been beyond the frontiers," says a contemporary, Lenet, "came back, one after another, and at the poor King's funeral we beheld all the people who had been banished, hung, broken on the wheel, beheaded, or imprisoned."

Mazarin, who never did anything foolish, encouraged the policy of good will, which would enhance the popularity of his Queen. Playing his game of humility, he welcomed every friend of the Queen as his own.

Mademoiselle de Hautefort arrived, only three days after the King's death. She proudly displayed a letter from the Queen, containing the words: "Come, my dear friend; I am dying with impatience to see you and to embrace you." She was warmly received, warmly embraced, and for a time she resumed her old laughing intimacy with her lady. But she was now twenty-seven, still unmarried, and the Queen liked younger maids of honor about her. Mademoiselle de Hautefort had become very devout and had developed a somewhat waspish mood. She soon recognized that the Queen confided more in Mazarin than in her. She did not like Mazarin, and, trusting in the old friendship, spoke loudly against him to the Queen. This was a serious mistake.

The Prince de Marcillac does not tell us of his feelings on seeing Mademoiselle de Hautefort again. Such intimate notes have no place in his Memoirs. But I think we may reasonably surmise that she caused small stir in his heart. A decade had passed since he had so adored her and she had played engagingly with his adoration. Both had changed. He was no longer inclined to worship humbly and hopelessly, and she would have found such mooning passion tiresome. Love, like life, cannot subsist without continual movement, and it ceases to live when it ceases to hope and fear.

Another woman out of Marcillac's past chose this moment to return. The Duchesse de Chevreuse had been watching French affairs from Belgium. At the death of Louis XIII she announced her return to France. The courtiers, already a little disturbed by Mazarin's importance, thought that the Duchesse would use her friendship with the Queen to oppose Mazarin and to aid the ascent of the Duc de Beaufort.

"I did not judge of her credit so highly as did others," says Marcillac. "The Queen spoke of her coldly to me, and I saw clearly that she would have liked to have Madame de Chevreuse's return to France delayed. The Queen even made trouble, in conversation, about letting her come to Court, after the express prohibition which the King had made on his deathbed. She told me that she was still fond of the Duchesse, but that, since she had lost her taste for the amusements which had bound the two together in their youth, she feared that she would appear changed to her friend. She said that she knew from experience how capable Madame de Chevreuse was of troubling the harmony of the Regency by her cabals. The Queen added that Madame de Chevreuse was no doubt returning with her mind embittered by the Queen's confidence in the Cardinal Mazarin and with the purpose of doing him harm.

"I spoke to her with perhaps more liberty than I should. I pointed out to her how much trouble and surprise an unexpected change would arouse in the public and her former servants, if they should see her first acts of power and severity directed against Madame de Chevreuse. I reminded her of the lady's faithful attachment, of her long services and of the lasting misfortunes which had ensued. I begged her to consider how she would be accused of inconstancy, and to think what an interpretation would be made of this inconstancy, if she should prefer the Cardinal Mazarin to Madame de Chevreuse.

"This conversation was long and agitated. I saw clearly that I was sometimes irritating her, but as I still kept a good deal of power over her mind, I obtained what I desired. She charged me to go and meet Madame de Chevreuse, who was returning from Flanders, and to persuade her to follow a course which would be agreeable to the Queen."

Meanwhile Madame de Chevreuse set out from Brussels, attended by twenty coaches filled with lords and ladies who went the first stage with her. She had to traverse the opposing battle lines in the perpetual war. Her coach passed the Spanish front, to a great doffing of plumed hats. Thence across the narrow no man's land to the French lines. There she was welcomed with equal courtesy. Her radiant smile had stilled the guns; once more Venus had vanquished Mars. At Roye she met her committee of welcome, Marcillac and Montagu, both her former lovers. Poor Montagu was restless. He was a postulant for the monastic life, and no doubt suspected that Mazarin had sent him on this mission with humorous intent.

Marcillac gave the Duchesse a good talking-to. He told her of the Queen's attitude, and warned her that things were much changed since her time. "I advised her to follow the Queen's tastes, since evidently she would not be able to change them. I pointed out to her that the Cardinal was not accused of any crime, that he had no share in the violences of Richelieu, that he was almost the only one who had any knowledge of foreign affairs, that he had no relatives in France, that he was too good a courtier not to pay her her due respects, and that I thought she ought to receive his advances, to support him if he did his duty and to keep him from being remiss to his duty. I added that there were few individuals whose probity and capacity were so well recognized that they should be preferred to Cardinal Mazarin. I urged her, above all things, not to let the Queen imagine that she was returning with the design of governing the Queen's mind, because that was the pretext the Queen's enemies most used to injure her. I said that she should apply herself solely to regaining in the Queen's mind and heart the same place that others had tried to take from her, and that she should put herself in a position to protect or destroy Cardinal Mazarin, as his preservation or destruction would be useful to the public."

Hoity-toity, thought Madame de Chevreuse. This solemn young man is telling me how to intrigue. Me!

But she told him that he was very sensible, and she would follow his advice to the letter.

She arrived then in Paris after ten years of absence. Her return was a social sensation. Her salon swarmed with callers, who were captured once more by her vivacious charm. Even the official *Gazette de France* remarked on the magic preservation of her beauty.

The Prince de Marcillac accompanied her to the Louvre. "Although she was received by the Queen with many marks of friendship," he says, "I had no great trouble in observing the difference between the joy the Queen showed on seeing her again and that which she had previously manifested in speaking of her. However, Madame de Chevreuse did not perceive this difference, and she thought that her presence would undo in a moment all that her enemies had contrived against her."

Madame de Chevreuse immediately threw herself headlong into intrigue. She allied herself to a party which was forming about the Duc de Beaufort as a nucleus. The members were called the *Importants,* because of the solemn, important air they affected in public. They paraded a Roman virtue, which was then much in the mode, but in fact they were mostly old friends of the Queen who were now disappointed at their lack of royal favor and were united by a jealous hatred of Mazarin. "To my misfortune I was one of their friends, without approving of their conduct," says Marcillac.

The *Importants* drew up a program. Châteauneuf, former lover of Madame de Chevreuse and former Chancellor of Louis XIII, should be brought back from his prison, and his influence would soon destroy that of Mazarin. (Unfortunately old Châteauneuf did not keep up with the times. His short jacket and tiny hat gave him the ridiculous air of a Pantaloon.) Suitable rewards should be given to the members of the cabal. The Prince de Marcillac should be made Governor of Le Havre.

The demands of the *Importants* were enormous. Naturally, in every case someone would have to be dispossessed of his post to satisfy them, and naturally the outcries of the dispossessed would be frightful.

Thus the Prince de Marcillac, from being more than half in favor of Mazarin, shifted until he was more than half in favor of the *Importants*. Both sides made him offers which neither side fulfilled. And both sides came to distrust him because he would not choose outright one course or the other. He balanced and hesitated. He displayed that indecision which was to grow until it became a mark of his character.

Of course more was at stake than the award of lucrative posts. The very position of France was at issue, though one would hardly suspect it in reading the memoirs of the courtiers. Mazarin held to the policy of Richelieu: to oppose forever the power of Austria, Spain, and the Papacy, to aid any allies, Catholic, heretic, or Turk, against them. The *Importants* were for peace with Spain and the Empire, even though such a peace would mean the subjection of France to Imperial policy. They proposed also to intervene in England, to establish Charles I on his throne, to punish the upstart Parliament.

Mazarin pursued his aim by dividing his enemies to conquer them separately. The three parties, those of Gaston d'Orléans, of the Prince de Condé, and of the *Importants*, were equal in greed and jealousy. Mazarin fomented their jealousies, tempted and never contented their greed. He strove to keep them forever at odds with each other, to prevent them from combining against himself and the Queen.

To gain his ends he used every means, and particularly the weapon of love. For these were the great days of great women. They sat in councils, they made policy out of caprice, they lectured their lovers on diplomacy. The lovers, educated in subjection by *Astrée*, accepted their subjection as in the natural order of things. "You are lucky!" said Mazarin, a little later, to the Spanish Minister. "In your country you have two sorts of women: plenty of coquettes, and a very few good women. The first think of nothing but pleasing their lovers, the second think only of pleasing their husbands; in both cases their sole ambition is for luxury and vanity. But our women on the contrary, whether they be prudes or light women, old or young, clever or fools, all want to interfere in everything. An honest woman will not go to bed with her husband nor a loose one with her lover unless he first tells her something about the affairs of state. They must know everything, see everything, be told everything, and what is worse they must do everything and muddle everything. We have some here who daily throw us into a greater confusion than ever there was in Babylon!"

Accepting the conventions of his Court, Mazarin wooed briefly the Duchesse de Chevreuse, and then thought better of it. His best policy, the policy to which he was constant, was to woo the Queen.

The relations between Mazarin and Anne of Austria have been much discussed, and they have never become entirely clear. Most students accept, on the basis of written evidence, that Mazarin possessed the Queen's heart. He was a handsome man with a rare captivating charm, and she was a lonely woman, isolated in a hostile Court. The two foreigners were leagued by every interest, by natural liking. To Mazarin alone could the Queen tell all, in her native Spanish. There were many rumors of a secret marriage (for Mazarin, though a Cardinal, was not a priest). The story of the marriage may be no more than rumor, but certainly the actions of the Queen and the telltale phrases of her secret correspondence with Mazarin can best be explained by the assumption that the two were lovers.

Now we are ready for the drama of the Regency.

CHAPTER VIII

The Disgust with Things

1643–1646

WE OFTEN persuade ourselves that we love people who are more powerful than ourselves, and yet it is self-interest alone which produces our friendship. We give ourselves to them not for the good we wish to do them but for what we wish to receive from them.

In the first months after the death of Louis XIII Marcillac waited on his Queen with an air of adoring self-satisfaction. He pictured himself as the ruler of her mind, hence the virtual ruler of France. He awaited momentarily the royal word which would specify her substantial reward for his long devotion. But the Queen did not come to the point. She paltered forever, and made no proposal at all suitable. She seemed actually to be forgetting her obligation toward her faithful servant, her martyr. Pride does not wish to be in debt, egotism does not wish to pay. Indeed, it is generally true that nearly everyone takes pleasure in acquitting himself of small obligations; many people are grateful for middling ones; but there is almost no one who does not show ingratitude for great ones.

Mazarin, posing as the mere executant of the Queen's will,

DISGUST WITH THINGS 95

befooled Marcillac with his affected simplicity, a delicate imposture. He was fawning and humble, and excessive in protestation of his humility. Humility is, however, often only a feigned submission, which one uses to subdue others. It is an artifice of pride which abases itself only to rise higher; and although this pride may transform itself in a thousand ways, it is never better disguised and more capable of deception than when it conceals itself under the face of humility.

At first Marcillac thought that he would make policy for obsequious Mazarin. As the Queen's intimate adviser, he would be above partisanship between Mazarin and his enemies. He would be the arbiter, the judge. He could deal with all parties and decide among them.

He was gradually undeceived. No one appealed to his arbitration. The Queen did not stand above Mazarin, she was his ally, always approving his smallest decisions.

The Queen reproached Marcillac because he was still on good terms with the Duchesse de Chevreuse and the *Importants*. "Not a day passed that I did not need to make some apology to the Queen," he remembers resentfully. "I had spoken for someone who was out of favor, or I had not been warm enough against some critic; I had laughed at a story which reflected on the inner circle or the Cabinet; I had justified some odious fault; I had walked down some street where there were suspect houses."

He became aware that the Queen no longer told him the essential secrets of her policy and her thought. She confided to him only the news that he had already heard whispered in the antechambers. At length he realized that he distrusted his idol, his adored Queen. Well, our distrust justifies the deceptions of others.

Reflecting on her forgetfulness of his dozen years of sacrifice for her sake, he felt that he had learned a lesson about courtly behavior. Men are not only capable of losing all memory of benefits and injuries; they even hate those who have obliged them and cease to hate those who have outraged them. Insistence on returning good and retaliating for evil seems to them a servitude hardly to be borne.

The Court was tense with rivalries in the summer of 1643. It is recognized that when hostile armies patrol a frontier within shouting distance one of the other, peace is at the mercy of an incident, and none can be too grotesque to start a war. The expected incident was the Affair of the Dropped Letters.

The new Duchesse de Longueville, who was a Condé, had, at her marriage, obliged her husband to give up his mistress, Madame de Montbazon. The mistress's pride was hurt, and not only her pride; she had received from the Duc de Longueville an annual present of 20,000 livres. Now Madame de Montbazon was the stepmother of the Duchesse de Chevreuse. She was, to be sure, twelve years younger than her stepdaughter; she had married Hercule de Rohan, Duc de Montbazon, when he was sixty. As he could hardly live up to his pretentious given name, she immediately embarked on a career of wide-ranging gallantry. Her distinguished roll of lovers includes Gaston d'Orléans and the Abbé de Rancé, founder of the Trappist order. Her adorers extravagantly proved their devotion; when she had a tooth pulled a lover had sixteen of his own extracted in sympathy.

"She was one of the most beautiful persons one could see," says Tallemant des Réaux, "and she was one of the great ornaments of the Court. She outshone all the others at the ball, and in the judgment of the Polish envoys at the marriage of Princess Marie [November 1647], although she was over thirty-five she still took the prize. But personally I wouldn't have agreed. Her nose was large and her mouth was a little drawn in. She was a colossus, and at that time she already had a little too much stomach, and breasts half again too large. It is true they were very white and firm, but they were all the less easily concealed. She had very white skin, very black hair, and a great air of majesty."

She was obviously lusty and demanding, gross, unscrupulous, the terror of well-married wives. "When she appeared at Court in her youth," continues Tallemant, "she used to say that one was good for nothing at thirty, and that she wanted to be thrown in the river when she reached that age. I leave it to you to judge whether she lacked gallants."

After the marriage of the Duc de Longueville she promoted to the rank of chief gallant the Duc de Beaufort. Thus she became a member of the *Importants* by sentimental bonds as well as by her family connection with Madame de Chevreuse.

Her chief enemy was the new Duchesse de Longueville, who had married her previous lover. There was an antipathy of character as well as of circumstance. Madame de Montbazon was big, hearty, violent, dark; Madame de Longueville was fragile, languid, mysterious, blond. And Madame de Longueville was nine years younger.

"One day when Madame de Montbazon was receiving in her bedchamber," says Marcillac, "and when many people of quality went to see her, among whom was Coligny [Maurice de Coligny, scion of the famous Huguenot family], someone carelessly dropped two letters which were well composed, passionate, done in a fine feminine handwriting. Madame de Montbazon, who hated Madame de Longueville, seized this occasion to do her an ill turn. She thought that the style and the handwriting might fit Madame de Longueville, although there was little resemblance and although in fact she had nothing to do with the letters. Madame de Montbazon informed the Duc de Beaufort, to involve him in the matter, and the two together plotted to spread the word that Coligny had lost Madame de Longueville's letters, which proved their intimacy. Madame de Montbazon told me this story before the report had gone far. I immediately saw all the consequences, and what use Cardinal Mazarin could make of it against Beaufort and all his friends. I did not then know Madame de Longueville well, but I was very close to the Duc d'Enghien and I was a friend of Coligny. I knew the malignant character of the Duc de Beaufort and Madame de Montbazon, and I did not doubt that this was a mischief they wanted to do to Madame de Longueville. Out of apprehension of the results, I did my best to persuade Madame de Montbazon to burn the letters in my presence and never to speak of them. She promised me to do so, but the Duc de Beaufort made her change again.

"She repented soon that she had not followed my counsel. The affair became public, and the whole house of Condé took it up, as was proper. However, the man who had in fact lost the letters was a friend of mine, and he was in love with the lady who had written them.[1] He saw that these letters would inevitably be recognized, since Monsieur le Prince de Condé, Madame la Princesse, and Madame de Longueville wanted to display them publicly in order to convict Madame de Montbazon of an ugly false assumption, because of the difference of handwriting. In this imbroglio the man who had lost the letters suffered all that a gentleman must suffer in such a case. He talked to me of his grief, and he begged me to try every way to extricate him from his painful stiuation. I served him well; I took the letters to the Queen, to Monsieur le Prince and Madame la Princesse; I showed them to Madame de Rambouillet, to Madame de Sablé, and to some close friends of Madame de Longueville, and as soon as the truth was fully

---

[1] They were written by Madame de Fouquerolles to the elegant Marquis de Maulevrier.

DISGUST WITH THINGS 99

known I burned them before the Queen, and thus delivered the two interested persons from mortal distress.

"Although Madame de Longueville was fully justified in public opinion, Madame de Montbazon had not yet made the public reparations which she owed. The conditions were long disputed, and all these delays augmented the bitterness."

Madame de Longueville and her mother, the Princesse de Condé, demanded of the Queen that Madame de Montbazon should make a public disavowal of her accusation. The Queen agreed. The three ladies and Mazarin, in an earnest council, composed a little speech of apology for Madame de Montbazon to recite.

The Court assembled in the Hôtel de Condé. Madame de Montbazon was presented. Under the concentrated gaze of the courtiers, she flipped open her fan, to which was attached a sheet of paper. From it she read her apology exactly. Her manner was not insolent; there was nothing tangible for which she could be reproved. Yet by the mere confident carriage of her head and body, by the mere fact of reading an evidently unfamiliar text, she made a farce of her humility. Her head not quite sufficiently bent, her assured but uninterested voice, revealed that she was thinking: "Je me moque de tout cela—this is all nonsense."

She had won the first engagement in the courtly war. But she lost the next.

A few days later, on 21 August 1643, Madame de Chevreuse gave a ladies' lunch to the Queen in the fashionable restaurant, Renard's, near the Seine's side (and on the site of the Orangerie on the present Place de la Concorde). The Princesse de Condé was bidden. She accepted the invitation, stipulating however that Madame de Montbazon should not be present. Madame de Chevreuse assured her that Madame de Montbazon was ill at her home. But when the Queen with the Princesse de Condé arrived at Renard's, they learned that Madame de Montbazon was inside, helping to receive the guests. The Queen was furious. The Princesse de Condé cried: "I am causing the trouble; I will go. Don't let me spoil the party." The Queen clutched her arm. No, she must not retire; she had come on the understanding that Madame de Montbazon should be absent.

The Queen sent in her order to Madame de Montbazon that she should allege a sudden illness and depart. Madame de Montbazon sent back word that, with all due respect, she was invited to luncheon in a public place. She had never felt better, and she would not depart.

This was outright defiance. The Queen, raging, put the Princesse de Condé into her own carriage and drove back to the Louvre, where presumably they had an improvised lunch. The Queen then sat down and wrote an order banishing Madame de Montbazon to her country house. She also deprived Madame de Chevreuse, who had organized the ill-fated party, of what little favor remained to her.

Behind the scenes, Mazarin, with a great air of trying to appease everybody, smooth everything over, had been working to bring about just this dénouement. By espousing the cause of the Condés, the Queen brought them solidly to her side. Circumstance—with Mazarin's aid—had succeeded in disgracing Madame de Montbazon, and with her her stepdaughter, Madame de Chevreuse, and her lover, the Duc de Beaufort, and all the party of the *Importants*. Mazarin had proved to the Court that the *Importants* would have no influence over the Queen. He might drive them to some desperate act which would bring them to the Bastille. Mazarin was delighted with the ladies' war.

Coligny, whose name had been publicly coupled with that

of the Duchesse de Longueville, had now an obvious duty: to provoke the Duc de Beaufort, lover of Madame de Montbazon, and if possible to kill him in a duel. But the protocol of gallantry demanded that he should wait a certain time, for an immediate challenge would be taken as an admission that he was Madame de Longueville's lover. (And was he, indeed? The pretty point is still disputed. He was at least her devout admirer, and she was at least his excellent friend.)

While Coligny waited for the proper time to elapse, Mazarin acted. He had learned that Beaufort, urged by the inveterate conspirator, Madame de Chevreuse, planned to assassinate him. In fact, three times Beaufort assembled his bravos to stab the Cardinal in his coach, but Mazarin, well warned, always had by his side some personage too august to be implicated. On September 3 Mazarin struck. Beaufort was arrested in the very Louvre and hurried off to the château of Vincennes, to a fetid prison room which was worth its weight in arsenic, as Madame de Rambouillet said. The rest of the Vendômes were banished to their country castle; Madame de Chevreuse was sent again to Touraine. With the patience of a spider she began reweaving her web.

"The imaginations of all men were seized with respectful astonishment," says the Cardinal de Retz. "Mazarin did so well, that he found himself at the top of the world, while all thought they had him at their sides." Mazarin was now master of France, and master he was henceforth to remain.

The Prince de Marcillac, like the others, did not yet fully realize the state of affairs. He was not closely enough bound with the *Importants* to share their disgrace, but he had not been sufficiently their enemy to keep all the Queen's favor. He believed fondly that Madame de Chevreuse was ignorant of the plot against Mazarin.

"I want you to have nothing further to do with the Duchesse de Chevreuse," said the Queen to him. "I want you to be entirely the friend of Cardinal Mazarin."

"I thank you respectfully, Madame," he replied, "for your confidence in my fidelity. I will never hesitate between my duty to Your Majesty and my friendship for Madame de Chevreuse, and I will scrupulously obey your commands. However, I beg you to consider that having been so long associated with Madame de Chevreuse in the service of Your Majesty, I cannot justly cease to be her friend, as long as she is guilty of no other crime than to displease Cardinal Mazarin. I should wish to be the friend and servant of the Minister as long as Your Majesty will honor him with her confidence, but as far as my personal relations with Madame de Chevreuse go, I respectfully request that I be permitted to follow my first engagements."

This reply, reported to Mazarin, was regarded as highly unsatisfactory. Marcillac followed, none the less, his policy of friendship with both Mazarin and the Duchesse de Chevreuse. He was putting the claims of old friendship above the claims of political self-interest. In so doing, he later concluded, he erred. "I found hardly more gratitude on her side for my ruining myself this second time in order to remain her friend than I had just found on the Queen's part; and Madame de Chevreuse in her exile as easily forgot all I had done for her as the Queen had forgotten my services when she was in a position to reward them."

The Affair of the Dropped Letters thus resulted in the triumph of Mazarin, in the disgrace of the Vendômes and their allies, and in the unsettling of Marcillac's position at Court. The Affair was now to end in blood.

Coligny, the offended partisan of Madame de Longueville and Marcillac's good friend, was chafing for revenge against the friends of Madame de Montbazon. As Beaufort had been packed off to prison, Coligny challenged one of the lady's secondary lovers, the Duc de Guise. Coligny was a poor swordsman, and he had just risen from a long illness. Guise was a mighty blade, a furious matamore. The two met, with their fighting seconds, in the Place Royale, the present Place des Vosges. It is said that Madame de Longueville watched her champion from a high window. The battle was a short one. Coligny lost his footing and fell to his knees. The Duc de Guise stepped on his sword, and said: "I don't want to kill you, but treat you as you deserve for challenging a prince of my birth, without my giving you cause." He struck Coligny with the flat of his sword. Coligny rose, seized his weapon, and attacked wildly. Guise wounded him in the shoulder, grasped his opponent's sword, wrested it from him, and with it pierced his arm. Meanwhile the two seconds had wounded each other severely.

Coligny's wounds, if not originally serious, rapidly became so. Mortification set in, as it so commonly did in the days before sterilization was comprehended. After lingering a few months, he died.

The duel caused an immense stir in society and at Court. The hatred of the parties was further exacerbated. Madame de Longueville, for whose good name a gallant gentleman had martyred himself, perhaps under her very eyes, capped herself with an aureole of tragic charm.

Meanwhile Marcillac found himself more and more isolated. He had tried to put himself above parties. Now he recognized that politics is a play of forces, and that parties constitute force, and that the man above parties, lacking force, comes to lack everything. Mazarin, with the force of the Queen behind him, was playing the role that Marcillac aspired to play, the role he envied.

It is a great folly to wish to be wise all alone.

Marcillac attended a country Christmas party of the *Importants*.[2] Madame de Chevreuse and the others reproached him bitterly for his lukewarmness. Playing upon his disappointments, they sought to bring him into their fold, but in vain.

The fact is, his position was so infirm that he was the object of forces, and was obliged to yield to the severest pressures. The strongest pressure determining his actions was now that of his father, the Duc de La Rochefoucauld. The Duke had followed the lead of his master, the Prince de Condé, and had cast in his lot with Mazarin. He went so far as to report to the Cardinal the fact that his son had attended the seditious meeting of the *Importants*.

"My family interest stifled my anger," says Marcillac. His father directed him to be outwardly obsequious to Mazarin, to doff his umbrageous manner, to work for a suitable reward. The most suitable reward would be the Governorship of Poitou, which the father had once held and which he had been obliged to surrender.

Marcillac followed the paternal advice, but not to the letter. His touchy sensibility and the demands of punctilious honor interfered with the pursuit of advantage. He alienated Gaston d'Orléans by refusing to give his favorite, the Abbé de La Rivière, more than a cold salute. His taste for intrigue led him still into dangerous associations. In February 1644 Mazarin's spies reported that he was intimate with an Italian ambassador who represented the Spanish interest. In September he was said to be protecting the chief spy of the malcontents. He was playing a precarious double game.

Mazarin picked off his enemies one by one. Mademoiselle de Hautefort, who was still maid of honor of the Queen,

[2] Montrésor, *Mémoires*, 352.

DISGUST WITH THINGS

sympathized with the Duc de Beaufort in his prison, and with the *Importants* in general. She interceded for them with the Queen, and when rebuffed assumed an air of disdainful silence. Her mute disapprobation provoked the Queen to fury. In a tumultuous bedroom scene, in April 1644, Mademoiselle de Hautefort was dismissed and banished from the Court. The Queen's old friends were disappearing, yielding place to the one new friend.

Mazarin harassed steadily the Duchesse de Chevreuse in her Touraine exile. He forbade her to visit her former intimate, Queen Henrietta of England, who had now taken refuge in France from her troubled country. He arrested Madame de Chevreuse's steward and physician, and learned from them many damaging facts about their mistress.

Madame de Chevreuse's natural recourse when alarmed was a romantic flight. In the early spring of 1645 she made her way secretly to St. Malo, with her daughter Charlotte. Disguised as sailors, the two embarked on a small vessel which would take them to Flanders. Madame de Chevreuse was extremely seasick. Fate made her woes grotesque, no longer pitiable, as they had been on her flight to Spain, eight years before. Her craft was captured by a patrol ship of the rebel English Parliament. It seemed for a time that it would go hard with the two dainty sailors, so indecent in seafarers' pantaloons. However, after many difficulties, the refugees were sent on their way to Flanders.

There are means of curing folly, there are none for straightening a warped mind.

Marcillac, at Court, found his position very tiresome. Rewards and honors were forever promised, forever postponed. He set his heart on the Governorship of Poitou. To obtain it, he must first receive the royal consent; he must then purchase the post from its incumbent, who made endless difficulties. The matter dragged on for months and years. "The Prince de Marcillac murmured publicly against the Queen," says Madame de Motteville. Thus he betrayed an impolitic exasperation. The shrewder courtiers regarded him with distrust, accusing him of dangerous ambition.

It was a pity that he thus undermined his position, for he had every quality for success at Court. He was unusually handsome; his manners were impeccable, and were based on the hidden sensitiveness which makes manners an expression of the spirit. He talked with rare wit and grace. He had observed much, meditated much. He surprised and often delighted people by his perception of their thoughts and feelings. And yet there was a certain noble superciliousness about him which chilled his friends, checked their easy sincerity. He asked the confidences of others, he would not give of his secret self.

He dared not, indeed, for he despised the trade of the courtier, with its mean obligations. One does not like to praise, and one never praises anyone without self-interest. Praise is a skillful, hidden, delicate flattery which satisfies the giver and the receiver in different ways: the second takes it as a reward of his merit, the first gives it to indicate his fairness and his discernment. Marcillac had found to his cost that plain speaking, truth-telling, was folly or worse, for few people are sensible enough to prefer the criticism which is useful to them to the praise which betrays them. He had learned not to be deceived by the modest disclaimers of the great, when showered with adulation. The refusal of praise is a desire to be praised twice.

Even in the midst of flattering he would defeat his own aims by a small sardonic smile revealing the inward sneer, as he reflected that flattery is a counterfeit coin which has currency only through our vanity.

At Court he came to be regarded as an outsider, a man without a future. In return, he regarded the Court and its denizens with increasing cynicism. Nor was he the only disillusioned observer. The worthy, honorable Madame de Motteville describes the Court at this period as a place where men thought it almost shameful to render the ladies some civility, a place where lawless ambition and avarice were the finest virtues.

For a relief from Court life, with its too evident revelation of mean purposes, Marcillac would visit the précieux salon of Madame de Rambouillet.

Preciosity was an effort toward distinction, in speech, thought, literature, manners. "Preciosity consists of the singular expression of a banal reality," says René Bray.[3] Fundamentally, he continues, it lies in the moral order; the précieux language is a consequence of this fundamental. The précieux choose a mode of action, and from this emerge their manners and their jargon. Thus there is an initial act of the will, which is anti-natural, anti-instinctive. The précieux attempted to elevate woman above the prevailing grossness of their world. In so doing they developed a social doctrine, opposed the subjection of women in marriage, proposed divorce, trial marriages, the restriction of births, eugenics.

Naturally they fell into excess and promptly became ridiculous; Molière hardly exaggerates, in his *Précieuses ridicules*. The effort toward distinction in manners soon overpassed distinction and tumbled into the absurd. A précieuse fainted on seeing a dog naked. Madame de Rambouillet's outrageous daughter commonly collapsed on hearing a grammatical solecism. The précieux became fantastic in speech. The feet were referred to as "the dear sufferers," the cheeks "the thrones of modesty"; sedan-chair bearers were called "baptized mules," while such a locution as "j'aime le melon" was proscribed, as debasing the word "aimer." Their poetic productions were painfully arch; witness *The Plaint of the Consonants which*

[3] *La Préciosité et les précieux*, 137.

have not the Honor of Entering the Name of Neufgermain.
The précieux gentlemen, covered with ribbons and fal-lals, stenched with strange perfumes, ogling and furnace-sighing, were the butts of every virile mocker.

Still, in the *chambre bleue* of Madame de Rambouillet, the worst absurdities were checked by the hostess' frown. Here one met the eminent writers of the time and the eminent amateurs among the nobility. One talked of life and letters, played literary parlor games, listened to music. One engaged in the pleasing rivalry of composition; the guests were called upon to write portraits and maxims, as well as occasional verses.

The Prince de Marcillac found such exercises congenial. The maxim especially was to his taste. He took pleasure in assembling a series of observations on human behavior, drawing from them a generalization, and expressing the generalization in abstract terms. He began to practice the literary form which he was to make peculiarly his own.

There was always a touch of preciosity in his mind. He had, after all, fed on *Astrée*, whose pastoral daintiness helped to determine the form of preciosity. His aristocratic fastidiousness was in sympathy with the précieux effort toward distinction. He shared with the précieux their psychological interest, especially their fascination with love, its nature, ideal form, and obligations. His own definition of love was probably acceptable to Madame de Rambouillet and her circle: "It is difficult to define love. What one may say is that in the soul it is a passion to rule; in the mind, it is a sympathy; and in the body, it is merely a hidden, delicate desire to possess what one loves after many mysteries."

Our François speaks of love with much assurance. Indeed, now that he is in his thirties, he can lay some claim to competence in the matter. In his youth he had known well love's aspect in mind and soul; now he is more concerned with love in the body. He is impatient of long-suffering fidelities, unrecompensed ardors. He is in the mood for simpler satisfactions. For when our merit declines, our taste declines also.

We have the testimony of his literary friend Segrais that he took his share in all the vices that reigned at Court. It was in this period of disillusionment, when his youthful idealism had drained away, that he turned to easy consolations, to the game of love. The game was an agreeable one, combining the pleasures of the hunt with those of intrigue, bringing triumphs marked by hours of bliss. The game was paid for by the degradation of his self in his own mind. He accepted the blame of inconstancy, and put himself in the class of the dissolute wastrels he had once despised. And yet, he reflected, there is an inconstancy which arises from the mind's lightness or weakness, which makes it accept all the opinions of others, and there is another inconstancy, more excusable, which comes from the disgust with things.

In his disgust with things he compiled a cynic's Art of Love. Women's severity, he noted, is an adornment, a spot of rouge, which they add to their beauty. Therefore he paid tribute to their beauty with false vows, with the prestige of his person and his intelligence, to capture their adornment of severity for a souvenir. Most women surrender rather through weakness than through passion; hence it is that ordinarily enterprising men succeed better than others, though they be not the most lovable. After the surrender, after the enthronement of male pride, the span of enjoyment is brief. It is more difficult to be faithful to one's mistress when one is successful than when one is cruelly scorned. Fidelity, constancy—these are worn-out words, demanding analysis. In fact there are two kinds of constancy in love. One arises from the perpetual discovery in one's beloved of new reasons for love, the other from the fact that one makes constancy a point of honor. In most loves, with most women, the new reasons do not appear, and love dwindles and dims. But love does not merely disappear. It leaves an ugly residue in the mind. There are hardly any people who are not ashamed of having loved, when they love no more.

These are the words and thoughts of a rake who scorns women and men and himself. Marcillac's acts, in these gray years, fitted his mean thoughts. Love was a happy hunt, with its long chase, its triumphant kill; and then the quarry became suddenly revolting, and was fit only to be tossed to the dogs.

With all his air of courtliness, the Prince de Marcillac, in society, was measuring and estimating possible victims. By conquering the greatest, the most beautiful, he would gain merit in the eyes of his fellows and in his own.

He dared to look speculatively on the Princess of the Blood, Madame de Longueville herself. She had reason to be grateful to him for his role in the Affair of the Dropped Letters, when he had cleared her of the authorship of those compromising missives. And perhaps Coligny had induced her to take the first step on the path of infidelity.

"The beauty of Madame de Longueville," he says, "her intelligence, and all the charms of her person attached to her all who might hope to be suffered by her. Many men and women of quality tried to gain her favor, and, not to mention the charms of such courtship, she was then so closely bound with her whole house and was so tenderly loved by her brother, the Duc d'Enghien, that one could be assured of the esteem and friendship of that prince when one was approved by Madame his sister. Many gentlemen tried this course in vain, and joined other sentiments to those of ambition. Miossens, who later became Marshal of France, persisted longest, and he had the same ill success as the others. I was one of his close friends, and he told me his designs. But these soon destroyed themselves. He recognized the fact, and he told me several times that he had resolved to give up the attempt. But vanity, which was the strongest of his passions, prevented him from telling me the truth, and he pretended to hopes which he did not actually have and which I knew well he had no reason to have.

"Some time passed in this way, and I finally had some cause to think that I could make a more considerable use than could Miossens of the friendship and confidence of Madame de Longueville. I got him to admit it himself. He knew the position I was in at Court. I told him my aims, saying that consideration for him would always restrain me, and that I would make no effort to establish any relations with Madame de Longueville unless he should give me liberty to do so. I admit that I expressly angered him against her that I might gain his permission, although I said nothing which was not true. He gave me entire liberty; but he repented having done so when he saw the results of this liaison."

Thus cynically, brutally—if he is telling us all the truth—Marcillac bargained with a rival for the right to seduce, or to attempt to seduce, the loveliest and proudest princess of the Court. He made a cool calculation of political advantage, to be gained agreeably by false vows, by such lies as a gentleman may tell to ladies but not to other gentlemen.

What hope had he of success? He knew well that the beautiful Duchesse had spent her youth in a Carmelite convent, that she had accepted the grim privations of the nunnery with joy. At her first ball she had even worn a hair shirt under her low-cut bodice. She was virtuous by instinct, pious by training. But Marcillac, with the cynicism of the disillusioned romantic, convinced himself that there are few honest women who are not tired of their trade.

He set himself to the task of seduction, inwardly applauding his own realism in a base world. Now that he knew the rules of the mean game, he would play it to the limit, and for the highest stakes. He silenced within himself the voice of his own youth, crying troubled words of the beauty of fidelity, sacrifice, the holy dream. He was practiced now in presenting to the world the face of love's sportsman, *l'homme à bonnes fortunes*. We are so accustomed to disguising ourselves from others that we end by disguising ourselves from ourselves.

He flattered himself that he was a man of his world. He knew his way around; he had learned how to profit by the folly of others; he knew his own mind.

But those who know their own minds do not always know their own hearts.

We are, naturally, ignorant of the date when his campaign was crowned with success. Madame de Longueville bore her husband a son in January 1646, and in June she left France to join him at the peace conference in Germany. It seems unlikely that she yielded to Marcillac in the interval. But he laid the ground; certainly he laid the ground.

And his wife, one may say; the Princesse de Marcillac, what of her?

She was doing her wifely duty. By this time she had produced three sons and three daughters. She came to Paris with her husband and performed her courtly obligations. She was a close friend of the young Princesse de Montpensier, the only child of Gaston d'Orléans by his first marriage, and with her she even engaged in a little mild plotting, at the behest of her husband, surely. We find her in March 1646 implicated in a ladies' intrigue to make peace and union between Monsieur and the House of Condé.[4]

Of her relations with her husband we know nothing and are reduced to speculation. If she reproached him for his notorious infidelities he had his answer ready: the violence one does

---

[4] Montpensier, *Mémoires*, I, 107 n.

oneself to be faithful is hardly better than an infidelity. Did she pay him back in kind? The gossip writers, alert for every misstep of the nobility, give us no hint. No doubt she preserved the honor of the La Rochefoucaulds, but no doubt perforce. Her husband may well have pointed out, in bitter bedroom scenes to the tune of tears and fury, that most honest women are hidden treasures, who are secure only because they are not sought for.

Yet all the little indications of his life show that he honored and respected his wife, and even loved her after his fashion. Perhaps he pays her an obscure tribute when he remarks that infidelities should properly extinguish love, one should not be jealous when one has reason to be. Only those who avoid giving cause for jealousy are worthy of jealousy.

And this too is, I think, a covert confession: "It is difficult to love those we do not esteem, but it is no less difficult to love those whom we esteem more than we do ourselves."

CHAPTER IX

Men's Valor, Women's Virtue

1646–1648

AMONG the honors to which Marcillac aspired was the commission of maréchal de camp, something like brigadier general. The Queen and Mazarin had promised it for years, and then managed to withhold even this wretched reward. In the spring of 1646 Mazarin again dangled it before Marcillac's eyes. A great campaign was in preparation, under the command of Gaston d'Orléans and the Duc d'Enghien, that famous general, the future Great Condé.

"But after all, a brigadier should be with the army," said Mazarin to Marcillac, in his frankest man-to-man manner. "And naturally we must have d'Enghien's approval. So, my dear fellow, you must join the troops and commend yourself to d'Enghien. If he will only make the recommendation we will ratify the appointment in a moment. Her Majesty and I are so anxious to do something really suitable for you . . ."

Marcillac was now used to hunting the real meaning under courtly words. He interpreted these to signify that since rumor reported Marcillac to be now on excellent terms with d'Enghien, Mazarin thought that Marcillac, to obtain his generalship, would support the Cardinal's interest in his dealings with d'Enghien, and that d'Enghien would regard the appointment as a favor to himself from Mazarin.

In Mazarin's words Marcillac could see only self-interest. And self-interest impelled his own response. He would go to the wars indeed, and fight and if need be die, a little for France, a little for honor, and mostly for advantage.

The war, the eternal war between France and the Empire, flared up as the destined term of thirty years approached. The peace commissioners, including the Duc de Longueville, were already in conference at Münster, and both sides wished to put themselves in the most favorable position for diplomatic bargaining. The French plan was to invade Flanders and to capture as many cities as possible before the peace commissioners should cry a halt.

Marcillac, having no rank, prepared to join the army as a noble volunteer. He made ready his gear, his horses, his elaborate dinner service with which to entertain his noble friends. For his steward and personal servant he borrowed his brother's valet de chambre, Jean Gourville.

Gourville was a keen, prepossessing young man, just twenty-one. His family, from the town of La Rochefoucauld, was in the service of the ducal family. Old acquaintance and common background gave him an easy familiarity with his noble master, and the familiarity is hard to distinguish from friendship.

Gourville turned out to be the ideal steward, the longed-for jewel. He foresaw and forethought, made his master as comfortable in the field as he would have been at home. Gourville even built for Marcillac little huts for shelter against the June heats of Flanders, and prepared nightly a fresh straw mattress.

Gourville tells a curious anecdote of this campaign, revelatory of his character and also of the usages of an aristocratic army. He had recklessly bathed his arms and legs in cool water, and in the morning he found himself almost paralyzed. "But as I saw that the sun was getting brighter I hoped that that would much relieve me. When they told me that the rear guard was setting out I had myself put on a horse, and having made a stick out of a pike-staff, I went on to rejoin Monsieur le Prince de Marcillac's pack-horses. Some time later I heard a shout behind me: 'Out of the way!' and at the same time I received a blow on the head from a cane. I turned around quickly and landed a blow with my stick on the neck of the man who had hit me, without knowing who he was. Immediately a lot of men surrounded me, and the Captain of the Duc d'Orléans' Swiss Guard seizing me by the hair to pull me down, I gave him such a blow with my elbow in his stomach that he let go. The Marquis de Mauny, Captain of the Guards for the Duc d'Orléans, recognizing me in this unhappy state, came to my aid, parted the throng and told me to escape, which I did with all diligence.

"There was much talk of this affair that evening, how extraordinary it was that one should have struck Monsieur's aide de camp, who was making way for him. At the same time I told my side, how I had been struck without my knowing who did it, and how, as I had a stick in my hand, I had returned the blow, not knowing who had struck me nor that Monsieur was present. Finally it was decided that the captain of the guards of Monsieur le Prince de Marcillac would take me to ask pardon on my knees of Monsieur le Comte de Chaumont, who had been put to bed. I told him that I was in despair at having struck him, not having recognized him. He told me that he pardoned me and showed me his neck and head, much bandaged, and he told Monsieur de Bercenay, who had brought me, that he was going to be bled for the third time. When I met him later I always pretended not to recognize him."

It was perhaps at this time that Gourville determined to rise out of the status of servant, whom any gentleman might hit and club, and to become a gentleman with the right to club others.

Gourville and his master saw some hot work in Flanders. The French reduced the fortified city of Courtrai and besieged Mardijk, not far from Dunkerque. The flower of the French nobility fought and died in arrogant, absurd escapades. Marcillac observed their valor with cool mockery. Vanity, the sense of shame, and especially temperament, often make men's valor and women's virtue.

On 13 August the besieged Spaniards in Mardijk made a sortie in force and took the first line of trenches. The French ran to arms at the noise of battle. (Bussy-Rabutin abandoned a field dinner where he was being entertained by six small fiddlers.) The Duc d'Enghien led the counterattack in person. Bussy-Rabutin found him in the trench, sword in hand, bloody to the elbow. "You are wounded, sire!" cried Bussy. "No," said the Duke, "it's the blood of those scoundrels."

The Spanish were thrown out of the trench with great loss, but with greater loss to the French. The Duc d'Enghien himself was disfigured by a pot thrown from the city's walls. Many noble gentlemen died that day. The state apartments of Fontainebleau soon resounded with the grief of highborn ladies.

Marcillac was in the thick of things, and at his side was his servant Gourville. (Gourville had already visited the front lines to find out if he would be frightened; he found he was not, particularly.) Marcillac fought with his usual self-conscious recklessness. As his reward he had three wounds, one of them, a musket ball in the shoulder, serious. Gourville applied first aid and got his master back out of danger. After a few days he arranged for a litter, slung between two horses walking in file, and thus carried Marcillac precariously to his Paris house. When sufficiently convalescent, Marcillac journeyed by easy stages to his home in Verteuil.

He had time aplenty to ponder on the behavior of men in the test of danger and death. Perfect valor and complete poltroonery are two extremes which are seldom reached. The space between the two is vast; it contains all the other degrees of courage. There is no less difference between these than there is between faces, between humors. There are some men who expose themselves eagerly at the beginning of an action and who then lose their hold and are easily daunted by the battle's continuance. Some are content when they have satisfied honor, as the world sees it, and do very little beyond. One may see others who are not always equally masters of their own fear. Others let themselves sometimes be overcome by general terror. Others join in a charge because they dare not remain at their posts. There are some whose courage has been tempered by the habit of minor perils, which prepare them for exposure to greater ones. There are some who are brave toward sword thrusts and who fear musket shots, and others who are intrepid toward musketry and are fearful of swordplay. All these courages of different sorts have one thing in common: night, augmenting fear and hiding good actions and bad, gives one freedom to act with more discretion. There is another and more general kind of discretion. For one does not see a man do all that he might do on some occasion if he were assured of returning from it. Thus it is visible that fear of death takes something from valor.

In Marcillac's case, the result of his valorous action was that he lost all chance of becoming maréchal de camp. The

Duc d'Enghien was not interested in the appointment of an invalided general; Mazarin seemed to have forgotten the whole matter.

Marcillac turned all his effort to obtaining the charge of Governor of Poitou, and at last he succeeded. According to the custom of the time, he was obliged to buy the post from the incumbent, the Comte de Parabère, with the authorization of the monarch. He was forced to pay Parabère 300,000 livres for the same governorship which the Duc de La Rochefoucauld had sold to Parabère for 250,000 livres only fourteen years before. There were bitter complaints and repinings in the La Rochefoucauld household, particularly since times were hard and creditors were pressing the ducal family. But somehow Marcillac raised the money, and in April 1647 he entered Poitiers as Governor General of the province, and received the formal homage of the local dignitaries.

One would say that he justified Mazarin's long hesitations, for he remained at his post of duty for only a month. It is, of course, easier to appear worthy of functions one does not possess than of those one exercises. Yet there was certainly here a culpable indifference on Marcillac's part to his obligations toward his royal master and toward his subjects in Poitou.

The fact is that he was impatient to be in Paris, for Madame de Longueville was about to return with her husband from the long peace conference at Münster.

Thus in May 1647 he reappeared at Court and resumed the limited daily round of the courtier. There was no further question of his rejoining the army. The Duc d'Enghien—whom we must henceforth term the Prince de Condé, for he had succeeded to his father's rank and names, in the confusing manner of the French nobility—was in Spain, striving in vain to reduce the fortified city of Lérida. The war was fought with a manner. After a hot attack, in which the French were repulsed, the Spanish commander sent to Condé, under a white flag, a present of iced lemonade and cinnamon water. But he sent no food for the starving French soldiers. (In general, the trade of death dealing was carried on with an elegance which has disappeared, now that wartime generals are businessmen on leave. There was a Marquis de la Trousse who, transfixing his foe, always shouted that he was very sorry. Off Naples in 1648 a looming naval battle was postponed by agreement for the Christmas holidays.)

The Court would not be saddened by the distant war. The Queen indulged her taste for the comedy, notwithstanding that seven doctors of the Sorbonne opined that playgoing is a mortal sin. Mazarin brought from Italy singing actors and stage machines and produced the first opera in France. Its reception was mixed, in part because the performance lasted six hours. One evening the nine-year-old King led a ballet. He wore black satin tricked with gold and silver, and plumes and ribbons of scarlet. On hot summer days the royal family bathed in the Seine at Fontainebleau, wearing long shirts of gray linen which reached to the feet. "La modestie n'y était nullement blessée," says Madame de Motteville.

For Marcillac the Court's festivities were of little moment. He was totally taken with his happy love for the Duchesse de Longueville.

When she returned from the peace conference at Münster she was in her twenty-eighth year and in the full bloom of her beauty. Her graceless husband was now fifty-two. Possibly she had had one lover, Coligny, who had died for her; but the *chronique scandaleuse* of the time, gleeful over every lapse from virtue, is in her case very reserved. Most of her affection went to her brother, the Prince de Condé, two years her junior. The two were joined in harmony of spirit, sweet understanding. Indeed it has been said that Condé was the one love of his sister's life. Her second brother, Armand, Prince de Conti, was now eighteen, just appearing in the world. He was an unhappy humped weakling, fit only for the Church. He adored his sister with a passion which the enemies of his house roundly called incestuous. But the enemies were seeking to discredit the family, not to propound the truth.

At any rate we see a union of brothers and sisters, warmly intimate, understanding one another intuitively, holding a common purpose in the glorification of the family. There could be no secrets among them.

Condé, accepting the peculiar code of noble honor of those days, would see nothing amiss in his sister's taking a suitable lover. "Let the girl amuse herself!" he would have shouted, in his famous coarse bellow. But Conti would be jealous, impotently jealous.

Until Madame de Longueville went to Münster she had apparently been content to play her social role as Duchesse, to produce two children for her husband, and to exercise her wit in the salons of preciosity. But at Münster, where she ruled as queen, she learned to share in the universal preoccupation with politics. She discovered that the game is far from dull, that it consists in the manipulation of men and of great properties for the advantage of one's country and one's party. The game can be played with the same rules for the advantage of one's family, of oneself.

Madame de Longueville returned to Paris in May 1647. She was pregnant, and she wished to bear her child at home. This third child, a girl, was born not long after.

Among the first to congratulate the mother was the Prince de Marcillac. He paid more calls than were prescribed by social usage. He wooed her, no doubt, according to ritual of preciosity, parading his haggard despair and abasement. At the proper moment he fell sobbing to his knees, proclaiming that the shafts from Madame de Longueville's eyes had pierced his heart, that only her mercy could stanch its wounds.[1]

How a woman is to be pitied when she is possessed by love and virtue together! Madame de Longueville was indeed virtuous. She had taken seriously her Carmelite education; she had been proud of her reputation at Court as the unapproachable princess. But now she was ready for love, she was in love. She was twenty-eight, remember, tired of unapproachability and tired of lovelessness. She felt perhaps that she had overdone her habitual disdainful smile. Marcillac was just turned thirty-four, an appropriate age for twenty-eight. He was a handsome man, possessing every courtly grace. He charmed as well by the air of melancholy mystery which had come with the disillusionments of time. His education by Madame de Chevreuse and other brilliant women had made him adept in the art of love. And he knew the simple truth, deeper than any of the voluptuary's devices, that the passions are the only orators that always persuade. They are like an art of nature whose rules are infallible; the simplest man who has passion persuades better than the eloquent man who has none.

She was persuaded by Marcillac's passion, and urged on by the cynical spirit of her courtly friends. Marital fidelity was held in no high honor; it was indeed regarded as mildly ridiculous. A beautiful passion, *un bel amour*, was the dream of these great idle ladies, married without their consent for considerations of money and place. Against the convention of infidelity, so loose and lewd, the Church fought valiantly. Madame de Longueville no doubt hung back long from the

---

[1] Some learned scholars place Madame de Longueville's surrender to amour in the winter of 1645–1646, before she went to Münster, before Marcillac went to war. The present supposition seems to me more likely, but naturally it is all guesswork.

sin of adultery. But the same firmness which serves to resist love serves also to make it violent and lasting, and weak people, who are forever agitated by passions, are almost never really possessed by love.

Whatever her reasons, she yielded. After yielding, she had her happy time. The pleasure of love is in loving, and one is happier in the passion one feels than in the passion one communicates. So says Marcillac, giving the lie to other casuists of amour.

What keeps lovers and their mistresses from being bored together, he says again, is that they are always talking of themselves. Yet the time comes when even such delightful subject matter palls. In passion's intervals, Marcillac and Madame de Longueville, François and Anne-Geneviève, turned naturally to politics and intrigue.

Which of the two was the dominant one? Madame de Motteville, who knew them both well, says that Madame de Longueville became ambitious for Marcillac's sake. Marcillac, she says, was more self-seeking than tender, and he wished to rise by her aid. Set with this his own account of his courtship, wherein he pictures himself as calculating coolly the advantages of a liaison and dissuading a rival with the arguments of a land promoter, a huckster. We have his own authority for regarding Marcillac as the cynical, even diabolical, seducer of Madame de Longueville, the director of her political action, the master of her mind. Such is the picture drawn by Victor Cousin in his study of Madame de Longueville, which, after a hundred years, remains the standard biography.

One may respectfully disagree. Madame de Longueville was no less ambitious than her brother Condé, says Madame de Motteville again, half contradicting her other words. She needed no suggestion from Marcillac to make her ambitious. The pride of the Condés, the greedy aspirations of her father, mother, and brothers, gave them all the habit of demanding, accepting, and demanding more. As Princes of the Blood, they deferred only to crowned heads.

Madame de Motteville tells of some of the curious squabbles of exalted rank. Mademoiselle de Montpensier, daughter of Monsieur, entered Notre-Dame with two persons of quality bearing her train. The Duc d'Enghien, who was holding his wife's train alone, immediately signaled to one of his gentlemen to assist him. The ladies, towing their trainbearers, swept to the canons' stalls. Mademoiselle knelt, contriving to leave a symbolic gap between herself and the Condés. Madame de Longueville nudged her sister-in-law, the Duchesse d'Enghien, made her move over and fill the gap. Mademoiselle wept and made a great deal of noise. On returning to her palace she insisted that as she outranked the Condés she should have a dais in the King's house, a carriage studded with brass nails, footmen with turned-up breeches, and that when Princesses of the Blood called, they should sit in chairs without arms while she should take an armchair. Peace was somehow made, only to be broken when the Princesse de Condé, Madame de Longueville's mother, entered a church with Mademoiselle and laid down her footcloth exactly on a line with that of Mademoiselle. Alternately the great ladies inched their footcloths forward. Their prayers that day cannot have carried much weight in heaven.

Pride and ambition were in the air that Madame de Longueville breathed. From my reading of the characters and of their actions I think that in her relation with Marcillac she was the dominator, he the dominated. I think she led him for the first time into open rebellion against his monarch, that she encouraged him to treason, that she forced him into positions he was unable to sustain. When their love, with the adventures of the Fronde, came to an untoward end, Marcillac brooded incessantly over her mistreatment of him, and he sought to justify himself in his embittered Memoirs. To Madame de Motteville and to others of the Court he dropped the slyest of hints to suggest that it was his ambition that governed Madame de Longueville, not his passion that served her ambition and that of her house.

But, Victor Cousin might well say, how about Marcillac's cynical confession of his cynical wooing of Madame de Longueville?

I think he was in fact cynical when he began his planned seduction. As his enterprise progressed, I think it turned to love, a great devouring love. In love he lost his cynicism and found again the romantic adoration he had tried to forswear. And when love was ended, he reviewed his past ardors with hatred in his heart for his partner and for himself. When he wrote his Memoirs, he chose to tell the world: "I seduced her for my libertine pleasure and for my worldly advantage. I was a cad, if you like; I was not a dupe." He could not bear to write the truth, which was, I think: "I came to adore her with all the remainder of my dreaming youth. I fondly thought, and I gave the world to believe, that I ruled her spirit. But it is harder to keep from being ruled than it is to rule. She used me as the instrument of her ambition, and then she deceived me and cast me off. I was her dupe and fool, but a fool for the last time."

It is a pity to let such forecasts cloud the lovers' joy. They had their happiness, their hours of perfect trust, delicious sharings of experience.

In their colloquies and lassitudes they confided to each other their hidden ambitions. Marcillac's ambition may seem strange. He longed for the *tabouret*, the Right of the Stool, for his wife. Possessing this right, she could drive into the very court of the Louvre, not dismount at the gate. She could then enter the Queen's presence, pull forward a stool and plump herself down, if the Queen was sitting in her armchair.

There was at Court a whole hierarchy of chairs, running from throne down through armchair with fringe, armchair without fringe, armless easy chair with fringe, without fringe, hard chair with arms, without arms, folding chair, *tabouret* or upholstered stool, hard four-legged stool, hard three-legged stool. The ritual of sitting was most important. (Is its symbolism more laughable than that of kneeling?) The right to enter the Louvre seated in one's coach, the right to sit on a tabouret in the Queen's audience room were marks of pride and precedence granted to a few great families, such as the Condés, the Rohans, and the La Trémoilles. The Duchesse de Chevreuse, herself a Rohan, possessed the tabouret by special decree of King Louis XIII. The La Rochefoucaulds, though Dukes and Peers, did not. The Princesse de Marcillac must perforce stand, while favored Duchesses ostentatiously pulled forward their stools. It is true that the Queen acted with much tact, refusing to sit in Madame de Marcillac's presence, sometimes standing for hours on end.

"I saw myself so far from substantial rewards," says Marcillac, "that I settled on this one." He had in fact no right to it. The La Rochefoucaulds had less claim to the honor of the Stool, by blood or by military achievement, than a score of other ducal families. And the Prince de Marcillac was not the head of his house, only the heir to the dukedom. If he should be singled out for the award of the tabouret, a swarm of others with equal claims would press them furiously. Let the Princesse de Marcillac once make contact with her upholstered stool and half the Court would rebel.

Marcillac was not very reasonable in his ambition, but one never desires ardently what one desires only through reason.

He longed for this distinction because it was unreasonable, because its possession would set him illogically above his brother princelings. He saw nothing ridiculous in the point at issue. He could not regard it with the hearty common sense of the Duc de Montausier, who said: "My wife has good legs; she can stand up all right."

Nor, curiously enough, did Marcillac see anything peculiar in the fact that he was enlisting his mistress' aid to obtain this signal honor for his wife. Nor, apparently, did the mistress or the wife find anything peculiar in the situation. It must be that the modern mind is peculiar.

Marcillac devoted himself to love and to his ambition, which took the form in his mind of an aureoled stool, enskied in glory. He besought the Queen for his privilege, with humility, anger, and reproach. The Queen, well schooled by Mazarin, said neither yes nor no. She half promised, she made qualifications and difficulties, but she made her good will manifest. She summoned her Minister, who supported her promises and made the most of his southern charm. It was, however, one of his best maxims that he should not hurry in distributing rewards, as ordinarily time would relieve him of such necessities.

The circumstances are not clear, perhaps because Marcillac did not wish them to be so. The suggestion is strong that despite all his past disillusionments he yielded once more to the blandishments of Queen Anne and Mazarin. They convinced him that he had cruelly misjudged their eagerness to serve him, that this time they were sincere, with only the truth on their lips. Now there was news of a rebellion of the common people, desperate against taxation, in Marcillac's government of Poitou. He must take charge immediately of the repression. Mazarin promised solemnly that as soon as Marcillac should return to Court he would receive ducal rank. Of course the formalities would take a little time; but when they were once initiated they would permit the award of the tabouret to Madame de Marcillac.

The position of Madame de Longueville and the Condés in the matter is obscure. The lovely Anne-Geneviève certainly supported Marcillac's campaign, which implied co-operation with the Court and with Mazarin. However, at this time the Condés were drawing away from Mazarin, and they would be careful not to commit themselves too far or to put themselves under obligation to the Minister.

It is likely that Marcillac concealed from Madame de Longueville the extent of his commitments to Mazarin. Perhaps he was playing once more the dangerous double game, putting a stake on both sides. But gamblers say you cannot win by playing both red and black. Every now and then the zero turns up to ruin you.

We have come to May 1648. In obedience to his orders from Mazarin, Marcillac set off for Poitou to repress the rebellion in his province.

Just before he left, Madame de Longueville informed him that she was enceinte, and, as the French neatly put it, by the works of the Prince de Marcillac.

In Poitou he found that the rebellion was no great matter. Here and there peasants and bourgeois were attacking tax offices and clerks, more out of desperate fury than from any reasonable hope of accomplishing anything.

He writes: "I don't deny that their wretchedness made me regard their rebellion with pity, and that I would have been glad if the relief granted them had been more proportionate to their ills. But duty had the better of compassion, and, not doubting that the gentlemen of the Parlement had done all that time permitted, I brought to my task all the vigor necessary to dissipate the storm which had gathered. I imposed some sort of justice on those who had wished to make justice for themselves, and more by prestige than by violence I reestablished the royal authority in less than a week, without its costing the life or the honor of a single one of the King's subjects."

These are the words of an honorable and compassionate man. A little later, in a pen portrait of himself, he said: "I am little accessible to pity, and I should be glad if I were not so at all." His free acknowledgment of his pity in his account of the Poitou rebellion makes clear that his pen portrait erred, as so many portraits do, by delineating the man one would wish to be, not the true man one would conceal.

In September Marcillac reported the happy suppression of the rebellion to Mazarin, in letters which breathe excessive ardor to serve the Cardinal, with protestations of passionate devotion which go well beyond the fulsome formulas of seventeenth-century politeness. Mazarin replied that he read Marcillac's letters aloud to the Queen, that she was touched by his zeal for her service, that indeed she expected nothing less from his deep affection for her.

The coruscating winged tabouret swam in Marcillac's vision.

And then in October he learned that the tabouret had been officially granted to the wives of six Dukes whose titles had not been registered by the Parlement. A tabouret had even been awarded to a mere Countess, of a princely house, to be sure. There was no tabouret for the Princesse de Marcillac.

The good things and the bad which happen to us do not touch us according to their importance, but according to our sensibility.

Raging and menacing, Marcillac abandoned the affairs of his province and hurried to Paris.

CHAPTER X

Ambition, the Soul's Activity and Ardor

1648–1649

Now, in 1648, Anne of Austria had ruled for five years as Regent of France, with Mazarin for her agent, master, and probably lover. She had preserved the monarchy for her ten-year-old son, but she had lost the affection of her subjects. She lived in a world of enemies, and to their number she was adding daily.

The fault was not entirely hers. Wretched Europe was in fever, in the mood of hatred. The Thirty Years' War was drawing toward its end. And thirty years of war had cost cruelly dear, in blood, treasure, and human happiness. The French naturally blamed their rulers, the Queen and Mazarin, for every mischance in the field and for every new turn of the financial screw.

The idea of revolution was abroad. The rebel English had taken their own King, Charles I, prisoner, and his head sat most uneasily on his shoulders. In France there were some to applaud in secret the actions of the hardy Englishmen.

Misery reigned in the cities and the fields. Not only had the war come high, but Richelieu's internal administration had been very costly. Mazarin imposed new burdens on the people as he discovered new necessities for government expenditure. Each exaction found its victims and made its enemies. Since we must always take a fellow man to task for our miseries, the country seethed with hatred for the Queen-Regent and her paramour, these foreigners bent on destroying France.

Among the bourgeoisie the opposition centered in the Parlement de Paris. This body bore little resemblance to the cognate English assembly. Its functions were mostly judicial. It had, however, the obligation of registering the edicts of the King before they became law, and by delays, remonstrances, and pettifogging it could cause the government at least some inconvenience. It was not a representative body; its members bought their posts like seats on the stock exchange, and made a respectable profit on the perquisites of office. Nevertheless, the *parlementaires* were on the whole worthy representatives of bourgeois traditions and principles. They constituted a check, though an ineffective one, to the arbitrary power of the monarch. Anne of Austria hated and despised them. She was accustomed to say that she would never permit such canaille to attack the authority of the King her son.

The bourgeoisie, as represented by the *parlementaires,* was animated by vague aspirations toward a liberalizing of the regime and toward the tempering of absolutism by parliamentary checks and controls. The bourgeoisie had the enthusiastic support of the commonalty, who knew little about government but who knew that times were hard and the taxgatherers savage in the pursuit of the uttermost farthing. The bourgeoisie made common cause with a large part of the nobility. Their eventual aims were divergent, for while the bourgeois sought a liberalization of the monarchy in the direction of popular rights, the nobility sought a restoration of its local powers and privileges. The two classes were united in their immediate aims, which were to dispossess the royal favorite and to divide the lucrative posts at Court among their number. The hatred for royal favorites is nothing but desire for favor. One's annoyance at not possessing court favor is consoled and softened by the expression of scorn for those who do possess it. We refuse them our homage, since we cannot deprive them of what brings them general homage.

The desire for favor and the denial of favor will cause many strange reversals of position during these embroiled struggles of the Fronde, will turn rebel into patriot, and the contrary. We need not follow the tergiversations of the noble turncoats in any detail. Indeed, Marcillac himself admits that it is almost impossible to write any history of the Fronde, since its movers, having acted according to bad principles, have taken care to hide the facts. But for even a bare understanding the position of the chief figures must be brought up to date.

After Louis XIV, heir to the throne, and his brother Philippe, came their uncle Gaston d'Orléans, Monsieur. Timorous, inconstant, unstable as water, slouching in the palaces with his hands in his pockets, maddening everyone with his idle whistling, he was regarded with universal distrust. He had still his importance, however, and his party, composed of the vassals on his far-flung estates and of a crowd of hangers-on who drew from him immediate advantage.

Gaston's only child by his first marriage was Mademoiselle de Montpensier, the Grande Mademoiselle, so called not because she was so great but because she was so tall. This mettlesome lady was now twenty-one, and filled with the fire which descended upon the heroines of the Fronde. Being of the blood royal on both sides, she had determined to marry her cousin Louis XIV, though he was eleven years her junior. The opposition to this proposal by the Queen, Mazarin, and the unhappy boy himself threw her into the ranks of the dissidents. Her position was complicated by the fact that she hated the Condés, the nearest rivals to her family's greatness. Each military success of the Prince de Condé against France's enemies was for her an occasion for tears and grief.

Condé himself was loyal to the Queen and her minister. For them, for France, and for the House of Condé he fought and won the last battles of the dying war. After each glorious campaign he returned to Court with new demands, for governorships, for profitable charges, and for honors. Mazarin groaned and wrung his hands, but was forced to yield. As soon as possible, he would again dispatch Condé to his armies in the field. Fortune sometimes uses our faults to elevate us; there are uncomfortable men whose merit would be ill rewarded if one did not wish to buy their absence.

Condé's sister, Madame de Longueville, felt no fidelity toward the Queen. The thought of leading a civil war allured her. "I don't like innocent pleasures," she once said, and here was a pleasure with all the charms of guilt. Rebellion was, indeed, a bad bargain for her. But I think that we need not look for reasonableness in all her acts. Like so many of her spirited companions, she wanted chiefly to play a leading role in a national melodrama, to quick-change her costume for successive scenes of dark plotting, loud battle, sweet love.

To aid her rebellious purpose she enlisted, naturally, her lover Marcillac. She had also the wavering adherence of her husband, who was convinced in her presence, a prey to dreadful doubts in her absence. She had the entire support of her brother, the Prince de Conti, now nineteen years old. Adoring his sister, he would accept from her any policy and any order. He was emulous of his brother Condé and burned to prove that he too, given the opportunity, could be a great general. Unfortunately he was no source of strength. Misshapen and a weakling, he was unfit for arms; he must make his career as a churchman. Says the Cardinal de Retz: "He was a zero, who only multiplied because he was a Prince of the Blood."

We must introduce also the Cardinal de Retz, at this time only Bishop Coadjutor of Paris, who will contribute all he can to France's troubles. Small of stature, shortsighted, bandy-legged, maladroit, too clumsy even to button his clothes, he was none the less a fiery duelist, and sometimes carried a loaded pistol under his cassock. (Beaufort prodded it genially, remarking: "There is the breviary of Monsieur le Coadjuteur.") He was the gallant of numberless ladies, all of them in a position to serve his political advancement. He sought to take Madame de Longueville from Marcillac, but unsuccessfully, as he admits. His ambition was great, and was directed to one end: to obtain the post of Prime Minister by the ousting of Mazarin. (Self-interest, which blinds some, enlightens others.) For nearly ten years he had been building up his own party, distributing money to proud, poor gentlemen, courting the Paris mob, toadying at need, plotting at need against those to whom he truckled in public. He was a convinced and conscious hypocrite, a prince of hypocrites. (But hypocrisy is an homage that vice renders to virtue.)

Retz's Memoirs are not only one of the important sources for the period, they are a masterpiece of cynical penetration and brilliant writing. Let us hear how he analyzes the character of our Marcillac:

"There has always been something about the character of Monsieur de La Rochefoucauld that escapes you. He has been trying to practise court intrigue from childhood on, disregarding, to be sure, minor interests, which have never been his weakness, but not being cognizant of great affairs, which have not been his strong point. He has never been capable of handling any important business, and I don't know why; for he had qualities which in anyone else would have made up for those he lacked. His view of things has not been far-reaching enough, and at the same time he didn't see what was close at hand. But his common sense, very sound in speculation, together with his graciousness, his insinuation and his admirable easy manners should have more than made up for his lack of penetration. He has always suffered from an habitual irresolution, but I don't even know what to attribute it to. It couldn't have come from the fecundity of his imagination, which is anything but active. I cannot ascribe it to the sterility of his judgment, for although this is far from noteworthy in action, he has a good fund of reason. We can see the effects of this irresolution, though we don't know its cause. He has never been a real soldier, although he was very much the fighting man. He has never been, of himself, a good courtier, although he has always had the firm intention of being such. He has never been a good party man, although all his life he has been bound up in party affairs. That air of self-consciousness and timidity that you see in him in civil life turned into an apologetic manner in public concerns. He always thought he needed to apologize; this fact, together with his Maxims, which do not indicate sufficient faith in virtue, and together with his habit of always trying to get out of affairs as impatiently as he had got into them, makes me think that he would have done much better to learn his own character and to confine himself to passing, as he could have done, as the most polished courtier of his times."

Here, then, are the chief performers in the tragicomedy of the Fronde.

A "fronde" is a slingshot. At this time gangs of young hoodlums would meet by the Paris walls and fight savagely with their slung stones. These embattled "frondeurs" aroused public concern. When courtiers and bourgeois began to form in political gangs, they naturally received the appellation which was in the air.

The first event to be recorded was the sensational escape of the Duc de Beaufort from the Castle of Vincennes, on 31 May 1648. Beaufort, heir of the Vendôme house, leader of the *Importants*, had survived five years in his unhealthy prison. His partisans succeeded in planting one of their own men among the prison guards, and Beaufort and his accomplice bound and gagged the warden, went over the walls with a smuggled rope, and were spirited to safety. Thus one of the leaders of discontent, the darling of the Paris populace, was at large.

At this time the Queen and Mazarin sent the Parlement and the bourgeoisie into a fury. They proposed to withhold four years' salary from the members of certain accessory administrative bodies. These bodies made common cause with the Parlement. They drew up a charter of liberties for the kingdom, designed to be a French Magna Charta. Mazarin was obliged to yield temporarily.

At the end of August came some news useful to the monarchy. Condé had beaten the Spanish in the decisive battle of Lens. In the ensuing outburst of patriotic good feeling Mazarin felt himself strong enough to strike a blow at the Parlement. He arrested Broussel, one of the oldest and most respected Councilors. Broussel was the idol of the people, for he was incorruptible, poor, and the flagellator of the rich for their luxury and wickedness.

The news of his arrest sped through Paris. The commoners, in the immemorial Paris way, tore up the cobblestones from the streets and built barricades. The Queen ordered her Guards to disperse the mob; the Parlement called out the militia. The two armed parties faced each other across the barricades. No one quite liked to start shooting. The *parlemen-*

taires imposed a truce. A deputation of their number marched to the Palais-Royal in their ermine-trimmed red gowns and demanded a hearing. Their threats won the day; the Queen was forced to order the release of Broussel. But the Queen was resolved to punish those who had flouted her authority and that of her Minister and her son, the King.

Marcillac was absent in Poitou during these exciting days. He was busy pacifying the miniature revolt in his province, in the Queen's interest. But when word arrived that several tabourets had been awarded, but none for the Princesse de Marcillac, he dropped all his duties and hurried to Paris. This was in December 1648.

He had his interview with Mazarin. A living picture of pride and reproach, he entered the presence. He expected that the Cardinal would be covered with shame and confusion at the sight of one he had treated so shabbily. "But he never seemed to me less embarrassed. He received me as if I had all the thanks in the world to make him, as if, out of generosity and modesty, he did not want to give me the opportunity to thank him. He overflowed with tender civilities; one cajolery topped another. Prepared though I was to receive painful shocks, I wondered if he was not trying to make the best of his promises for the future, to make me think that though I was the last to be rewarded I was first in his intentions. But seeing that none of his fine speeches came to the point, I recognized that he was merely trying to pass off in vain expressions of good will an interview to which he would avoid giving any consequence for weeks to come. I realized that he was thinking that afterwards I would myself find it awkward to complain about what my long acquiescence would seem to have approved.

"That made me resolve to make him declare himself in whatever way and at whatever cost."

Marcillac did his best to pin down his slippery adversary. Mazarin tried to persuade him that the right of the tabouret was in itself a matter of no importance. Marcillac exploded with anger. "He proposed to me nothing more pleasing than to despise what I had not obtained, and what he did to dispose me thereto was to exaggerate with his Italian eloquence the glory of my birth, and to insist that he considered me superior to such mean considerations. In short one would have said, to hear him talk, that it was a great advantage to my wife not to dare to go to Court or to be obliged to stand up in a place where thirty other women were sitting down."

After all, what embitters us so against those who try their sharp practice on us is the fact that they think themselves cleverer than we are.

Marcillac took his rancor and his wounded pride to Madame de Longueville. From her he received every womanly consolation. It is a curious situation: the mistress, eight months pregnant with her lover's child, sharing his anger at the affront to his wife.

She was in fact delighted at Marcillac's clean break with Mazarin. This fitted perfectly her own mood, for she had been very busy plotting against the Minister. Pregnancy merely added piquancy to the conspiratorial gusto of the heroines of the Fronde.

(Those scholarly swains who still serve the Duchesse de Longueville accuse Marcillac of being her evil genius, who turned her from her natural virtuous bent to make her aid his petty ambitions. But note that Marcillac was in Poitou from May to December of 1648. There he acted with apparent sincerity in the interests of the Queen and Cardinal. Only when they disappointed him in the matter of the tabouret did he return to Paris. There he found Madame de Longueville implicated in a full-fledged conspiracy. He took his part in it, but as a subordinate, not as a director. He put his ambition at the service of his lady's.)

Madame de Longueville reported that Retz, the Bishop Coadjutor, had come to see her, and that an agreement had been made. She had guaranteed that her husband, her brother Conti, and others would cleave to the Parlement and defend Paris in case of trouble. Broussel and others promised the support of the Parlement; Retz vouched for his own adherents. The Bishop then tried in vain to interest the Duchesse in a bout of love, to sauce their conspiracy. The benefice, he notes in his Memoirs, was not vacant, though it was not being regularly served.

It was understood that Marcillac, the holder of the benefice, would join the cabal. Even had he wished, he could not abandon his mistress, swelling with his child. She fascinated him again, as she always had. And now she offered him the promise of high deeds. She was on the outs with her brother the Great Condé, but she would soon win him over. With the aid of Retz, of the Parlement, of all the French who hated Mazarin, the Regency would be overthrown and the party of right thinkers would rule. The way of ambition lay open; the way of prudence, of moderation, was not to be thought of. In fact, moderation cannot claim the merit of combating and vanquishing ambition, for they are never found together. Moderation is the soul's languor and sloth, as ambition is its activity and ardor.

There was indeed a base material difficulty in Marcillac's path. He had no money, and his father, bitterly opposed to this dangerous adventure, would give him no supplies. In this shameful pass he had recourse to his valet de chambre, Gourville. No, Gourville was no longer valet; he had doffed the livery for the fustian of the bourgeois. He had a magic way with money; he understood the world and the ways of men; and he would dare all for the welfare of the house he served. He knew what to do. He speculated in wheat, which the fear of the coming troubles rendered feverish, and soon he turned over a pretty profit to his master. He also turned over, on the side, a pretty profit for himself. In his dealings he made the acquaintance of the sharp men of affairs at Court, who regarded him with the greatest esteem. One of them said to Marcillac: "The next time you have any business, send me that man with the red coat."

While the malcontents prepared for violence, the court party strengthened its defenses. Its greatest weakness was the vulnerability of the young King, ill guarded in the Palais-Royal, in the midst of Paris. At any time the troublemakers might seize the King's person and make him sign whatever proclamations they pleased, announce to the world that a new Regency, the only legitimate one, was established, the Queen exiled, Mazarin proscribed with a price on his head, and long live the King!

Mazarin moved first.

On 5 January 1649, the eve of Epiphany, the Queen was very merry with her waiting women. She divided a Twelfth-night cake with them and with her sons, and she had the lucky bean. The Court retired.

At three in the morning the Queen roused her sons, descended the private staircase which led to a postern door, and so joined a carriage waiting at the gate of the Palais-Royal garden. Mazarin, Gaston d'Orléans, and a few others followed in their own carriages. The Prince de Condé summoned Madame de Longueville. She refused to move, alleging that she was near her term and that a journey in the ill-sprung coach over cobbled roads might prove disastrous. The excuse, excellent as it was, hid her purpose to remain with the rebels at all costs. Her husband was absent in his governorship of Normandy.

Finding her obdurate, Condé went to the bedroom of his young brother Conti, of whose fidelity he had every suspicion. He pulled Conti from his bed, thrust him peremptorily into the waiting coach. Conti, bewildered or timid, submitted to his masterful brother. He was soon to hate himself for his weakness and for the suspicion which he read in others' minds, that he had basely abandoned his sister.

The little procession, headed by the royal carriage, trotted westward, through Neuilly, Nanterre, Rueil, to the old château of Saint-Germain, a dozen miles from Paris.

The palace was bitter cold, most of the windows were void of glass, there were no beds or other furniture, for in those days even kings carried their equipment from one lodging place to another. A few cots and straw mattresses were found for the King and for some of the highest-born.

The plan was that Condé and his small faithful army should screen the gates of Paris and prevent the arrival of food for the populace. Give Paris a few days of hunger, vowed Condé, and it will find its loyalty again.

When the Parisians awoke, they learned that the King and Court had fled. Surprise cannot last long. The Parlement met, issued a sharp denunciation of Mazarin, forbade any soldiers to approach within twenty leagues of the capital, put its militia on a war footing, manned the Paris gates. The Parlement made clear that it was not rebelling against its King. It demanded merely that the rebellious Minister, Mazarin, return the King to his loving subjects.

The noble allies of the people declared themselves. There

was the great semi-independent Duc de Bouillon; there was the Bishop Coadjutor, Retz; highest in rank was the Princess of the Blood, the Duchesse de Longueville.

She was frantic with anger because Condé had carried off her faithful brother Conti to Saint-Germain. She was no less annoyed because her husband, the Duc de Longueville, who was supposed to be a rebel leader, was somehow deflected to Saint-Germain. Conti and Longueville must at all costs be rescued from the Court and brought to Paris, to assume their proper roles as virtuous defenders of the people's rights.

Who could restore them to their conspiratorial duties? Who but the faithful, the heroic defender of desperate causes, the Prince de Marcillac?

Wild rides in the service of gallant intrigue were always to Marcillac's taste. He took horse, with Gourville at his side. A chit from his mistress passed him through the Paris gates. He came to Saint-Germain, and was admitted on some specious excuse. To his irritation, the Court did not seem to take him quite seriously. Cardinal Mazarin led him aside. "Bring me out some money on your next trip, won't you, my dear fellow?" Marcillac refused haughtily, and Mazarin chuckled in his crimson sleeve.

Marcillac found occasion to plead with Longueville and Conti to join the Paris rebels. Longueville wrung his hands, regretting that he had ever let his wife entangle him in conspiracy. Marcillac feared that he or weak-willed Conti would disclose all to Condé. They must be irretrievably implicated in the revolution. But they hung back, fearing to take so bold a step.

Marcillac sent Gourville to Paris to report. "One may think it strange," he says, "that I confided a matter of such weight to Gourville, who was then very young and little known. But as I had tested his fidelity in other circumstances, and as he had a very bold and ingenious mind, all those whom I dealt with trusted him, and it was on the strength of his reports that we acted in concert."

Gourville, who had so recently doffed his lackey's livery, was now intriguing with all his power, for he knew that by such dangerous courses alone he might rise to be a person of condition. He carried the message to Madame de Longueville without mishap. The rebel council decided to offer Conti the post of general in chief if he would return to Paris. Thus he would oppose in the field his brother Condé. No matter; the appointment would probably appeal to his ambition.

Gourville was given this message to carry to his master in Saint-Germain. He had some trouble in leaving the city. But as he was a member of the militia he mounted guard with his company and succeeded in slipping away and galloping to the royal castle.

"It was immediately settled," he says, "that Monsieur le Prince de Conti would leave that evening at about eleven, with Monsieur le Prince de Marcillac and Monsieur de Noirmoutiers, and that horses would be held ready for them at the drinking trough near the Castle. [The Duc de Longueville was also of the party.] After this was resolved, Monsieur le Prince de Marcillac talked to me for a long time, to inform me of what he wanted me to say in Paris in case he should be taken prisoner, as he had no doubt he would be beheaded. After he had told me many fine things, I took it on myself to tell him that if he wanted them to be known by the person to whom he ordered me to tell them [Madame de Longueville, of course], he had better write them down, because I did not intend to abandon him in case of capture, and there was every likelihood that if he should be beheaded, I would be hung.

"When the hour set for the departure drew near, Monsieur le Prince de Marcillac, imagining that Monsieur le Prince de Conti would have some trouble in walking as far as the horse trough, told Monsieur de Berquigny, his first squire, to mount and take a led horse and join him in the forecourt outside the castle gate. Monsieur le Prince de Marcillac proceeded there and dismounted, and then went near the gate to see when the Prince de Conti would emerge, for he had not been warned of this arrangement. Chance would have it that a man came out carrying a torch, and Monsieur le Prince de Marcillac had to hide to avoid being recognized. At this instant Monsieur le Prince de Conti emerged, accompanied by Monsieur de Noirmoutiers, who was supporting him, because he could walk only with difficulty, to go to the horse trough and mount his horse."

Conti, Longueville, and Noirmoutiers, failing to find Marcillac at the rendezvous, decided to ride to Paris without him. Marcillac, after an agony of waiting, learned that he had missed them, and hurried on with Gourville to catch them up.

The Duc de Longueville was bitterly torn by conflicting purposes. On the way to Paris he halted and said to Conti: "Sir, let us return to the King and not set fire to all four corners of France, as will indubitably happen through this schism." But the young prince, who, says Madame de Motteville, "was more complaisant toward his sister than the husband was toward his wife, would hear nothing of it, and firmly withstood the laudable sentiments of the one who had the honor to be his brother-in-law. As for the Prince de Marcillac, I don't doubt that he entered gaily on the crime of lèse-majesté and that this journey seemed to him the most beautiful and glorious action of his life."

At any rate, as Gourville concludes the story, the Prince de Condé was extremely angry against the Prince de Conti, and still more so against Monsieur le Prince de Marcillac. Condé lost no opportunity to sneer at his ill-graced brother. In the

King's bedchamber at Saint-Germain he noticed a monkey chained to an andiron in the cold hearth. He bowed low to the monkey, exclaiming: "Hail to the generalissimo of the Parisians!"

In Paris all the new noble generals demanded from the city rewards commensurate with their rank, if not with their military record. The Parlement regarded their new-found zeal for parliamentarism with distrust. It was not sure its money was well spent.

In this moment of chill, Madame de Longueville, or some acute adviser, conceived a diplomatic master stroke. She drove to the Hôtel de Ville with the Duchesse de Bouillon by her side, each with a small son in her arms. The Duchesses entered the assembly hall amid a great flurry. They announced that their husbands, to demonstrate their profound trust and affection for the Parisians, had determined to confide to the citizens as hostages their dearest possessions, their wives and children. The citizens were moved to tender tears, most particularly by the mute propitiation of Madame de Longueville's advanced pregnancy. "Imagine," says Retz, "these two ladies on the balcony of the Hôtel de Ville, the more beautiful in that they appeared *négligées,* which in fact they were not. Each held in her arms one of her children, as beautiful as their mothers. The Place de la Grève was filled with people up to the roofs. All the men shouted with joy, all the women wept with emotion. I flung five hundred pistoles out the windows of the Hôtel de Ville."

The two ladies insisted that they had come to lodge in the Hôtel de Ville until the troubles should be over, with Right on its throne. The *parlementaires* were embarrassed, alleging that they had no means of properly accommodating such grand personages. The ladies, not to be daunted, sent home for their beds.

In another room of the Hôtel de Ville the high posts of the rebellion were being awarded. The bourgeois looked glumly on the chief contenders for generalship: Conti, a weakling who walked with difficulty; Bouillon, whose gout was so bad that day that he had to be supported by two retainers; and d'Elbeuf, a shifty timeserver, who had already fought for Spain against France. Without enthusiasm, the Parlement chose Conti and made the other two his Lieutenant Generals. To Marcillac was given one-third of a Lieutenant-Generalship, certainly one of the most peculiar military ranks on record. The other two-thirds of the appointment were given to Noirmoutiers and another. How the military trinity was to operate is not made clear. What only is clear is Marcillac's disappointment. Again, despite all the high promises made, he was relegated to a minor rank, while the important posts went to men whom he despised—and envied. We often draw vanity from even the most criminal passions, but envy is a timid, shameful passion that one never dares avow. What is worse, our envy always outlasts the bliss of those we envy.

Marcillac was in a touchy mood, ready to take and give offense. A casual remark of Bishop de Retz made of him a lifelong enemy. Retz tells how Noirmoutiers, in his shining steel cuirass flowered with tender ribbons, paid his respect to Madame de Longueville and her ladies in the Hôtel de Ville. "This mingling of blue scarves, ladies, cuirasses, fiddlers in the reception room and trumpeters in the square, made a spectacle which belonged rather in novels than elsewhere. Noirmoutiers, who was a great reader of *Astrée*, said to me: 'I can imagine that we are besieged in Marcilli [referring to an episode in *Astrée*].' 'You are right,' I answered. 'Madame de Longueville is as beautiful as Galatée; but Marcillac is not so fine a gentleman as Lindamor.'" The remark was overheard. "I have never been able to guess any other reason for that first hatred Monsieur de La Rochefoucauld felt toward me."

The new commanders set promptly to work. The fortress of the Bastille, held by the King's men, was summoned to yield. It was then, as in 1789, the symbol of arbitrary and unjust power. For the looks of things its commander waited until half a dozen cannon balls had rebounded from its walls, and then surrendered. "It was an amusing spectacle," says Retz, "to see the women at this famous siege bring their chairs into the Arsenal garden, where the battery was placed, as if they were going to hear a sermon."

Everywhere the women! They were in the thick of things, directing and misdirecting, making policy for advantage or caprice, bedding gloriously with their heroes.

Their servants, their agents, were the young nobles, perfumed and beribboned, whose long well-tended curls brushed the steel of their cuirasses. Warriors in laces, they were called. At their ladies' feet they sighed and postured, plucked from their puffed sleeves a scented sonnet bewailing the assassination of their hearts by the deadly flash from the adored one's eyes. Then the alarm would sound. These finicking fops would spring to horse and fling recklessly into battle, and would return—if they returned at all—with all their finery smutted with blood.

With the intrigues of policy and ambition were entangled the intrigues of love, spite, hate. When each lady must plot for the advantage of her husband's house and at the same time for the advancement of her lover, the interpretation of her aims and deeds baffles the historian.

Madame de Longueville, almost ready to be brought to bed, had the difficult task of advancing simultaneously the interests of the Duc de Longueville, the Prince de Conti, and the Prince de Marcillac.

Marcillac suffered at being relegated to the second rank of

command. His umbrageous spirit was constantly offended because he was overlooked, because he heard a reference to some secret decision which no one had thought to confide in him. He inspired a certain distrust in the inner circle. One never quite knew what he was thinking. The Bishop Coadjutor called him, by antiphrasis, "La Franchise," Old Frankness, Earnest Frank, for frankness was the quality he conspicuously did not possess.

He found himself assigned to minor tasks. His special duty was to rouse opposition to the government in his home country of Poitou. Naturally he was removed from the governorship by Mazarin, but he could still play upon the grievances of his friends and his multitudinous relatives with hortatory letters.

Another aspirant to supreme command arrived in Paris. The Duc de Beaufort, who had been in hiding since his escape from Vincennes, offered his sword and his personal charm to the rebellion.

Meanwhile Condé threw a cordon of loyal troops around Paris, to check the transport of food to the city. He had only about 6000 men, too few to make an effective blockade, but enough to harass the food convoys, to increase the risks of the suppliers, and to justify a shocking increase in prices.

The rise in the cost of bread provoked the populace, already exasperated by the many discomforts of life. To be cold and hungry in a Paris January tests the stoutest spirit. The chill rains fell; even the Seine was in a surly mood, rising above its banks and invading the riverain areas, so that one did one's errands in those streets by boat, but, says Madame de Motteville, with no Venetian pleasure.

The people were in an ugly mood. They blamed all their troubles on Mazarin and the court aristocracy. The King's servants, wearing his livery, were hunted through the streets. Poor Madame de Motteville was driven by a mob into the church of Saint-Roch, where High Mass was in progress. She knelt before the altar; a harridan tore off her mask, crying: "She's a *mazarine!* Kill her! Tear her to pieces!" As the rabble poured into the church, the priest halted his Mass. He succeeded in calming the people and in hustling Madame de Motteville into the safety of a confessional.

Strange gallows-bird characters appeared as agents of the Fronde, broke into great houses in the name of the people, and departed with sacks of silverware. In their enthusiasm they often mistook the homes of honest bourgeois for those of the noble enemy. The ardor of the bourgeois for rebellion began to cool.

Condé's besieging army seized some strategic suburban villages. The hungry people of Paris grumbled more and more. Their generals proposed dashing sorties against Condé. The citizens held back, dreading a full-scale battle against disciplined, well-equipped troops. The noble officers became very scornful of their rabble soldiery and dubious of the outcome of their enterprise.

Bishop Coadjutor de Retz, who had staked everything on the rebellion, made heroic efforts to bring it to success. He raised at his expense a regiment, which, since Retz was titular Bishop of Corinth, was called the First Corinthians. He proposed that the chalices, monstrances, reliquaries, and crucifixes of the churches be confiscated and melted down, but the laity thought his proposal impious.

As morale sank, Madame de Longueville played another masterly stroke. On January 28 she bore a son in the Hôtel de Ville. The father of her son was the Prince de Marcillac.

The great heart of Paris was deeply moved. Madame de

Longueville asked the Provost of Paris Merchants to be godfather, with the Duchesse de Bouillon as godmother. Thus was symbolized the unity of classes in a common war.

An imposing procession set out from the Hôtel de Ville, including the municipal magistrates, the councilors, the ushers in their robes, the city's archers wearing red and blue plumes. The Provost of Merchants walked with the Duchesse de Bouillon, holding her hand. Madame de Longueville rode in a padded carriage, holding up her newborn son to the applauding crowd. Fife and drum corps played the cortege to the church, where the Bishop Coadjutor waited. The godfather named the child Charles-Paris, "because of the place where he was born and in conformity with the custom always observed of giving children names suitable to the circumstances and accidents of their birth, to preserve the memory of it to posterity."

The Duc de Longueville received the compliments usual for a father. The actual father was once more disregarded, relegated to a minor role. He had to crane his neck to see the baptism of his own son. The happiness of the day was bitter to him.

The Bishop Coadjutor concluded the ceremony by flinging many pistoles to the cheering throng.

The Duchesse de Longueville sent her son to the family town house, to be tended by nurses wet and dry, and gave herself up to the delights of politics. "This princess took so much pleasure in the brilliant deliberations which went on under her eyes," says her contemporary biographer, Villefore, "that in spite of the precautions necessary after the incommodities of childbirth she hardly lost a day when she did not listen to reports and state her own views, although she was naturally very delicate. But joy gave her strength."

On 9 February Charles I, King of England, was beheaded

by his subjects.[1] The news, brought to Paris by galloping couriers, cast a chill over the Court, where England's widowed Queen and her two sons had taken refuge. However, those in power did not much fear that the French, schooled in respect for the divine right of kings, would follow the example of the heretic English. The Court was chiefly concerned because its poverty prevented it from draping all its horses in mourning black, as the etiquette of royal death prescribed.

Did the news from England in fact provoke mutinous mutterings of emulation among the commoners of Paris? There is some evidence of it, but on the whole strangely little. The masses had it firmly fixed in mind that they were rebellious only against the King's false ministers, and that they were loyal to the person of young Louis. "Querimus nostrum regem," read the device on the Frondeurs' banners.

The beleagured Parisians occupied themselves by making sorties to bring in food convoys. In some of these they were successful; in others they were overmastered by Condé's men.

On 19 February, says Marcillac, he went on such an expedition with his brother, the Chevalier de La Rochefoucauld, and with faithful Gourville. "The Marquis de Noirmoutiers went out with seven or eight hundred horse and some infantry to escort a large convoy which was coming in from the Brie region. I went to meet him with nine hundred horse to facilitate his passage, which the Comte de Grancey was trying to prevent with an equal number of cavalry and two regiments of infantry. The Marquis de Noirmoutiers and I were half a league apart, and we had agreed to aid each other in case the Comte de Grancey should attack either of us. Noirmoutiers sent me word to advance, as he was going to be charged upon, and I did what he asked. But the Comte de Grancey, learning

---

[1] On 30 January, say the English. But England still used the Old Style reckoning; France had adopted the Gregorian calendar.

that I was advancing, dropped his purpose of attacking Noirmoutiers, and turned toward me, to attack me alone. Noirmoutiers saw him make this evolution, but instead of doing for me what I had done for him, he continued on his way with the convoy and did not concern himself about a battle which he made so unequal by his retreat.

"The Comte de Grancey and I marched against each other with an equal number of cavalry, but with a great difference in the quality of the troops. He had besides two regiments of infantry, as I said. I made my first line of five squadrons and my second of four, commanded by the Comte de Rozan. As the Comte de Grancey was a thousand paces away from his infantry, I made all possible diligence to charge him before the infantry should arrive. When we were only twenty paces apart we found a ravine which separated us. We went along it for two hundred paces to pass around its upper end, and in this space of time part of the Comte de Grancey's infantry had time to come up. At the first volley all my troops fled and my horse was killed, and those of the Chevalier de La Rochefoucauld and of Gourville were killed too. One of my gentlemen dismounted to give me his horse, but I could not make use of it because one of the squadrons pursuing our fugitives was too close. The Comte d'Hollac, who was at its head, and three other horsemen came up to me, shouting to me to surrender. Determined not to do so, I went up to him, and, trying to run him through the body, I merely pierced his horse's shoulders, and my sword ran against his saddle and was bent by it. He fired at me point-blank. The shot was of such violence that I fell to the ground. His whole squadron, almost passing over me, fired at me. Six foot-soldiers arrived and seeing that I was well dressed, argued over my loot and disputed as to which one would kill me.

"At this moment the Comte de Rozan charged with his

second line against the enemy. The noise of their firing startled these six soldiers and they fled—I know no other reason why. Although my wound was very serious, I summoned up enough strength to stand, and seeing a horseman near me about to dismount, I took his horse from him and his sword too. I wanted to join the Comte de Rozan, but as I went toward him I saw that his troops were following the example of mine, and it was impossible to rally them. He was captured and wounded, and he died soon after.

"I joined the Comte de Matha and we arrived together in Paris. I asked him to say nothing of what he had seen Noirmoutiers do, and I made no complaint against him. I even put a stop to the punishment of the troops who had abandoned me, and I saved a percentage of them from being shot.

"My wound, which was serious and dangerous, deprived me of the means of seeing for myself what happened in the rest of this war, whose events were hardly worthy of being recorded."

An indication that men know their own faults better than is commonly believed the case is that when you hear them talk of their own conduct they are never wrong. The same self-love which ordinarily blinds them then enlightens them, and gives them such just opinions that it makes them suppress or disguise the slightest things which may be condemned.

Retz's account of the same action suggests that Marcillac's self-love had enlightened him so far as to make him suppress or disguise some of the circumstances.

"Noirmoutiers left with two thousand horsemen," says Retz, "to bring into Paris a convoy of five hundred cartloads of flour, which were at Brie-Comte-Robert, where we had a garrison. As he had information that the Comte de Grancey was coming from Lagny to oppose him, he detached Monsieur de La Rochefoucauld with seven squadrons to occupy a defile by which the enemy were obliged to pass. Monsieur de La Rochefoucauld, who had more courage than experience, was carried away by his ardor. He did not limit himself to his orders; he left his position, which was a very advantageous one, and charged the enemy very vigorously. As he was engaged against old soldiers and his own were new, he was soon overcome. He was wounded by a very severe pistol-shot in the throat. . . .

"The convoy would infallibly have been lost, if Noirmoutiers had not arrived with the rest of the troops. . . . He brought the convoy back to Paris without losing a single cart."

Of course, Marcillac was present at the battle and Retz was not. Of course, the two were jealous rivals, and Retz may well have weighted his account in Marcillac's disfavor. And yet Retz's account is more coherent, more in accord with normal military practice, than is Marcillac's. Notice that Marcillac assumes that he and Noirmoutiers were of equal authority, that their mutual communications were requests. But according to Retz, Noirmoutiers was in command and issued orders which Marcillac disregarded. One would think that Retz is reporting the understanding of the Paris committee.

Marcillac's wound preserved him from the danger of compromising himself. On the very day of the Brie-Comte-Robert expedition a Spanish envoy appeared before the Parlement, proposing military and financial aid from Spain against the wicked Cardinal Mazarin. The bourgeois and commoners hung back. They were sick of war, they distrusted their noble allies, and they were offended at the idea of a pact with the traditional enemy. The nobles, however, were inclined to favor the acceptance of Spanish aid. The nobility has always been drawn toward localism and internationalism: localism, the interest of the noble patrimony; internationalism, the interest of the noble caste, which readily overpasses the frontiers. Between localism and internationalism mere nationalism may be suppressed. The gentry, with their incessant talk of honor, referred mostly to personal and family honor, not national loyalty. Retz says frankly: "A prince of the blood should rather make civil war than abate anything of his reputation or his dignity."

But Marcillac, lying in his bed with a bullet wound in his throat, which was tended with the painful and ineffective devices of the time, could not have betrayed his country had he wished. He was in a mood of weak despondency. The councils met and made policy without concern for him, almost as if he did not exist. He reflected sadly that the man who thinks he can find in himself such resources that he can do without the world is much mistaken, but the man who thinks that the world cannot do without him is much more so.

His sick heart was full of regrets. He longed mostly for peace. A messenger from Gaston d'Orléans called on him on 24 February, only five days after the disastrous expedition. Retz reports the conversation (he had it direct from the messenger's mistress, who was one of his own troop of adoring ladies). "Flamarens [the messenger] found him in bed, in great distress from his wound and very sick of civil war. He told Flamarens that he had only got into it in spite of himself, and that if he had returned from Poitou two months before the siege of Paris he would certainly have prevented Madame de Longueville from embarking on that wretched business, but that I [Retz] had made use of his absence to get her embroiled in it, together with the Prince de Conti; that he had found the engagements in such an advanced stage that he could not break them; that his wound was again a new obstacle to his purposes, which were and would always be to reunite the royal house; that that devil of a Coadjutor did not want peace, and he was always hanging at the ears of the

Prince de Conti and Madame de Longueville to cut off all suggestions of peace; that his illness prevented him from acting upon them as he would have done otherwise; and that, if it weren't for his wound, he would do everything that one might require of him." (The "one" must mean the Queen and the Court party.)

The words have the ring of truth. (And they support our contention that Madame de Longueville was the dominant in their relationship.) They have the sound of the sickbed reflections of a man who is too weak to dissemble, a man who has played and lost, and who now longs chiefly for repose for his pain. One should deal with fortune as with one's health: enjoy it when it is good, have patience when it is bad, and never take violent remedies save in extreme need.

A few days later Retz suspected that Conti, prompted by Marcillac, was in secret negotiation with the Court. Again, on 4 March, he shows Conti at a loss in the council, "because he had not consulted his oracle." On the following days he says: "Monsieur le Prince de Conti and Madame de Longueville, inspired by Monsieur de La Rochefoucauld [i.e., Marcillac], wanted to bind themselves to Spain almost without restriction, because the measures they had thought of taking with the Court, by the agency of Flamarens, having fallen through, they threw themselves desperately to the other extreme, which is the character of all weak men."

It is possible that the three went over to the policy of rapprochement with Spain. Such revulsions on the part of angry and emotional people are familiar enough. However, Retz's accusation is unsupported by other evidence. It is possible, but, I think, unlikely.

At any rate it turned out that it made no difference what policy Marcillac and the nobles would choose. The leaders of the Parlement went directly to the Court and proposed peace. Thereupon the nobles crowded into the negotiations, each presenting his grievances and his demands. The fantastic rewards they asked for ceasing to rebel against legal authority show well their greed and rapacity, which are not obscured by all their fine talk of honor and fidelity. Madame de Longueville presented Marcillac's bill. He should have his governorship of Poitou restored, and the command of the Fusiliers with a salary of 18,000 livres, and of course the famous tabouret for his wife.

Mazarin yielded to the Frondeurs' exigencies. He had long since learned that he could please people by making them promises. He could please himself by not keeping them. "Time and I will arrange things," he used to say; *il tempo ed io*.

The Peace of Rueil was formerly declared on 30 March 1649. The conspirators had their promises, but they had actually lost, for Mazarin remained unscathed as Minister. The peace was well received in Paris, save among a few wrongheaded, or forward-looking, radicals, who put up cries of "We want a Republic!"

On 1 April the leading Frondeurs, among them the Prince de Marcillac, with his bandaged throat, paid their proper calls at Saint-Germain. The Queen received them with great hauteur, but Mazarin was as smiling and ingratiating as ever. He could not seem to bear a grudge.

It was, incidentally, All Fools' Day.

The courtiers who had remained faithful to the Crown stood by with ugly looks. They had benefited not at all from their fidelity, while the troublemakers had received the promise of large rewards for their return to duty. There were many bitter words *sotto voce*, and much shaking of noble heads. A lesson for the future had been taught them.

This was the end of the First War of the Fronde, often

called *la Fronde parlementaire*. It seemed to Marcillac, as to many others, a foolish war, all plotting and bluster. Nothing had been achieved. The noble conspirators had revealed themselves as frivolous, ineffective, mercenary, treacherous to their country. If Marcillac had shown himself in no better light than the others, at least he was conscious of a meaning in his conduct and in theirs. He was still learning about life. He had now seen civil war from the inside, and he knew how to esteem it and the actors in it. Great, splendid, dazzling actions are represented by political men to be the effects of great designs, whereas they are ordinarily the effects of humors and passions. Thus the war of Augustus and Antony, which is ascribed to their ambition to master the world, was perhaps only the effect of jealousy.

CHAPTER XI

The Land of Egotism

APRIL 1649 – JANUARY 1650

THE Peace of Rueil turned out to be merely an armed truce, as any wise observer might have predicted.

For a time good feeling was the fashionable air at Court. Mazarin had the outward adhesion of the important leaders, Gaston d'Orléans, the Condés, the men of the Parlement. Only the Duc de Beaufort, Retz, and a few others remained publicly unreconciled. The rabble of Paris also, having received no rewards, could not change so readily from hate to love. Mazarin and the Court dared not enter their capital city for months. In many an evil tavern ragged proletarians began to mutter of beheading their tyrants and setting up a republic. Pamphlets were passed from hand to hand, praising the courage of the revolutionaries of England and Venice. Footmen wearing the King's livery were beaten in the streets, and, says Montglat in his Memoirs, "people said that kings were no longer in fashion, that they were all right for the bad old days. Men talked openly of a republic, of liberty, alleging the example of England. They said that the monarchy was too old, that it was high time it should come to an end."

The murmurings of the lowly did not disturb Mazarin unduly. What concerned him more was the attitude of the Prince de Condé. This arrogant noble was deeply conscious of the rights of the Blood and conscious of the Court's debt to him for his resounding victories against Spain and for his effective throttling of the Paris rebels of the First Fronde. Regally ambitious, he made incessant demands upon the Cardinal for honors, grants of territory and office, privileges for his followers. He made his demands offensively, with the strong-blooded man's humorous contempt for the weakling. Mazarin found the payments to Condé awkward. He dodged and doubled, threw his favor as far as possible to Gaston d'Orléans' party in order to provoke as many jealousies as possible.

Whatever discovery we may have made in the land of egotism, there still remain many unknown territories.

The situation was agreeably complicated by the appearance of the Duchesse de Chevreuse in France, shortly after the Peace of Rueil. She had spent the months of the First Fronde in Brussels, actively rousing Spanish aid for the rebels. On her arrival in Paris the Court refused to receive her, and ordered her to her suburban castle of Dampierre. But Mazarin thought that since she must intrigue, it would be advisable to have her intrigue for his side. He made to her some tempting proposals. She cast up the arguments of advantage. Condé's party was riding high, carrying everything before it. She revolted at the thought of joining the triumphant procession. It is, in fact, more often through pride than through lack of penetration that we oppose so obstinately the accepted views. We find the first places taken on the good side, and we don't want the last places.

Madame de Chevreuse listened to Mazarin complaisantly. Her allies, Beaufort, Retz, and others of the Old Fronde, as they were called, were disturbed by the rising power of Condé.

She proposed to make a bridge between the Old Frondeurs and Mazarin, in the hope of bringing Condé low. She acted with her accustomed competence and by her usual means. But as she was now forty-eight, she had difficulty in using seduction in the service of ambition. She found a surrogate, turning over her beautiful twenty-four-year-old daughter, Charlotte de Chevreuse, to Bishop Coadjutor de Retz.

Their are few women whose merit lasts longer than their beauty.

Her understanding with Mazarin now justified her reception at Court. The Queen, her old playmate and companion, received her coldly, and refrained from embracing her. Afterwards Her Majesty remarked that Madame de Chevreuse had kept hardly any traces of her former beauty. It was evident that Madame de Chevreuse could not hope to regain her former mastery over the Queen's mind.

Marcillac, meanwhile, was living in a state of provisional satisfaction. He had again his governorship of Poitou, which returned revenue without requiring his presence. He had the promise of the tabouret for his wife. With the powerful backing of Condé he would surely secure the fulfillment of the Court's promise.

He had the honor of a distinguished liaison. The Duc de Longueville, alone in all France, was ignorant of his wife's infidelity. But Condé accepted it comfortably. He admitted Marcillac to the family councils, wherein the two brothers and the sister plotted their aggrandizement. Marcillac shared in the Condés' domineering pride, and strove to outdo his mentors. (We arrogate to ourselves the defects opposed to the ones we possess; when we are weak, we boast that we are obstinate.)

He was happy in the tender dealings of his love. Madame de Longueville's alluring languor, hiding her steely core of will and purpose, made a fitting match for his outward air of courtly competence, beneath which lived his brooding, self-questioning insecurity. The two could play together the précieux games they delighted in, analyzing their love and their hearts. When she asked the inevitable question: "Are you really true to me in your secret self?" he could ingeniously reply that constancy in love is a perpetual inconstancy, by which the heart attaches itself successively to all the qualities of the loved one, giving the preference now to one quality, now to another; so that this constancy is merely a fixed inconstancy, concentrated upon a single subject.

But there were cold aftermoments, when he sat alone with his sad heart from which all ardor had fled, when he remembered his sighs and protestations almost with shame. Examining his own actions and those of his companions, he reflected that there is no passion in which love of self reigns so mightily as in love. One is always more disposed to sacrifice the repose of one's beloved than to lose one's own.

For the moment, however, he strove to serve his lady's interests in the land of egotism. His actions at this period are very obscure. Retz tells us that since the Prince de Conti's rewards were slow in coming from the Cardinal, Marcillac tried for a time to impose Conti upon the still unreconciled Frondeurs, so that Mazarin would have to buy him back. If Marcillac made such an effort, nothing came of it. Again on 15 June 1649 we find him present with Conti at a political dinner given by one of the Bouillons, which was enlivened by the twenty-four violinists of the King.

Three days after the Bouillon dinner there was a great to-do in Renard's fashionable restaurant. A party of friends of the Queen and Mazarin were dining peaceably. The Duc de Beaufort entered, and after some high words he flipped the tablecloth from the table, upsetting the dishes and wine on the guests' finery. Swords flashed out; there were many challenges, followed by a few duels. The mood of the gentry became tense. Beaufort and Retz paraded Paris, each with a hundred armed gentlemen and fifty liveried servants behind his carriage.

In September of this year we get a glimpse of the plotters at work. Gaston d'Orléans was very limp in his loyalty to the Court. He was governed, however, by his favorite, the Abbé de La Rivière, who had more to gain by fidelity than sedition. Madame de Longueville, Marcillac, and Conti, who had "vast designs," sought to bring over Monsieur by tempting his favorite. They offered to La Rivière the post of Prime Minister, to replace Mazarin, if he would persuade his master to rebel. But La Rivière found the proposition too hazardous. The only thing he wanted anyway was a Cardinal's hat. Says Madame de Motteville: "This proposal to make him Prime Minister, which was chimerical in itself, must have seemed so to the person to whom it was made, and it is to be presumed that the impossibility of it was evident to Madame de Longueville, the Prince de Conti and the Prince de Marcillac. They no doubt made it to the Abbé de La Rivière on the principle that one must chance everything with those who possess great ambition, because it is easy to dazzle them by showing them the ways of gaining what they desire. It makes no difference if the ways are good; their passions ordinarily prevent them from examining the means, and the slightest hope deprives them of sound reason."

Marcillac was deputed to make a second effort to win over La Rivière. He whispered his proposals in La Rivière's ear one day at Court, under the very eye of Her Majesty. "This second attack was more vigorous than the first. The Queen perceived it, and as the Prince de Marcillac was suspect to her because of his close attachment to Madame de Longueville, she asked the Abbé de La Rivière what they had been talking of together. He dissimulated, and replied coolly that they had talked in general terms about the present situation."

To be sure, Marcillac himself tells a different story. He says that the overtures were made by the Abbé de La Rivière. But as nothing came of the proposed plot, we may be pardoned for not examining it in detail.

Mazarin, thoroughly aware of the cabals forming against his rule, cast about for new allies. He dealt with the Duc de Vendôme, father of the Duc de Mercoeur and his junior, the Duc de Beaufort. He proposed that Mercoeur should marry his beautiful, well-dowered niece, Laure Mancini. The elderly Duc de Vendôme was tired of factionalism, and he had a ducal eye for a good marriage. He gave his consent to the match. Beaufort was, however, outraged.

Condé's party took alarm. The elevation of the Vendômes threatened the Condés, and menaced especially certain privileges of the Duc de Longueville. Madame de Longueville summoned Marcillac to her assistance. The mistress had aided the lover in obtaining honors for the lover's wife; it was only fair that the lover should now serve the interests of the mistress's husband.

Here as elsewhere we see Madame de Longueville as the fount of ideas and the source of action. Madame de Motteville, a keen observer, says that Condé permitted himself to be led by this Princess to do what he would never have done of his own accord. Condé, who had at first carelessly approved the marriage of Mercoeur and Mazarin's niece, now revoked his approval. He upbraided Mazarin in public with his usual coarse and violent language, and proclaimed that he would not again salute him or speak to him. With his princely hand he pulled the Cardinal's little goatee. "Good-bye, Mars!" he shouted, and turned on his noble heel. He went off with a roar of laughter, to repeat his witticism to all his friends.

To any gentleman, and particularly to a southern Italian, such an offense calls loudly for vengeance. But for the moment Mazarin bided his time, and devoted all his effort to making friends of the Old Frondeurs and the Parlement of Paris, at the same time trying to break up the precarious harmony between Gaston d'Orléans and the Condés.

Pretending that his memory was short, that a tug at the beard was no more than an excellent jest, Mazarin obtained a specious reconciliation with Condé. Marcillac, with the perspicacity that comes after the fact, gives us a shrewd analysis of the Cardinal's behavior at this period. "The Cardinal, easily banishing all remembrance of the obligations he had toward the Prince de Condé, remembered only the annoyances he had received from him, and on the pretext of a sincere reconciliation he lost no opportunity to take advantage of Condé's too great confidence. He soon recognized that Condé's designs went no farther than to frighten him. He thought he should confirm Condé in this way of thinking and pretended to fear him, not only to prevent Condé by these means from taking more violent steps against him, but also to execute more surely and easily the project he was preparing against Condé's liberty. With this purpose, all his speech and action showed dejection and fear. He talked only of giving up politics and leaving the Kingdom. Every day he made some new proposal to the friends of Monsieur le Prince de Condé to give him carte blanche. Things went so far that he agreed that henceforth there would be no award of provincial governments, important posts, charges in the King's household or offices of the Crown without the approval of Monsieur le Prince, Monsieur le Prince de Conti, and Monsieur and Madame de Longueville, and that an accounting of the administration of the finances would be rendered them. These promises, so extensive and given in such general terms, had all the effect that the Cardinal could hope. They dazzled and reassured Monsieur le Prince and all his friends. They confirmed everyone in the opinion they had conceived of the Cardinal's discouragement, and they made even his enemies desire to keep him in place, through their belief that they would gain their own advantage more easily in the weakness of his ministry than in a more vigorous and better established government. In short he gained with much address the time he needed for the designs he was forming against Monsieur le Prince."

A part of his deep plotting was his announcement of the award to the Prince de Marcillac of the privileges so long sought. Marcillac might at last enter the Louvre courtyard in his coach, and his wife might gloriously sit on her stool in the Queen's presence.

Marcillac had his moment of radiant joy. But alas, it was only a moment. It was fated that the tabouret was to be forever proffered to Madame de Marcillac and forever withdrawn, to the sound of ghostly laughter, as she was about to depress her princely posterior. The nobles of the Court, of whom some dozens had a better right to the tabouret than did Marcillac, rose in a fury of protest. Mazarin knew, of course, that they would do so. Marcillac accuses him of stimulating the protest, but indeed Mazarin had no need to suggest or stimulate.

The nobles met in private conclaves and drew up a Humble Remonstrance, couched in language far from humble. They demanded that the award of the tabouret to Marcillac be revoked, and that other similar awards made in previous years be likewise annulled. Marcillac and by extension his protectors the Condés found themselves the objects of widespread rancor.

The new enemies were both those who thought themselves passed over and insulted by the award, and those who had received recent favors and now saw themselves threatened with the loss of them, thanks to the agitation Marcillac had aroused. Of these last was Madame de Montbazon, that coarse and hearty baggage, who had recently obtained a tabouret for her daughter. She proclaimed to all ears that she was going to cut off the Prince de Marcillac's *je ne sais quoi* and send it to Madame de Longueville in a silver dish.

Marcillac, alarmed at the outcry and unwilling to embarrass his patron, went to Condé and offered to withdraw his claim. But Condé felt that if he should consent to the annulment of the award to his protégé he would sustain a distinct loss of face as a party leader. His *gloire,* that interest of prestige which so concerned the heroes and heroines of Corneille, was implicated. He promised to support Marcillac through thick and thin.

The offended nobles presented their formal protest to the Queen, and threatened to summon the States-General, which had not met for thirty-five years. The Queen was disturbed; there was no telling what forward schemes the States-General might propose. The matter was getting out of hand. She yielded to the nobles, and revoked all the tabourets and other exceptional privileges which had been granted since the death of Louis XIII. Perhaps this revocation had been her aim, or Mazarin's aim, in making the award to Marcillac. But she now frankly hated him, says Madame de Motteville.

The result, which Mazarin must have foreseen, was a severe blow to the prestige of Condé. He had lost with the Court without making a corresponding gain with the enemies of the Court. In the world of intrigue, honest purpose has no merit.

Many of the shrewd gamesters among the great shifted their stakes, to play on the Cardinal's side.

Marcillac was in a passion of rage, not against the nobles who had balked him—they were merely defending their own interests, properly enough—but against the Queen and Mazarin. He could not admit that the good we have received from a person should make us respect the harm he does us. The injury done him was a wound to his pride. He had thought himself sharper than his opponent, and that is a sure way to be deceived. He felt himself ridiculous; nothing could be less tolerable for a La Rochefoucauld. Those who are taken in by our own finesses seem by no means so ridiculous as we appear to ourselves when the finesses of others have captured us.

In his swelling anger he found a recourse unusual for his times. He sat down to write a record and defense of his actions in the affair of the tabourets. Except for possible contributions to the budgets of précieux salons, this is his first literary effort, at any rate the earliest that remains.

"I do not presume enough upon my virtue," he begins, "to dare to allege that I would have hated Cardinal Mazarin if he had loved me. Perhaps he would have done things in my interest which would have disguised from me all we have seen him do against the interests of the State, and a false constraint would possibly have made me die in an evil cause wherein signal obligations might insensibly have engaged me. I admit then that he may say that I would have been his friend if my misfortune had so willed it that he had been my friend, that I would have defended his crimes if there had been reason to believe that I would have profited by them, and in short that I could have committed great injustices lest it might appear that I would have committed acts of great ingratitude."

It is very *fin*, very subtle. He has learned from the précieux to weigh motives on featherweight scales, to analyze character with the utmost cunning. The reader of today finds the *Apologie de M. le Prince de Marcillac* in the great tradition of French literature, which is forever concerned with the psychological examination of difficult states of spirit. But perhaps it is too *fin*. By dint of weighing motives, Marcillac overlooked some of the most obvious ones. We may understand from the *Apologie* that this introspective analyst, a player of systems, would be no match in action for Mazarin, a more instinctive gambler.

The *Apologie* is frank and revelatory. The paragraph quoted is evidence of Marcillac's effort to see clear in himself, to admit his shortcomings of character, to tell his truth. He admits too much. Already he sees his inward self too lucidly, with a masochistic pleasure in its defects. He knows already that we try to do ourselves honor for the faults we do not wish to correct. Too significantly he entitles his outburst his *Apologie*. A La Rochefoucauld should not apologize. This he soon realized; he did not publish the *Apologie*, though it is evidently written with the printer in view.

I like to think that it was Madame de Longueville who dissuaded him from publication. She knew by instinct that such a querulous complaint was unsuitable for her noble lover. Let him justify himself by the sword, if need be, not by parading his disappointment in words. He was too much inclined to be miserable anyway; did he enjoy being wretched?

He thought it over, and found a new commentary to make on his state of mind, and this, as usual, he could put to the account of humanity. "Those who think they have merit take pride in being unhappy, to persuade others and themselves that they are worthy of being the butts of Fortune."

He destroyed his *Apologie*. It survived in a single copy which a friend preserved, fortunately for us. For it is, say the

French professionals of letters, "one of the first models of French prose of the seventeenth century, natural, sinewy, firm and free in movement." [1] Again, "It is indeed the first model of true classic prose, that of the gentleman, adapting himself in turn to all manners and dialectics, those of eloquence and irony." [2]

Having discharged his bile in written words, Marcillac now gave himself utterly to the pleasing business of intrigue. The situation was briefly this: the Queen and Mazarin had determined to bring low Condé and his party, because their power was great and their demands greater. Gaston d'Orléans, previously on good terms with Condé, had turned jealous, and saw in the chance of Condé's downfall an opportunity to be first at Court. The Old Fronde, Retz, Beaufort, Madame de Chevreuse, had tried to join forces with Condé and had been rebuffed. They now made a secret rapprochement with Mazarin, in order to humble the haughty Condé. Retz was certain that with Condé out of the way he would be able to outwit Mazarin and dominate Gaston d'Orléans, become, in short, master of the realm. His ally Madame de Chevreuse pictured herself as again ruling the mind and action of the Queen. "Her hope was the better founded," says Madame de Motteville, "in that she and her cabal proposed in the future to possess the Queen by force, and consequently with the more surety."

Condé refused to heed the hints that were dropped of the coalition against him. Only great men have the right to have great faults. Condé's great fault was his contempt of lesser men, his unwillingness to explore their minds to discover their mean purposes. "He would rather win battles than hearts," says the Duchesse de Nemours, who was the daughter of the

[1] J. Gourdault, in *Oeuvres de La Rochefoucauld*, II, 436.
[2] G. Grappe, *La Rochefoucauld*, 58.

Duc de Longueville by his first marriage. "In matters of consequence the three Condés liked to infuriate people, and in ordinary life they were insufferably unpractical. They wore such a mocking air, they said such offensive things, that people could not endure them. When one paid them a visit they showed such scornful boredom, they indicated so openly that they were inconvenienced, that it was not hard to conclude that they were doing everything possible to hurry the guest away. No matter what one's rank, one waited endless hours in Condé's antechamber, and often after a long wait he would dismiss all his callers without having seen them. The Princes were merciless toward those they disliked, and they were incapable of any gratitude for services rendered them. Thus they were equally hated by the Court, the Fronde, and the common folk, and no one could get along with them. All France suffered impatiently this behavior, and especially their excessive pride."

Marcillac was dimly aware of the set of events. He advised Condé never to go to the Royal Council with Conti and the Duc de Longueville. The presence within Mazarin's power of the three titular leaders of the Condé party might tempt the Minister too far. Condé laughed off the warning.

On 14 January 1650 the Cardinal concluded a secret pact of alliance with Retz and the Duchesse de Chevreuse. He now felt strong enough to strike.

He asked Condé offhandedly to sign an order for the arrest and imprisonment at Vincennes of a notorious rebel. The order included the provision that troops should be stationed at strategic points to check any attempt at rescue by the populace. Condé signed, unconcerned.

On the morning of 18 January (as Madame de Motteville tells the story), Condé called on the Cardinal in his study in the Palais-Royal. Mazarin abounded with civilities, and asked especially that the Duc de Longueville should be present at the afternoon meeting of the Council. Condé strolled to the fire, and observed the Cardinal's secretary writing busily at his table. The secretary fumbled with his papers, slid them under a cover, talked with embarrassed volubility.

Condé had midday dinner with his mother. She was oppressed by some presentiment or some warning given her. She warned her son to be on his guard, for surely the Court had turned against him. Condé treated the maternal timorousness with good-humored scorn.

After dinner he went with his mother to the Queen's bedchamber to pay his respects. The summons to the Council came. Condé left his mother with a casual adieu. He was never to see her again.

Condé found Mazarin in a nearby room and began to upbraid him for the unfulfillment of certain promises. He shouted so loud that the Queen feared something had gone wrong with the plans.

The Prince de Conti and the Duc de Longueville entered the room. Mazarin said to an aide: "Everything is ready. Tell Her Majesty that she may come to the Council." This was the signal that the Queen should give the last orders.

"Do your duty," said the Queen to the Captain of the Guards, Guitaut. She took the eleven-year-old King into her oratory, bade him kneel and pray for the success of her enterprise.

Guitaut entered the Council Room. Condé, thinking that he came to ask some favor, asked him what he wanted. Guitaut answered: "Sir, what I want of you is this. I have an order to arrest you, your brother the Prince de Conti, and Monsieur de Longueville." Incredulous, Condé replied: "What, Monsieur Guitaut, you are arresting *me!*" Then, after a moment: "In the name of God, return to the Queen and tell her that

I beg to speak to her." "It will be no use," said Guitaut, but to oblige Condé he went to do his bidding.

Condé turned to the others, his face distorted. "Gentlemen," he said, "the Queen is arresting me! And you, brother! And you, Monsieur de Longueville!" He asked the Chancellor and another gentleman to crave an audience with the Queen and the Cardinal. They left the room obediently.

Guitaut returned with the message that the Queen would not see Condé, and had bidden him execute her orders. Condé mastered himself. He said calmly enough: "Well, I am willing, I obey. But where are you going to take us? I hope it's some warm place."

"My orders are to take you to Vincennes," said Guitaut.

"Very well," said Condé. "Let's be going." He started for the door which led to the Cardinal's apartments. "Not that way," said Guitaut. "I have Comminges and twelve men posted there." Condé turned to the company with a tranquil face and made his farewells, asking all to remember him and to testify on all occasions, like the gentlemen they were, that he had always been a loyal servant of the King.

Guitaut summoned his guards and conducted the Princes to the waiting carriages. The Prince de Conti said not a word and offered no resistance. The Duc de Longueville, who was old and lame, had to be supported, for he was overwhelmed, picturing death before him.

Condé marched to the coach door with a soldierly step, and waited there for the others. He tried to learn from Guitaut whether the imprisonment was a prelude to execution, but Guitaut knew nothing beyond his immediate orders.

Guitaut bade his brother, Comminges, take his place beside Condé.[3] To dodge any possible hindrance, the party took a

---

[3] This Comminges was an amusing fellow, and a scholar in the many idle hours afforded by guard duty. He was sent by the Maréchal de Bas-

roundabout route over very bad roads. Troops of soldiers were posted along the way, according to the orders Condé himself had signed, not knowing their purpose.

The drivers whipped their horses over the frozen ruts of the side roads. At one point Condé's coach upset. "As soon as it tipped over," says Madame de Motteville, "Monsieur le Prince, whose physique, agility, and address were incomparable, found himself out of the coach in open country. More quickly than a bird from its cage he dodged his escorting guards and began to flee. Miossens ran after him and stopped him on the edge of a ditch wherein he was about to throw himself. Said Condé: 'Don't be afraid, Miossens; I'm not trying to escape. But really, you see what you could do if you wanted to.' Miossens replied that he begged the Prince very humbly not to ask him a thing which he could not do as a man of honor; he was sorry to be obliged to such fidelity, but he had to obey the King and Queen.

"When the carriage was righted, Comminges ordered the driver to go at top speed. Monsieur le Prince burst out laughing: 'Don't be afraid, Comminges, nobody is coming to my aid. I assure you that I have taken no precautions against this journey.' He then asked Comminges what he thought of his imprisonment, for as for him, he could not guess the reason. Comminges said that he knew nothing of it at all, but he was bound to believe that the Prince's greatest crime was like that of Germanicus, who became suspect to the Emperor Tiberius because he was too worthy, too great, and too much beloved.

---

sompierre to tell Madame de Villars that he did not love her. Madame de Villars attempted a dramatic suicide by swallowing her diamonds. Comminges took her by the throat and forced her to disgorge. He counted the diamonds and found one missing. He nearly strangled poor Madame de Villars before he obtained the last one. He pocketed the lot, regarding it in the nature of treasure cast up by the sea, so to speak.

"On entering the castle of Vincennes, Condé seemed somewhat moved, and he asked Miossens to assure the Queen that he was her very humble servant. When they arrived in the room they were to occupy, they found no beds there. The three prisoners were obliged to amuse themselves by playing cards. They passed the whole night in this occupation, and Comminges told me that it was with much gayety and repose of mind. The Prince de Condé, rallying the Prince de Conti and the Duc de Longueville, said a thousand agreeable things. In addition to the card playing, Monsieur le Prince had a great dispute with Comminges on astrology. And I have heard from this same Comminges, who spent a week with him, that he had never passed such pleasant hours as those in which he enjoyed his conversation, and that if he had not been touched by compassion for the Prince's misfortune he would have liked to spend the whole time of the Prince's imprisonment with him."

Meanwhile the Queen prayed earnestly in her oratory until news was brought her that the Princes were safe in jail. She and Mazarin congratulated each other. Gaston d'Orléans cried jubilantly: "There's a fine bag! They have taken a lion, a monkey, and a fox!"

But jubilation did not last long. For the signal was given for the Second War of the Fronde.

CHAPTER XII

Love of Glory,
Fear of Shame . . .

JANUARY 1650 – FEBRUARY 1651

THE news of the arrest of the Princes ran with the wind through the swarming streets of Paris. The populace, uncertain as to the political significance of the imprisonment, recognized that any bold stroke, whether of repression or rebellion, was an occasion for rejoicing. The little men emerged from their dark dens, built bonfires in the streets, danced around them, slaked and encouraged their thirst by visits to the wineshops. Just so had they celebrated Condé's great victories at Rocroy, Nordlingen, and Lens.

Faithful Gourville brought the news of the Princes' arrest to Marcillac. Gourville was now a substantial man, the friend of substantial men. He had wormed his way into the confidence of Mazarin, who knew a good man when he saw one. But like his noble mentors he was capable of playing a double game. When he learned that his old master was threatened, he ran to give warning.

"The order is out for your arrest," said Gourville. "Now that the chiefs are taken, their dangerous servants will be taken too. You must escape, you, the Duc de Bouillon, the Vicomte de Turenne."

"And Madame de Longueville?"

"Naturally she will be taken too. She is ordered to report to the Queen in the Palais-Royal. There she will be informed of the Queen's will."

Marcillac did not hesitate. He made all haste to the Hôtel de Condé. There he found Madame de Longueville, stunned by the turn of fortunes. She must flee, he told her, flee into Normandy, her husband's province. She must rouse the Parlement of Rouen to espouse the cause of the Princes; she must take possession of the fortresses of Normandy, particularly the stronghold of Le Havre.

There was no time to lose, and none was lost. Madame de Longueville kissed her children good-bye, most warmly the year-old son fathered by her lover. Marcillac bundled her into the coach of her good friend Anne de Gonzague, Princesse Palatine, and drove with her to a small secret house which the Princesse Palatine kept as a hideaway from prying eyes. The house was brilliantly illumined with torches, to indicate joy at the Condés' downfall.

When night fell the Princesse Palatine's coach set cautiously forth, bearing Madame de Longueville and her sulky stepdaughter, Mademoiselle de Longueville, who hated her, but hated the prospect of imprisonment more. Before and behind the coach rode a number of well-mounted horsemen, amply cloaked and hatted, putting on an air of having met by the merest coincidence. Among them were Marcillac and Gourville. The party passed a Paris gate, whether by deception or bribery. It traveled all night, and reached Rouen on the following day. The ladies emerged, bruised and lightheaded from a headlong hundred-mile journey in a tossing, ill-sprung coach.

The Parlement de Rouen assembled to greet the wife of its liege lord. Madame de Longueville took a high tone with the lawyers and magistrates, summoned them to aid their imprisoned master, to rebel against Mazarin's authority. The magistrates immediately conceived manifold objections, they paltered and appealed to law and precedent. Finally they respectfully prayed their lady to retire from her city.

"We are wasting our time here," said Marcillac. "Let us get on to Le Havre, and make sure of its citadel."

But at Le Havre the Governor—who had received his appointment by Madame de Longueville's special favor—refused to receive her. She could not, after all, storm a fortress barehanded. The little party, now looking ominously like a band of refugees, made its way to Dieppe. There it was received at least with courtesy. Mademoiselle de Longueville, irked by the long flight, broke away from her stepmother and took refuge in one of her family's country houses.

Madame de Longueville, Marcillac, and Gourville took counsel together. It was decided that Marcillac should hurry to his homeland of Poitou and rouse its nobles to rebellion. Gourville should return to the service of Mazarin, pursue his own advancement, and help the cause when occasion should arise. Madame de Longueville would look to the defense of Dieppe against the royal authority.

Let us now follow for a moment the adventures of Madame de Longueville. As supreme commander in Dieppe she organized its preparations for defense, with her own hand trained the cannon on the tower of the castle. But when a royal army approached, the citizens, insensible to her conquering eyes and lordly smile, announced their fidelity to the King. Madame de Longueville and a few faithful gentlemen and waiting women slipped out a postern gate and rode to a nearby port where a small vessel had been stationed to await them. The sea was high and embarkation difficult. A sailor took the Duchesse in his arms to carry her out to the ship. A wave caught them; he staggered and dropped her into the sea. She was rescued and brought dripping to shore. With her women, she rode the rest of the night to a secluded friendly house and there hid for a fortnight. She was told that the captain of her escape vessel had been bought by the Cardinal; if she had not been doused in the sea she would have been carried straight to prison. One of her agents then made a discreet bargain with an English sea captain in Le Havre, paying him well to save an unhappy young gentleman who had fought an unlucky duel. Madame de Longueville, in man's disguise, came to the rendezvous without mishap and was borne to Rotterdam, in the Spanish Emperor's dominions. Thence she went to Stenay, a semi-independent state between France and the Spanish Netherlands which was ruled by the Lorraine family. Here she was welcomed by the Vicomte de Turenne, a junior of the Lorraine house. He had long been sighing for a glance of mercy from her radiant orbs.

Marcillac, meanwhile, made his way to Poitou. Disdaining the safe way by sea, he passed through Paris, and no doubt did a little conspiratorial business there.

Jogging along the familiar homeward way, he had plenty of time to reflect on the events of the previous days. The imprisonment of the Princes gave him a great opportunity, for he was outranked by few among Condé's friends still at liberty. He could rise as far as his courage, decision, will, and luck would bear him. There are no accidents so unfortunate that clever men may not draw some advantage from them, and none so fortunate that imprudent men may not turn them to their own prejudice. He must prove himself one of the clever men of the world, bold, fierce of will.

And then he would fall into a weary fit, the old self-questioning mood he so hated and feared. Did he in fact possess that grim force of will one recognizes in simple people, who progress toward their ends with animal sureness? On the battlefield he had proved his valor to men's eyes, but had he proved it to his own heart? And what is valor? Love of glory, fear of shame, the purpose of winning fortune, the desire to make one's life comfortable and agreeable, a longing to bring others low, are often the causes of that valor so celebrated among men.

Nay more, the passions often engender their contraries; avarice sometimes produces prodigality and prodigality avarice. One is often firm from weakness, and audacious from timidity.

He had, to be sure, love, the love of the highest and worthiest lady of France. He had her fidelity, no doubt; but here he was riding west while she was escaping eastward, toward a refuge with the ardent Turenne. Would her fidelity match his? When one is in love, one often doubts what one most believes. Ambition perhaps ruled the love in her heart. Her arrogance was awkward, uncomfortable, and probably unwise. Her passionate delight in mastery had proved impolitic at Rouen, Le Havre, and Dieppe. Was this rebellion of hers likely to result only in her destruction? And in his destruction also, and the ruin of the great house of La Rochefoucauld? Was he, indeed, a dupe?

All passions make us commit errors, but the errors that love makes us commit are the most ridiculous ones.

Marcillac arrived in Verteuil to find his father in his last agony. A few days later, on 8 February 1650, François V de La Rochefoucauld died. The Prince de Marcillac became at that moment Duke François VI de La Rochefoucauld. At last and henceforth we may refer to him by his ducal name.

Immediately afterward he learned that in company with

Madame de Longueville, the Duc de Bouillon, and the Vicomte de Turenne he was formally declared guilty of lèse-majesté, a hanging crime. But not a shameful one; Madame de Motteville tells us that lèse-majesté was regarded rather as an honor than the contrary.

The new Duc de La Rochefoucauld had no time for repining at the news, and none for grief at his father's death. He had had a splendid idea. His messengers went out through all the country of Poitou, summoning his faithful vassals to the funeral of Duke François V. The gentlemen were bidden to come well mounted, armed, and equipped for a campaign.

The funeral was a memorable one. The ducal hearse was followed by two thousand horsemen and eight hundred foot soldiers clad in leather and fustian, bearing their martial harness. The interment was unwontedly gay. The soldiery ate and drank at the new Duke's expense. They cheered their master, cried confusion on Mazarin, promised to undertake any deed of adventurous sedition. (One can hardly find any ungrateful men as long as one is in a position to confer benefits.)

La Rochefoucauld's first enterprise was to assail the strong city of Saumur. He was delayed, however, by various politic considerations, and during the delay many of his gentlemen had second thoughts about the course of events and disappeared without taking leave. When La Rochefoucauld at length arrived before the city he found it too strongly held by the King's men to be taken by storm. More of his gentlemen found urgent reasons to return to their estates. It is ordinarily only in minor matters that we take the chance of not believing in appearances.

It is not my intention to follow in any detail the obscure, embroiled military history of this Second War of the Fronde. It is an affair of endless, aimless marches, of threats and counterthreats, of mysterious strategy entangled with more mysterious plots and counterplots. For La Rochefoucauld it was a period of vexation and disappointment, of splendid plans forever going awry, of high hopes constantly dashed.

La Rochefoucauld and the Duc de Bouillon, brother of Turenne, became coequal generals of a rebel army operating in the southwest. In May 1650 they succeeded in entering Bordeaux, where they were received with enthusiasm by the turbulent populace but with hostility by the well to do, who saw their fine houses threatened. La Rochefoucauld sent his brother-in-law, Sillery, to Spain to beg aid. Spain promised much and did little. In the whole war, La Rochefoucauld complains, the rebels received only 220,000 livres from the Spanish.

La Rochefoucauld makes this note in his Memoirs in the most casual fashion, with no suggestion that he considers an accord with Spain blameworthy or that he thought himself guilty of treason in inviting the traditional enemy into France. The mind of the high nobles was still marked by their feudal inheritance. Condé regarded himself as almost an independent prince, above the laws of the realm, possessing the right to make war on his cousin the King, if his own majesty was infringed. His vassals owed their first duty to Condé, not to France. La Rochefoucauld, as Condé's agent, felt himself to be within his rights in inviting the King of Spain to come to the aid of the Prince de Condé, as any noble might come to the aid of another noble. His invitation was not treason against France but lèse-majesté against his King. Of lèse-majesté he was already proclaimed guilty, and the guilt made no spot on his ducal honor.

La Rochefoucauld was merely following an example set by greater than he. Indeed, nothing is so contagious as example. We never do great deeds of good or evil without producing others of the same sort. We imitate good actions out of emulation and bad ones out of the iniquity of our nature, which shame had kept prisoner and which example sets free.

The royal army assembled in force outside Bordeaux, with Cardinal Mazarin observing the operations. The twelve-year-old King himself was present for his instruction, and also to be a discouragement to rebellion. For France loved the handsome, spirited boy. Even at the siege of Bellegarde in March of this year 1650, the embattled rebels ceased firing at his appearance and cheered him long and loud before again working their guns against his army.

Within Bordeaux, Bouillon and La Rochefoucauld put the citizens to the fortification of their city. The great ladies, the Princesse de Condé herself, gave the example, carrying token baskets of earth. The generals regaled the workers with wine, the ladies brought fruit and confitures. In the evenings the Princesse de Condé entertained with elegant collations on her galley, promenading the river.

In September the King's army attacked Bordeaux. According to all testimony La Rochefoucauld performed prodigies of courage. Three times, with a band of Condé's guards, he recaptured a half-moon fortification, built largely of wine casks and manure, protecting one of the city's gates.

But it was the vintage season, and all Bordeaux's citizens were agitated by a compelling need to pick and press their grapes in the surrounding vineyards. They soon had a bellyful of insurrection. Disregarding their noble defenders, they sent a deputation to the royal camp to seek terms.

La Rochefoucauld and Bouillon were forced to recognize their defeat. They paid a humble visit to the Cardinal. He received them with his usual smiling courtesy. He invited them, with a third rebel, Lenet, to step into his coach. He remarked, with a laugh: "Who would have believed a week ago that we four would be riding today in the same carriage?" "Everything happens in France," replied La Rochefoucauld; "Tout arrive en France." The casual phrase has had a great fortune. It is in every *Dictionnaire de Citations*, and on the lips of unnumbered Frenchmen.

La Rochefoucauld and Bouillon argued earnestly for the release of the Princes, alleging that as long as they remained in prison they would be the core of dissension, the pretext for every malcontent's opposition to authority. But the Cardinal would grant nothing, not even promises.

This war in the west ended, then, disastrously for La Rochefoucauld, as for his Princes. He learned that the royal army had seized his castle of Verteuil, had robbed and gutted it, and had driven out his mother, his wife, and his children. The most he could gain for himself was the assurance that he would not be pursued for the crime of lèse-majesté, and that his post of Governor of Poitou would be restored to him in a year if his conduct during that period should be exemplary.

Meanwhile in the east the war continued. Madame de Longueville ruled the little court of Stenay and plotted endlessly with Spain and with likely troublemakers in France. Her devoted slave, Turenne, made incursions into French territory, but gained more booty than adherents. Great general though he was, he possessed insufficient force to make head against the rising power of Mazarin.

At Court, a gradual shift of position was visible to shrewd eyes.

I must remind you (for even the actors themselves became confused in their mazy conspiratorial dance) that the Old Frondeurs, Retz, Beaufort, and Madame de Chevreuse, had joined Gaston d'Orléans and made friends with Mazarin, in order to bring low the party of Condé. The Old Frondeurs had gained their end, the imprisonment of the Princes. Now they found that Mazarin's power was intolerably enhanced. Swollen with success, he treated the Frondeurs with hauteur. Says La Rochefoucauld: "The Frondeurs thought that he would cease to hold them in consideration because he was ceasing to have need of them; and fearing that he would bear down upon them in order to rule alone, or in order to sacrifice them to Monsieur le Prince de Condé, they entered into negotiations with some partisans of Monsieur le Prince." The Frondeurs were, then, shifting to Condé's side, to make common cause against the mighty Cardinal.

La Rochefoucauld had retired to his estates in early October, to tend his ruined affairs, to patrol resentfully his sacked castle of Verteuil. About the first of the new year, 1651, he received an urgent message from the Princesse Palatine, Madame de Longueville's closest female friend. He must come to Paris incognito and give counsel as to what should be done for the imprisoned Princes.

La Rochefoucauld hurried to Paris. He learned that the Princesse Palatine, as the agent of the Princes, was ready to sign a treaty with the Frondeurs on their behalf and with their assent. The treaty stipulated that the Prince de Conti should marry Mademoiselle Charlotte de Chevreuse, that Madame de Chevreuse's ancient lover, Châteauneuf, should replace Mazarin as Prime Minister, that Monsieur should rally to the side of Condé, that Retz should receive the Cardinal's hat at the earliest opportunity. The position of Retz was somewhat quaint. He feared that Conti would enter the Church and gain the cardinalate he coveted for himself. Now Mademoiselle de Chevreuse was notoriously Retz's mistress; he celebrates her charms in most ungentlemanly fashion in his Memoirs. It seemed to him both politic and amusing to fob off his mistress on Conti and thus debar him by marriage from a churchly career. The fact that Conti was a tottering hunchback counted for little with the promised bride, her lover, and her broad-minded mother.

La Rochefoucauld, in secret conference with the Princesse Palatine, opposed the signing of this treaty with the Frondeurs. He disliked and distrusted them personally; he feared the alliance by marriage of the Condés to the ever dangerous Madame de Chevreuse. He thought it much better policy to attempt a reconciliation between the Condés and Mazarin. In his heart of hearts he was sick of the sedition to which he was bound by his devotion to Madame de Longueville. As Madame de Motteville says with her usual penetration: "The great lords always find their advantage in cleaving to the King and his ministers; it is from this source alone that they can receive favor and benefits. The Duc de La Rochefoucauld thought rightly that by reestablishing peace and union between Monsieur le Prince de Condé and Monsieur le Cardinal he might receive an important reward, and he saw with pleasure that on this occasion his interests and his duty coincided."

The Princesse Palatine yielded to La Rochefoucauld's arguments. She informed Mazarin that he was in Paris and craved a secret audience. The Cardinal bade him come by night to the private door of the Palais-Royal. (All the great palaces seem to have had their unguarded secret doors, for intrigue or for escape.)

At the appointed hour La Rochefoucauld knocked discreetly at the private door. Keys turned noisily. The door swung open to reveal the Cardinal, alone, in his undress, a candle in his hand. "I could have run him through and left him dead, and escaped scot-free," says La Rochefoucauld. But he also reflected that the Cardinal could have greeted him with a pistol shot.

Mazarin, fawning and friendly, led the way to his private apartments. He overwhelmed his guest with flattering words, said even: "I shall put in your hands the entire arrangement of the marriages of my three nieces, to prove to you, by this singular mark of my confidence and esteem, the preference I would show you over all my other friends." La Rochefoucauld, who knew only too well the value of the Cardinal's promises, put the case to him. The Frondeurs were about to desert Mazarin; it was to his interest to release the Princes and make a reconciliation with the still powerful house of Condé. "These words disturbed the Cardinal," says La Rochefoucauld. "But nevertheless he could not make up his mind on the spot. He would not give a final answer until the next day. But his natural irresolution and his ignorance of the state of affairs made him lose, to no purpose, the opportunity of making a conclusion."

The farewells were said. The Cardinal conducted his guest to the private door. In the corridors La Rochefoucauld caught the curious looks of Mazarin's guardsmen in their crimson and silver uniforms, their red-and-white-plumed hats. He could almost feel, behind his back, the master's signal, the heavy hand laid on his shoulder. But Mazarin made no move, and after the proper civilities La Rochefoucauld found himself safe in the open street.

There was something admirable, he thought, in Mazarin's frank and loyal reception of him. The trouble is, it is so hard to judge whether an open, honest, sincere action is the result of probity or of astuteness.

For two days he awaited a message from the Cardinal. As none came, he reluctantly accepted the opposing policy of the Princesse Palatine. He signed the secret treaties binding him to support the interests of Monsieur and the Frondeurs, in return for their alliance with Condé.

Now matters moved fast. Gaston d'Orléans came out openly in favor of the release of the Princes. The Parlement warmly agreed. The nobility assembled and passed vigorous resolutions in favor of the Condés. Everyone pointed at Mazarin as the villain who alone kept their darling nobles in confinement. The bourgeoisie took arms and guarded the Paris gates. The common folk, recognizing that a little tumult would be favored by the great, paraded the streets, shouting "Death to Mazarin!"

Men did not foresee, says the contemporary Montglat, "that to release Condé in such a manner was to let out of his cage a raging lion who was going to devour everyone, and who, to have revenge for his imprisonment, would set fire to every corner of the realm."

Mazarin was filled with terror and bewilderment. He could not understand how in a moment he had descended from his secure position in control of France to become the universal enemy. Only the Queen—was she, in fact, his secret wife?—remained faithful to him. And she was terrified by the shouting throngs without the palace, by the menace within. She had found the Cardinal's portrait adorned with a rope around his lordly neck.

Mazarin concluded that his only recourse lay in flight.

On the night of 6 February 1651 six men, identically bearded, wearing red jackets and plumed hats, left Paris by several gates. One of them was the Cardinal himself, the others were his decoys.

The date was a happy one for La Rochefoucauld, for on that day he was invested with his title of Duke and Peer, and he received once more his governorship of Poitou, in advance of the time set by Mazarin.

The Queen was now in the hands of the friends of Condé. She made a fumbling effort to escape and follow the Cardinal. Being easily prevented by her guardians, she resigned herself sadly to the new set of affairs. On 10 February she signed an order bidding La Rochefoucauld and two others proceed to Le Havre and release the Princes from their prison, to which they had been transferred from Vincennes.

On the following day La Rochefoucauld and his party set forth. Gourville, the respected man of substance, accompanied his former master. They trotted comfortably for two days. La Rochefoucauld rehearsed the drama of release, the cries and tears of joy.

A few leagues from Le Havre he turned in to the château of Grosménil for an hour's rest and refreshment. And there he found, gaily dining, the Prince de Condé, and Conti, and the Duc de Longueville.

Mazarin, in defeat, had managed to score a little victory of prestige. The Queen had informed him secretly of her order for the release of the Princes. He had hurried to Le Havre and had presented the Queen's message to the castle warden. Entering the captives' apartment, weeping copiously, he embraced them one by one. He then invited them to a formal luncheon, in the course of which he explained the innocence of his motives and his desire for the protection of the Condés, now that they were to regain all their old eminence and more. The Princes were polite, according to the world's usages, but cool toward their host's effusiveness. When he set them on their horses, he went so far as to kiss Condé's boot.

La Rochefoucauld had missed his dramatic opportunity by only six hours. Mazarin had stolen the show.

CHAPTER XIII

Stratagems and Treasons

FEBRUARY – SEPTEMBER, 1651

THE Princes—Condé, Conti, and Longueville—rode to Paris, over the frozen roads, in La Rochefoucauld's coach. The villages acclaimed them with bonfires, in which straw effigies of Mazarin, clad in old red dresses, were joyously burned. La Rochefoucauld and Gourville reviewed the recent past, and gave the Princes good counsel for the future. The Princes were much struck by Gourville's vigorous sagacity. Before long the former valet was dining at the Prince de Condé's table.

When the cavalcade came near to Paris it was met by Gaston d'Orléans, Beaufort, and Retz. After the proper embraces, these three hastened to claim full credit for the release of the Princes and the downfall of Mazarin. The file of carriages entered the city through cheering throngs. The people of Paris greeted the Princes with an enthusiasm equal to that which they had displayed for their imprisonment. The coaches rolled to the Palais-Royal. There the Queen received the liberated nobles, making her compliments with evident effort.

This, says La Rochefoucauld, was Condé's great opportunity. He could have demanded and obtained the immediate installation of Gaston d'Orléans as Prime Minister, for Mazarin was in flight, his friends mute, the Queen sunk in despair. But Condé did not realize his opportunity, or if he did he balked at elevating his rival, Monsieur, who was so closely bound with the hated Frondeurs, Retz, Beaufort, Madame de Chevreuse. In great affairs one should apply oneself less to creating opportunities than to making the best of those which present themselves. Condé revealed, not for the first time, a fatal lack of cold political calculation. To be a great man, one must know how to profit by all one's fortune.

The Queen was in mortal alarm for fear that Condé, on his tide of power, would put her in a convent and perhaps postpone the official majority of her son, who was to become absolute ruler at the end of this his thirteenth year. Concern for Mazarin, hunted over the border, weighed on her heart. She said to her confidante, Madame de Motteville: "I wish it were always night; for though I cannot sleep, I love silence and solitude, because in the daytime I see only people who are betraying me."

She tried valiantly and well to play the game of intrigue, to divide her enemies by rousing their ready jealousies. She summoned the Princes, with La Rochefoucauld, to a private conference. She poured flattery on Condé, and he took it with a satisfied smile. (If we did not flatter ourselves, the flattery of others could not harm us.) She offered many large rewards in return for the Princes' faithful friendship. She pointed out, however, that the proposed marriage of Conti and Mademoiselle de Chevreuse, which would yoke the Princes to the Frondeurs, seemed to her most unwise.

Nothing was concluded at this meeting, but the news of it promptly reached the Frondeurs, and aroused in them some quick distrust of Condé. They invited him to a conference, and there the scheme of a popular uprising against the Queen was broached. Condé discouraged the proposal. "I don't know anything about fighting with roof-tiles and chamberpots," he said. The Frondeurs' distrust of him was heightened.

The Frondeurs hastened the marriage of Conti and Mademoiselle de Chevreuse as best they could. Since the two were nearly related, a papal dispensation was necessary, and the Pope would not be hurried. Meanwhile, to Condé's fury, the Prince de Conti fell in love with his promised bride. He announced even that he would marry her without the Pope's permission. His conduct was regarded by all as most extraordinary.

It was at this juncture, in March 1651, that Madame de Longueville returned from her year's absence in Stenay.

Her joy was great to be again in Paris, reunited with her two brothers. Perhaps there was a momentary pleasure even in reunion with her husband. And certainly she contrived some hours of bliss with La Rochefoucauld. But these hours must have been few, for her husband, who had the rare distinction of being still ignorant of her liaison, would not take lightly an affront to his honor.

The lovers found themselves a little estranged by the eventful year of separation, by the multitude of experiences unshared. Madame de Longueville's arrogant self-esteem grated on her lover. He gave her some good advice about her conduct, which she heeded not at all. On her part, she saw all too well La Rochefoucauld's infirmity of purpose, his wavering prudence. "She began even to be a little disgusted with him," reports her stepdaughter, who was certainly in a good position to observe.

It is almost always the fault of the one who loves if he does not recognize when one ceases to love him. So La Rochefoucauld later reflected, recollecting his blind confidence in those days. Nay more, in love the one who is cured the first is always the best cured.

La Rochefoucauld shook his head at her behavior. She carried things with a high hand, offending her husband, her brothers, Condé's wife the Princesse. She went so far as to announce to the Queen the hour when she would pay her ceremonial call, and then she came two hours late. It is true that in the Queen's presence she was seized by a fit of trembling and was unable to speak. Condé was most annoyed, and surely La Rochefoucauld felt shamed for her. There was a family quarrel. Condé refused to heed his sister's counsel, and looked coldly on her lover.

Her chief foe was Madame de Chevreuse, whom she had many reasons to hate. And now Madame de Chevreuse's daughter, shameless as her mother, was to marry the Prince de Conti! Thus she would take precedence over Madame de Longueville, step before her at every public function! It was not to be endured. The marriage must not take place.

The means to check it lay ready to hand. Madame de Longueville began to scatter sly remarks about Mademoiselle de Chevreuse's virtue. She was the trull of the Bishop Coadjutor. Retz himself was the most indiscreet of men; he was still slipping into Mademoiselle de Chevreuse's room almost every night. The delightful story was soon on every tongue. Condé was furious that such a butt of gossip was to enter his arrogant house. The Queen saw her advantage, offered fine governorships to Condé if he would break off the marriage. In so doing he would of course break his alliance with the Frondeurs.

Madame de Longueville gained her end, which chimed with Condé's tendency to cleave to the Court against the Frondeurs. Condé called in his brother, and with brutal mockery recited Mademoiselle de Chevreuse's list of lovers and gave scabrous details of her current relations with the Bishop Coadjutor. "You think your fine face and figure have won her," he said. "If you marry her you will grow horns to hang mitres on!"

Conti was first incredulous, then crushed, then furious against the girl who had cheated his honest love. He agreed to the rupture of the marriage.

The news was brought to the fiancée by an uncomfortable envoy. He found Mademoiselle de Chevreuse dressing before the fire in the presence of the Bishop Coadjutor. (It is a pretty domestic scene.) She merely laughed at the embarrassed message. Doubtless she preferred her pleasure to her pride, a vigorous clerical lover to a warped husband who could barely walk a hundred yards.

But Madame de Chevreuse flew into a violent rage, and swore deathless enmity to the Condés.

Now the parties took new positions in the formalized ballet of power. Condé, having alienated the Frondeurs, asked great rewards of the Queen. The Queen, prompted by daily letters from Mazarin in Cologne, disavowed her promises, for fear that the Great Condé would become too great. The Frondeurs sought to make peace with the Queen, in order to make an end of Condé. Condé, his pride ruffled, his greed disappointed, began to think once more of rebellion against the Crown, to possess himself of the prestige and rewards he coveted.

What causes men's disappointment about their recompenses for favors done is the fact that the pride of the giver and the pride of the receiver can never agree about the value of the favor.

Madame de Longueville espoused her brother's dissatisfaction and urged him warmly toward civil war. She had her private reasons. The Frondeurs, in revenge for her revelations about Retz and Mademoiselle de Chevreuse, had opened her husband's eyes about her love for La Rochefoucauld and her gallantries with Turenne. The Duc de Longueville demanded that she join him in Normandy, whither he had now retired. The thought of returning to her husband filled her with disgust. But in a war, a jolly war, she would ride with her brother, guide his thoughts, play the delightful game of domination and intrigue. And she would come dramatically to her lover's side, surprising him in the creaking bedchambers of country castles, in wind-blown tents on fields prepared for battle.

"The ladies," says Madame de Motteville, "are ordinarily the first cause of the great upsets of states; and wars, which ruin kingdoms and empires, nearly always arise from the effects of their beauty or their malice." This is a typical seventeenth-century judgment (and a far cry indeed from the economic determination of modern theorists). It was normal and proper for beauty to upset states. The bold, imperious women did no more than was expected of them, making policy by day and love by night, while statesmen and generals put history in service to the heart aflame.

Madame de Longueville rallied her forces. She had the adhesion of the powerful Duc de Nemours, for Condé had taken his mistress, Madame de Châtillon, and Nemours thought that only a war would separate the two. She had the somewhat reluctant aid of Bouillon and La Rochefoucauld, for they had learned the facts of civil war in the previous year. Says La Rochefoucauld: "They had just had experience of the number of insurmountable troubles and difficulties to which one exposes oneself in sustaining a civil war against the King's presence. They knew how one is threatened by the infidelity of one's friends when the Court offers rewards and furnishes pretexts for the return to duty. They knew the weakness of the Spanish, how vain and deceptive are their promises, how their true interest was not to have either Monsieur le Prince or the Cardinal control the State, but only to foment disorder between them, in order to draw advantage from our divisions." But, as he further confesses, he could not express his repugnance for rebellion openly; he was obliged to follow the opinions of Madame de Longueville.

His lady was already bound by contract to the Spaniards. They reminded her that they expected her to live up to the terms of her agreements. She sent her agents to Flanders, and, on her brother's behalf, she made the alliance even closer. The Spanish promised, as usual, much more aid than one could reasonably expect, in case Condé should take up arms against the Queen.

La Rochefoucauld disapproved of such stratagems, for stratagems and treasons come only from lack of ability. His objections were not, however, moral. Long years in the atmosphere of the Court had stilled any youthful scruples, as they had withered his illusions. Men would not live long in society if they were not dupes, one of the other.

The Queen, coached by daily letters from Mazarin, followed the old precept of dividing to conquer. She showed all her favor to the Frondeurs, none to Condé. News was brought to Condé that she was planning his arrest, even his assassination. Was the rumor true? It would appear unlikely, for the Queen's two purposes were to obtain the return of Mazarin and to preserve the authority of her son until he should be of an age to rule, and these purposes would be ill served by the elimination of Condé and the elevation of Gaston d'Orléans and the Frondeurs. She had once tried imprisoning the Princes, and had been none the more secure therefor. Much better to keep the Frondeurs and the Condés at each others' throats.

But Condé, bitterly remembering his year in jail, believed

the rumors. One cannot console oneself for being deceived by one's enemies and betrayed by one's friends, and one is often happy to be so by one's self.

Condé cast about for allies. He was reconciled with his sister, after their family tiff, and for her sake he admitted La Rochefoucauld to his intimate councils. He sought to patch up matters with the Duc de Longueville. He took his sister on a conciliatory visit to her husband in Rouen, in June 1651. According to court gossip the visit passed off pleasantly, but the Duc de Longueville laid down the law and insisted that if his wife should return to Paris, La Rochefoucauld must leave the city. Madame de Longueville promised, but with a mental reservation. She was more than ever resolved upon war, which would serve her restless ambition and her love.

On the night of 6 July urgent word was brought to Condé that two companies of the Guards had assembled, no doubt to seize him in his town house. In fact, it later appeared that the Guards' only intention was to smuggle some contraband wine into the city. But our wisdom is no less at the mercy of fortune than is our property. Condé rose, and with a half dozen of his followers rode toward the gate of Saint-Michel. On the way he heard a great clatter of horses' hooves. "The Guards!" he cried; "ride hard!" He and his men made for the open country.

The clattering horses turned out to belong to a party of peaceful egg and chicken dealers, hurrying to get a good place in the markets.

Condé rode to his château of Saint-Maur, on the outskirts of Paris. The die was cast; public notice was given of his break with the Queen. He established a little court at Saint-Maur, with his mistress, Madame de Châtillon, for queen. There were hunts by day and balls, comedies, and gaming for high stakes in the evening. The food was of a rare succulence. Sedition was subtly confounded with pleasure.

Condé summoned Madame de Longueville and La Rochefoucauld, and attempted to constitute a firm and faithful party. But he recognized that the powerful nobility was tepid in his favor, nor was he himself quite ready to risk all in a civil war. He saw about him mostly, says La Rochefoucauld, "those uncertain people who always offer themselves at the beginning of intrigues, and who ordinarily abandon or betray according to their fears or their interests. . . . He saw that the Duc de Bouillon was quietly detaching himself from the party, that Monsieur de Turenne had made up his mind to have no further dealings with it, that the Duc de Longueville wished only to live at ease and was too angry with his wife to share in a war of which he thought her the principal cause."

Condé had, however, a mortal aversion for prison life, and he knew that if he should be again arrested he would be more harshly treated than before, and probably would never issue alive from his jail. Madame de Longueville played upon his fears and urged him to open rebellion. She liked the exciting thought of war, and was sure that her wonderful brother would conduct it to victory. She knew too that only a war would save her from her tiresome husband, who was demanding ever more loudly that she return to his side. Normandy would be her prison; she feared it as her brother feared a castle dungeon.

La Rochefoucauld's situation was difficult indeed. His interests and his good sense counseled a reconciliation with the Court, the acceptance of the Queen's promises, fallacious though they might prove to be. Condé was half inclined to agree. But Madame de Longueville received any suggestion of accommodation with scorn and anger. There were high words and tears in the Château de Saint-Maur. La Rochefoucauld's prudence seemed to her infirmity and cowardice. And he, knowing well the ways of the world and of the heart, divined the source of her noble protestations. Whatever care we may take to cover our passions with appearances of piety and honor, they always are visible through the veils.

La Rochefoucauld did his best to combine two incoherent purposes: to re-establish friendship with the Court, and to prevent Madame de Longueville from being returned to her husband. His behavior was puzzling, to his contemporaries as to us. Says Retz: "Every morning he would make an embroilment and every evening he would work for a reconcilement." He hurried to and fro, interviewing the Queen, Monsieur, all the men in place, bearing proposals soon disavowed, making promises soon forgotten. The task of intrigue and universal befuddlement was beyond his powers. His brother-in-law Sillery wrote to him, indeed: "There is no one on earth easier to fool than you are."

Mazarin, over the border in Cologne, watched sardonically. In his secret correspondence with the Queen, he nicknamed La Rochefoucauld "le Rocher," the Rock. (As Retz turned his first name François into "La Franchise," Old Frankness.)

La Rochefoucauld now had a superb idea. He proposed that Madame de Longueville, Condé's wife the Princesse, and his son the Duc d'Enghien, should remove to the stronghold of Montrond, a few miles south of Bourges. The chief reason he alleged was that Condé should not be embarrassed by the presence of the ladies and his heir when he should rise in rebellion. The real aim was that La Rochefoucauld should not be embarrassed in his efforts to make peace, while at the same time he would separate Madame de Longueville from her importunate husband. Madame de Longueville let herself be persuaded by her lover's argument. (Whatever distrust we may have of the sincerity of those who are speaking to us, we always think they speak more truly to us than to others.) The two ladies and the young heir departed from Saint-Maur on 18 July 1651.

La Rochefoucauld found that the absence of Madame de Longueville did not make his project of reconciliation any the easier. Spirits were aroused; hot tempers burst into flame. La Rochefoucauld's carriage was three times attacked. Though he had no proof, he blamed Retz's bullies, for the Coadjutor hated him, accusing him of being the agent who had broken the marriage of Conti and the episcopal mistress. La Rochefoucauld's pride returned all Retz's hatred. A man often thinks he is leading himself when he is led, and while in his mind he tends to one end his heart constrains him insensibly to another.

Condé would abate nothing of his pretensions and his magnificence. He entered Paris with La Rochefoucauld and fifty or sixty well-armed gentlemen and took his place at a session of the Parlement. His only purpose in so doing was to provoke and infuriate the Court and the Frondeurs, and in this he succeeded.

It is not enough to have great qualities; one must have the government of them.

Discovering that he could visit Paris with impunity, Condé took great pleasure in braving his enemies. He added to the number and the flamboyance of his liveried servants, and marched to his town house with princely pomp. His train exceeded that of the Queen and Monsieur. He held "le haut du pavé," forcing everyone to turn out for him. He visited the Parlement, and there behaved with contemptuous arrogance. He insulted Gaston d'Orléans, who had recourse to his usual method of avoiding unpleasantness: he took a mighty purge and went to bed.

La Rochefoucauld struggled in vain against this set toward violence. Retz says that within the Condé party there was "an inexplicable chaos of intentions and intrigues, not merely distinct, but opposed. I know well that even those who were the most deeply engaged in their cause could not disentangle the confusion." Condé himself was not sure what he wanted. "He was preparing for war," says La Rochefoucauld, "although he had not yet entirely formed the design of fighting."

On Saturday, 19 August, the Parlement met in the great hall of the Palais de Justice. Condé, supported by La Rochefoucauld, accused Retz of double-dealing. Retz replied with spirit and with no proper deference. High and angry words were shouted, such words as prelude bloodshed. The hall was cleared; the parties left, swaggering and defiant.

Retz spent the week end assembling his gentlemen allies and his hired bravos. He even hid a stock of grenades in the Palais de Justice buffet. On Monday, when the Parlement reassembled, he posted his men strategically within the building, so that they could take the enemy from the flank. The eager hotheads of the Court chose their sides. Retz tells us that the ruffling Marquis de Canillac came to him to offer his sword, but when he saw the Marquis de Rouillac, he bowed deeply, and said: "It is not just, Monsieur, that the two craziest men in the kingdom should be on the same side; I am off to the Hôtel de Condé."

Monsieur took more medicine and went to bed.

When Condé and his imposing train arrived at the Palais de Justice, they found knots of resolute gentlemen holding the doorways and stairheads. Plumed hats swept low in greeting, but there was mockery in the extreme of deference. Condé took his high seat in the great hall, and Retz the place reserved for the Bishop Coadjutor. La Rochefoucauld disposed his men as best he could. The Councilors of the Parlement sweated in their ermine-furred red robes, and not from the August heat alone.

"This is more an armed camp than a temple of Justice!"

cried Condé. "I do not conceive how there may be men in France so insolent as to try conclusions with me!"

Retz made him a reverence. "I most humbly beg Your Highness to pardon me if I say that I think there is no one in France who would be so insolent as to venture to try conclusions with Your Highness; but I am persuaded that there are some who, through their dignity, can and should yield the wall only to the King."

"I will make you yield the wall!" shouted Condé.

"That will not be easy."

Tumult filled the great hall. The Presidents of the Parlement flung themselves between Condé and Retz, ordering, begging, that the Palace of Justice be cleared of armed men.

Condé nodded. He turned to La Rochefoucauld. "Bid my friends depart," he said. La Rochefoucauld bowed and started for the door.

Retz sprang to his feet. "And I will ask mine to retire," he said.

The words, he confesses, were a mistake, for it is never permissible for an inferior to make himself equal in words to one toward whom he owes respect, however much he may equal him in action.

The nobles, conscious of the impropriety, looked at Retz in fury. "You are armed, are you?" said one to him. "Can you doubt it?" he replied with a smile. And this he recognizes to be a second error, for an ecclesiastic should not admit he is armed, even when he is in fact. There are matters concerning which the world wants to be deceived.

Retz walked with his best dignity to the door of the great hall and passed beyond into the Ushers' Chamber. There he met La Rochefoucauld returning from his mission. La Rochefoucauld may best tell his own story.

"At the sight of the Coadjutor all the men of his party drew their swords without knowing the reason, and the friends of Monsieur le Prince did the same. Everyone ranged himself according to the party he served, and in a moment the two bands were separated only by the length of their swords, although not one made a thrust or discharged a pistol. The Coadjutor, seeing so much disorder, recognized his peril, and to escape it tried to return to the great hall; but on arriving at the door of the hall, by which he had emerged, he found that I had taken possession of it. He tried hard to open it, but as only one side of it opened and this I held, I shut it on the Coadjutor as he was re-entering in such a way that it caught him with his head on the side of the Ushers' Chamber and his body in the great hall."

The door was a great double one. La Rochefoucauld, in the Ushers' Chamber, held both halves, with Retz's furious face pilloried a few inches from his own. He succeeded in fastening the catch which held the halves of the door ajar.

Hatred glared at hatred, while the men of both parties stayed their hands, irresolute. "Your daggers!" cried La Rochefoucauld to the noble partisans who had remained in the great hall beyond the door. "Stab the *bougre* while I hold him!"

But none of the gentlemen quite liked to sink their poignards in the Bishop's back. This would be a cowardly assassination of a high cleric wearing his episcopal robes. And Retz, after all, was another gentleman. And the high court of justice commanded its own respect. Condé's men looked to their master, and received no affirmative nod from him.

La Rochefoucauld held the door and called for murder. A member of the Parlement shielded Retz with his cloak. Another hardy member, who was in the Ushers' Chamber, shoved La Rochefoucauld from behind and shook his hold. La Rochefoucauld sensed general condemnation, suddenly lost his assurance. The hardy member of the Parlement released Retz from his durance. All the cooler heads commanded that swords should be sheathed.

Retz caught his breath, straightened up, turned to the Parlement, and seized the advantage presented to him. He humbly begged the Parlement's pardon for the scandalous scene provoked by his enemies. By his self-control and by his control over his men he had prevented a sacrilegious murder, an affront to God's majesty, the pollution of the very temple of justice with blood, perhaps even an outbreak of civil war.

He swept out of the hall, with all the honors of the engagement. La Rochefoucauld caught him and hissed in his ear: "We shall settle this privately, with our two swords!"

"Be calm, my friend Sincere Frank," replied Retz in carrying tones. "You are a coward and I am a priest. There will be no duel between us."

The dangerous moment was past. Both parties returned to their headquarters, to wait on events.

When La Rochefoucauld's wild fury was spent, he must have recognized that he had grievously erred. He had come within an ace of provoking a war with the worst possible precipitating cause, the assassination of a high prelate in the very face of the Parlement. He had misjudged the moment and the temper of his friends. What had seemed to him, in his passion, a glorious opportunity was felt by all to be wicked folly. His act had been grotesque, as had been the very posture of his intended victim. He had been ridiculous, and ridiculousness dishonors more than does dishonor.

All our qualities are uncertain and doubtful, in good as in evil, and they are almost all at the mercy of chance.

He was invaded by a sense of solitariness. In the pinch, all his courtly polish, so carefully cultivated, availed him nothing. He was alone. Other men acted by some secure common instinct, but he, when he trusted to instinct, met only the reproof of the banded world. Men were united against him, for they all knew some mysterious rule which he could never fathom, which they could never tell him. He was a fool. There are people, he reflected dolorously, who are destined to be fools, who not only commit follies by their choice, but who are constrained to commit them by Fortune herself.

There are men who accept the world, knowing themselves to be its happy initiates. Such was Retz. There are others who are forever outside, and who spend their lives seeking union with mankind, as the mystic seeks union with God. Such was La Rochefoucauld, and indeed so are most of the men the world remembers.

La Rochefoucauld, oppressed by the sense of his isolation, was forced to retire to the refuge of his own heart. What ordinarily hinders us from displaying the depths of our hearts to our friends is not so much our distrust of them as the distrust we feel of ourselves.

The grotesque affair of the Palais de Justice had a grotesque sequel. On the following day Condé, crossing Paris in his coach, with La Rochefoucauld and other gentlemen, encountered an ecclesiastical procession. Behind a knot of clerics bearing holy jeweled reliquaries marched Bishop Coadjutor de Retz in his pontifical vestments. Condé and his companions descended, according to propriety, and knelt on the dirty cobbles of the streetside. As the Bishop passed the kneeling nobles he raised his hand and traced in the air his benediction, with such an air of apostolic unction! Condé and La Rochefoucauld bowed their heads, raging. Retz had spoken truly. He held "le haut du pavé"; he had brought the Prince of the Blood to his knees.

Events now moved fast. Paris was in a state of alarm; even the artisans carried muskets to their shops. Condé had lost prestige; he was regarded as the chief enemy of the public peace. Too proud to make any overtures to the Court, he sought to find allies among the dissatisfied and the rebellious.

King Louis XIV attained his thirteenth year on 7 September. He was now of an age to rule, for kings mature more quickly than common men. Condé chose this inopportune moment to pay a visit to the Duc de Longueville in Normandy. The Queen was furious at the absence of the great Prince of the Blood from the celebration of the King's majority. She said ominously to Retz: "Either Monsieur le Prince will perish, or I will."

Conti and La Rochefoucauld represented Condé, however inadequately, at the ceremonies. They occupied the posts assigned by precedence in the Sainte Chapelle. The Chancellor solemnly conferred upon the King absolute power over his subjects. La Rochefoucauld, in his turn, knelt, kissed his master's hand, and swore eternal fidelity. He then engaged in whispered conversations with his fellows, urging them to revolution.

At Condé's direction, he made lavish promises of land and honors to the disaffected. He brought over the Duc de Bouillon and certain others. Meanwhile the Court affronted Condé by making new appointments without his approval or cognizance.

On 12 September (or thereabouts) Condé sent to Conti and La Rochefoucauld a peremptory order to join him south of Paris and to proceed with him to the family stronghold of Montrond, near Bourges. The Third War of the Fronde was about to begin.

CHAPTER XIV

Glorious Crimes

SEPTEMBER 1651–1653

CONDÉ and his friends were received at Bourges with the wild delight the populace accords to any brilliant spectacle which justifies shouting and drinking and which remits momentarily from toil. Condé was encouraged, despite all his knowledge of the fickle mob. (The most subtle folly is made of the most subtle wisdom.) He pushed on to Montrond, where his sister, his wife, and his small son awaited him.

The family, with La Rochefoucauld, assembled in council. First, should they continue the course toward war, or should they backwater, attempt further negotiation with the Court? Madame de Motteville says outright that Madame de Longueville determined her reluctant brother to choose war. La Rochefoucauld bears her out, though perhaps he is an interested witness, anxious to put all the blame on his faithless lady. He himself hung back, dodged the fateful decision as much as he dared. He remembered only too well the disappointments and frustration of the previous civil broils. The pillaging of Verteuil lay on his heart. It seems clear that he was dragged into the new war by his imperious mistress.

War being once decided, a summary plan of operations was drawn up. The Duc de Bouillon should command Condé's faithful troops in the northeast, in the region of Stenay. Condé himself would proceed to Bordeaux and rouse its hot-headed people. Thus a pincer movement could be inaugurated against Paris. Spain would surely come to the rebels' aid with troops and money.

The council drew up a proposal of terms for the Spanish King. This document is still preserved. It is written in La Rochefoucauld's hand, and his signature follows those of the Princes. The moral question of enlisting the old enemy of France did not arise. Condé was commonly termed "magnanimous," great-minded, and magnanimity despises all, to gain all.

The day after the council, Condé and La Rochefoucauld departed for Bordeaux. They left behind them in Montrond Madame de Longueville, Conti, and the Duc de Nemours, brother-in-law of Beaufort and rival of Condé for the favors of Madame de Châtillon. Nemours was a cherubic, golden-haired young man of twenty-seven, the ladies' darling. Mazarin referred to him as "Le Joli," Pretty Boy. His agreeable task was to watch over Madame de Longueville. She, five years his senior, was much taken by his winsome charm. The two found themselves isolated in a country castle, far from their legal mates and from the mates recognized by social convention. These full-blooded nobles had not the habit of denying their desires. *Ce qui devait arriver arriva.*

Meanwhile Condé and La Rochefoucauld rode to half-ruined Verteuil. Madame de La Rochefoucauld greeted her lord submissively. The ducal vassals were assembled, and many gentlemen were persuaded to join the rebellion.

Condé and his party, which steadily increased in size, hurried on to Bordeaux, arriving on 22 September 1651. The effervescent mob acclaimed Monsieur le Prince, and the Parlement received him kindly. He seized the available royal revenues, raised troops, a sorry lot, and tempted the local nobles with rich promises.

Gourville was dispatched to Paris as high plenipotentiary of the party. Here was a further step in his ascent from lackeydom. He found the Duc de Bouillon a prey to new hesitations, and persuaded him to cast in his lot once more with the rebels. But Bouillon's brother, the great general Turenne, would not be seduced. The offers of the young King seemed to him more secure, and Madame de Longueville was no longer by his side to make his policy. She, no doubt, screamed of ingratitude; but gratitude is like the good faith of merchants: it is good for business. We do not pay because it is just to acquit ourselves, but the more easily to find lenders.

Gourville had another mission: to abduct Bishop de Retz, who was now nominated by France for the cardinalate. Gourville showed less than his usual efficiency, and let his victim slip through his hands. Retz says that Gourville's attempt was no mere abduction; he accuses La Rochefoucauld of trying to have him assassinated. But even with allowance for La Rochefoucauld's abiding hatred, we may feel that he would not have commissioned such a dark deed, nor indeed would the murder of the prelate have brought advantage to his party.

The young King opened hostilities, inaugurating his reign with war. He marched to Bourges in October. The city received the mettlesome boy with an enthusiasm exceeding that which it had shown to Condé, three weeks before. In nearby Montrond, Conti, Nemours, and Madame de Longueville took alarm. They made their way to Bordeaux to join Condé.

La Rochefoucauld, reunited with his mistress, was troubled by her airy, chilly attitude. He was, however, too occupied with the war to concern himself much with her new mood or even to see her frequently.

A small Spanish fleet had anchored in the river below Bordeaux, though its aid was mostly moral. Many of the southwestern cities came over to Condé, but some strong places held out against him. Cognac was occupied by a royal garrison. La Rochefoucauld was sent to besiege it, but before he could reduce it a large relieving army forced him to retire. Condé was furious with him.

There were other military mishaps. The King's generals with their well-trained troops outmaneuvered Condé and his haphazard levies. Condé's conquering star seemed false to him. His noble allies hung back, waiting to see more clearly the outcome of the war. The military record is one of mysterious strategic marches, of threats unfulfilled through weakness.

There are crimes which become innocent, even glorious, through their brilliancy, their number, and their excess. Hence it is that public thefts are clevernesses and the unjust capture of provinces is termed "making conquests." But the contrary is also true; with failure, high deeds again become crimes, not even glorious.

In the northeast, Bouillon did not stir. As soon as he was left alone, he was troubled by anxious afterthoughts and forethoughts. At length Condé, in anger, removed him from his generalship and sent Nemours to take his place.

Madame de Longueville, whose affection for the Pretty Boy was now public, could not be consoled for his absence. She was convinced that her lover would soon find his way to the empty arms of Madame de Châtillon, who had left him for Condé.

La Rochefoucauld did not assume the warm place quitted by Nemours. His pride was too deeply touched, his love wounded to death.

The pains of these days inspired in him later a throng of dolorous commentaries. His mistress had befooled him long, and his kind friends had made sure that he would be the last to learn of his comical situation. But perhaps we should not be offended that others hide the truth from us, since so often we hide it from ourselves. Perhaps even Madame de Longueville thought her deception was a kindness to him, since we are sometimes less unhappy at being deceived by our beloved than by being undeceived by her. And of course their love was itself a deception of the ridiculous Duc de Longueville, whose simplicity had seemed to the lovers so amusing. But the slightest infidelities one does to us are more reprehensible than the greatest that one does to others.

He realized that he had long been jealous of his Anne-Geneviève, during the interminable separations of the Fronde. He had been darkly suspicious during her yearlong stay with Turenne at Stenay. He had been ruffled by her open favors to Nemours. Jealousy feeds on doubts, and it either becomes a fury or it ceases, as soon as one passes from doubt to certainty.

Clearly his love was at an end, for one pardons as long as one loves. But did he not deceive himself in so magnifying his lost love? Had not love created a simulacrum of habit and then quietly slipped away? The mind cannot long play the character of the heart. His mistress had been exacting, and her demands had increased as ardor diminished. One is almost equally difficult to content when one is much in love and when love is dying. Recently he had been irked by his lady's regal manner, her ambition, her vanity. He smiled sourly. What makes the vanity of others insupportable is that it wounds our own.

The agony in his heart was real, the torture cruel. But was it really love that bled? Or merely jealousy? Jealousy is always born with love, but does not always die with it. What makes the pains of shame and jealousy so acute is that vanity cannot serve to bear them.

What was it, this pain, with its strange intermissions of numbness? Was it perhaps something he had induced in himself, to prove his sensibility? There are certain tears which often deceive us ourselves after having deceived others. At any rate there could be no return for his proud heart. It is impossible to love a second time one whom we have really ceased to love.

He turned from stricken love to deal with battle and intrigue. He felt somehow set free to devote himself entirely to the service of ambition. In the human heart there is a perpetual generation of passions, so that the ruin of one is almost always the establishment of another.

Bad news and good for the rebels came from Paris. Retz had paid for his cardinalate by making a pact with the Queen, in which he promised to favor the return of Mazarin to France. At Retz's urging, the Parlement registered a royal decree, in December 1651, declaring Condé, Conti, Madame de Longueville, Nemours, and La Rochefoucauld rebels and criminals, to be stripped of all their honors, offices, and governments. While the Parlement hesitated whether or not to permit Mazarin's return, the redoubtable Cardinal entered France at the head of a mercenary army which he offered humbly to his monarch. He joined the King and the Queen Mother in Poitiers, within striking distance of Bordeaux.

To set against this bad news was the report that Monsieur had taken fright at the alliance of the Queen, Mazarin, and Retz. With his considerable following, he came over to the side of Condé, being careful, however, not to commit himself too far. He put at Condé's disposition his private army, billeted along the banks of the Loire near Orléans. Condé accepted the aid most gratefully, but without illusions as to Monsieur's motives. "A fool hasn't the stuff in him to be good," says La Rochefoucauld.

The situation in the midwinter of 1651–1652 stood thus: Condé had three armies, one in the northeast under Nemours; one in the Orléanais under Monsieur's general, the Duc de Beaufort, brother-in-law of Nemours; and one in the southwest, around Bordeaux, under his own command. He had the alliance of Monsieur and a good number of Old Frondeurs, and the general sympathy of the Paris Parlement and people, who could not forget their long hatred for Mazarin. Against Condé were arrayed the King, the Queen Mother, and Mazarin in Poitiers, Retz (who received his Cardinal's hat in February), Madame de Chevreuse, and all the nobles who were averse to rebellion or who were betting on the King and Mazarin to win. Among these latter was the Duc de Bouillon, who chose this moment to abandon his generalship under Condé for a better offer from the King's side.

During the winter months Condé, Conti, and La Rochefoucauld fought vaguely up and down the southwest country, like the Andabates, those Roman gladiators who battled blindfold on horseback. The rebels were ill equipped and supplied. At Miradoux they were obliged to pay their soldiers to run into the moat and rescue their own cannon balls. Madame de Longueville queened it in Bordeaux. She allied herself with the vile mob, which was infected by revolutionary ideas from its contact with English sailors, boasting of the beheading of their King.

Madame de Longueville's arrogant rule of Bordeaux, her delight in the huzzas of the vulgar, offended Conti and provoked a complete break between the two, erstwhile so devoted. There were other emotions at work in Conti's mind. His affection for his sister was bruited to be more than fraternal. Though he had become reconciled to the almost official liaison of Madame de Longueville with mature La Rochefoucauld, he was bitterly jealous of her infatuation with Nemours, who was not far from his own age. "Perhaps through loving her too much he sometimes hated her," says Madame de Motteville. "For, wanting her to prefer him to everyone, he was afflicted to see that he did not have a sufficient share of her secrets." La Rochefoucauld's hints are as broad. "The true cause of the Prince de Conti's lassitude with the war was his animosity against Madame his sister, which would throw him into a fury of hatred and jealousy toward her more excusable in a lover than in a brother."

La Rochefoucauld, the lover, could thus find his own hatred and jealousy excusable. He had other excuses. He managed to see some letters Madame de Longueville had written Condé, in which she sought to undermine Condé's confidence in him. She had then forgotten all his sacrifices for her, his ruined fortune, his demolished home. He now hated her, frankly. The more one loves a mistress, the more one is ready to hate her. His persistent rancor was later condemned by the worldlings as unseemly in an *honnête homme*. They could not know the rage of his hidden fire.

By the end of March 1652 Condé became impatient with the conduct of his war in the north. Nemours had marched his army from the northeast to the Orléanais and had combined with the troops of his brother-in-law Beaufort. Neither had any other qualifications than noble birth for generalship. And the two hated each other more than they loved Condé. The master's presence was necessary, to drive and to inspire. He resolved to join the Orléans armies. To do so he must traverse half of France, comfortably held by the King.

On Palm Sunday Condé announced casually to his staff in Agen that he was off to Bordeaux for a couple of days. This was a blind to hide his real purpose. Once outside the city, he was met by La Rochefoucauld and his eighteen-year-old son, the new Prince de Marcillac, and by the Marquis de Lévis, three other gentlemen, a valet de chambre, and the invaluable Gourville. The Marquis de Lévis had a royal passport permitting him to return to Auvergne with his servants. The party took the names of the servants listed. Condé was modestly dressed in gray with a beet-colored jerkin and a black scarf. His hair was cut short and he wore a pair of large false mustaches tied with black ribands—rather showy adornments for a servant, one would say.

The gentlemen rode by day and by night, seldom halting for more than two hours. The tender Prince de Marcillac was in agony, and gave Gourville a great deal of trouble. They went east through rugged country. At eight o'clock on Monday morning they reached Cahuzac, a good hundred miles from Agen. The village was a fief of La Rochefoucauld's. Says Gourville: "A man who was leaving the town told me that a company of cavalry had just entered, so I told the gentlemen to take a road to the right which would lead them to a small farm five or six hundred yards from Cahuzac. Finding there some officers of Monsieur de La Rochefoucauld, I made myself known and asked the officer to be so kind as to go elsewhere, which he promised me to do after he had baited his horses. I obtained some baskets of bread, wine, boiled eggs, nuts and cheese, and had them taken to the barn, where I found the whole band asleep. After eating, they slept another hour. The horses having had their fill of oats, we continued on until late at night and entered a village where there was an inn. We stayed there three or four hours. Finding nothing but eggs there, Monsieur le Prince de Condé took it upon himself to make an omelette. When the hostess told him that he had to turn it over to cook it properly, and when she had shown him more or less how to do it, he tried to turn it over, and dropped the whole mess neatly into the fire. I asked the hostess to make another and by no means to entrust it to that cook.

"We always had an extra horse for the guides we took on from time to time. However hungry our gentlemen were, they were still more desirous of sleeping on the straw we had brought with us. As for me, I took care of the horses and of the dealings with our hosts, so that I had very little time to rest. . . .

"On Wednesday we started about three in the morning. Seeing that we were approaching a fairly large place, I asked our guide if we were to pass through it. He said no, that we should pass near the gate at the left, and that the river was so close there that there was hardly more than the width of the road below the walls, and that when he had passed there a few days before it was guarded. I then put on a white scarf, the royal colors, which I had provided for myself. Seeing some men standing in front of the gate, I asked them not to let any of those who were following me enter the city, and I was fully obeyed. We passed by and baited our horses in a large village, where a peasant said to Monsieur le Prince that he knew him well, and in fact called him by name. When I heard this I started to laugh, and some others coming up, I told them what had happened. With everybody joking about it the poor man did not know what to believe.

"When we were ready to leave, Monsieur le Prince de Marcillac, who had hardly eaten at all and had gone to sleep, was awakened and bidden to mount, but he was so sleepy that it seemed he had lost all consciousness. Two gentlemen pulled him to his feet, but as soon as they let go of him his knees would collapse. Finally I threw a lot of water in his face, and that brought him to and he was put on his horse. We started off.

"Most of our horses were very tired, and when we passed an important-looking noble dwelling we learned its master's name, and Monsieur de Chavaignac said he knew him well and we might find some horses to buy there. In fact he bought two which he brought to us, and we recognized one which had been in Monsieur de La Rochefoucauld's stable not long before. . . ."

According to other chroniclers the party halted for a night at a château, taking false names. At dinner the conversation turned gaily on the liaison of La Rochefoucauld and Madame de Longueville. Condé and La Rochefoucauld were obliged to contain their fury and laugh at the salty jests.

Gourville continues: "We slept in a château which belonged to Monsieur le Marquis de Lévis. There most of the gentlemen slept between sheets, for the first time since their departure. Monsieur de La Rochefoucauld was attacked for the first time with gout, rather severely. I worked all night to make for him a great stocking which buttoned up the side, and which much relieved him. All the gentlemen except Monsieur le Prince were so tired that they could hardly stand up when they dismounted.

"Next morning Monsieur le Prince de Marcillac gave his horse its head and it got into some water with very muddy footing beneath, and he fell into it and got soaked up to his neck. A little while afterwards we came across a sabot-maker's place. The Prince de Marcillac dismounted and so did I, and I pulled a shirt out of a pack-roll I had behind me (I had put in two shirts for Monsieur his father and two for him) and I made a fire with the scraps and shavings of the sabot-maker. I soon dried his clothes, and it did not take us long to rejoin the gentlemen, who were going at a walk while we trotted."

The party crossed the Loire at an unguarded ferry near La Charité, and slipped past that royal stronghold. Indomitable Gourville was detached and sent galloping on to Paris.

Now they were in the heart of the enemy country, for the Court, with the King and Cardinal Mazarin, was at nearby

Gien. A stray horseman recognized Condé's valet de chambre and hurried to report to headquarters. The Cardinal immediately sent out patrols. Condé's guide led him, out of ignorance or malevolence, within a league of Gien. But chance or his star preserved him from the patrols, and he passed the city safely and arrived at the camp of his own army, on the edge of the Forest of Orléans.

He was received by his men with transports of joy. It was high time indeed that he should arrive, for his two generals, the brothers-in-law Beaufort and Nemours, were at each other's throats.

Condé learned that there had just been great doings at the city of Orléans. Monsieur's daughter, the Grande Mademoiselle, had thrown herself impetuously into the war. She was moved in part by spite, for she had confidently expected to marry Louis XIV, and the King, now thirteen, refused outright to espouse his strapping cousin, who was nearly twenty-five. To teach Louis a lesson and to satisfy her romantic impetuosity, she had herself commissioned a colonel in her father's rebel army, took two ladies as aides-de-camp, and had her portrait painted in a martial casque. Nor would she confine herself to honorary glory. Joan of Arc had taken Orléans, and so would the Grande Mademoiselle. She proposed the operation at a staff meeting, in which she was obliged to separate the two generals, after Beaufort had slapped Nemours' face and Nemours had knocked off Beaufort's blond wig. As the generals could come to no agreement she was forced to take Orléans singlehanded. She bribed her way into the city by a convenient postern. Then with her small escort she paraded the streets before the nonplused citizens. She had taken Orléans, and who could henceforth prate of Joan of Arc?

Condé, disregarding Mademoiselle's conquest, hastily organized his troops and attacked the King's men under Turenne, a general who was fully his match. There was hot action at Bléneau. La Rochefoucauld joined in the derring-do, despite his weariness and his gout, and the young Prince de Marcillac killed his first man.

Condé then made a bad mistake. Instead of staking all on the annihilation of Turenne's army, he chose to go to Paris with La Rochefoucauld, to entangle himself in negotiations, in which inevitably he was worsted. After many tergiversations he proposed a peace with the Court. He would consent to the return of Mazarin and would humbly submit to his King, if his party should receive specified great rewards and indemnifications. For La Rochefoucauld he asked ducal honors equaling those of Bouillon and Guémené, plus 120,000 crowns for the purchase of the governments of Saintonge and the Angoumois.

Gourville, who had so lately been contriving stockings for La Rochefoucauld's gout and drying shirts for his young master, was chosen to negotiate with Mazarin. None but he could so well match finesse with finesse. As he had guarded Condé's life on the roads with his sleepless vigilance, so he would guard his interests. Here was a heady elevation indeed. His universal competence brought him universal respect. "Under a crude and simple appearance he hid much intelligence, skill and sharpness," says Madame de Motteville. "He was born for great things, being eager for every task and animated by the pleasure of giving pleasure and of doing his work well. He had much constancy and genius for intrigue; he knew how to make his way by rough, circuitous roads as well as by the highways. He almost always convinced people of what he wanted them to believe, and usually found ways of attaining whatever he undertook."

In Mazarin, however, Gourville met more than his equal. The Cardinal half promised, half fulfilled, and played for time. *Il tempo ed io.* At least, Mazarin conceived a great respect for the negotiator. Whatever should happen, Gourville's fortune was assured.

In fact, everyone wanted peace, except Madame de Longueville in Bordeaux and spiteful Retz, but everyone wanted it on his own terms. Chief among those who desired the glory of making peace was Madame de Châtillon, the common mistress of Condé and Nemours. She was gulling her *amant en titre*, Condé, for the benefit of her *amant de coeur*, Nemours. If her behavior was ignoble, I fear that La Rochefoucauld's was even more so. He says outright (using the modest third person): "The Duc de La Rochefoucauld thought that the intervention of Madame de Châtillon might remove all the obstacles to peace. With this thought in mind, he encouraged Monsieur le Prince to come to an agreement with her, and to give her the property of Marlou as her own. He also disposed Madame de Châtillon to deal kindly with Monsieur le Prince and Monsieur de Nemours, so that she could keep them both; and he got Monsieur de Nemours to stomach this liaison, which he should not have taken amiss because he was kept fully informed and because it served to give him the principal share in public affairs. This plan, which was set on foot and carried on by the Duc de La Rochefoucauld, gave him almost complete control over those concerned. . . ."

It was an ingenious scheme. By its means La Rochefoucauld gained indirect power over the Prince de Condé. He had his vengeance on Madame de Longueville by binding her lover, Nemours, to her rival, Madame de Châtillon. His vengefulness toward Madame de Longueville and the ill will of Madame de Châtillon and Nemours alienated her from her brother, Condé. (Nemours took his proxenetic role hard. Once, watching Condé cozen his mistress, he scratched all the skin off the back of his hands without realizing it.)

But La Rochefoucauld's scheme was an ugly one indeed. There are evil-sounding names, in French and English, for the man who deals in women's love to his profit. This is the pass, then, to which has come the young knight out of *Astrée*, the faithful paladin of love, the Queen's martyr. The world has soiled him, and he has soiled himself. And by his candid admission of his turpitude he reveals that he does not understand the world's judgments, the world itself. He has never understood them; he never will.

While Condé, in Paris, dallied with his darling, the Cardinal was winning time and strengthening himself in the field. Turenne, unopposed by any good general, gained success after success. There was a delightful episode at Etampes, a little south of Paris. The Grande Mademoiselle paid a call on Turenne. She was to be sure a colonel in the opposing army, but among people of rank hostility does not count socially. Turenne and his generals turned out to receive her with all honor. She remarked that she would like to see a battle. Turenne, the soul of courtesy, ordered an attack on the city. About twelve hundred men were killed. It was very thrilling.

Condé suffered other misfortunes. He counted heavily on the aid of Monsieur's brother-in-law, Duke Charles of Lorraine. Charles had lost all his lands; his whole wealth consisted in a well-trained army of 8000 men, with excellent artillery. Duke Charles marched to Paris and was welcomed by Condé with great festivities. He then received a thumping sum from Mazarin, and turned around and marched home again. It was an admirable operation for Duke Charles; he had been very well paid by both sides, and his precious army was intact.

The Parlement and the Paris mob became discouraged and discontented with Condé. His negotiations for peace seemed to come to nothing. It was high time that he should take personal command of his troops and gain one of his resounding victories.

Through the day and night of 1 July 1652 Condé moved his army of six thousand men around the walls of Paris, heading for a strategic position in the open country. Turenne learned of the move and saw his opportunity. In the early morning of 2 July he brought up twelve thousand men to block the operation. Condé retired to the Faubourg Saint-Antoine, just outside the eastward walls (and, of course, within the present city limits). He hammered on the gates and summoned the citizens to give him entrance. But the burghers refused. They had no wish to see a great battle in their streets. They held their gates against friend and foe.

Condé turned against his attackers. At least, he had his rear secure against the city battlements. His position was a tangle of narrow streets between the walls of convents and country houses, with here and there some open areas. Above him, within the city, rose the high towers of the Bastille. He threw up hasty barricades and manned the house windows with sharpshooters. It was a good position for a desperate stand. In street fighting the advantage lies with the defense.

Turenne brought up his artillery. He promised the King and Mazarin a great battle, and placed them on the height of Charonne, whence they would have an excellent view.

At nine in the morning he attacked with great violence. His men were fresh, while Condé's troops were tired from their all-night march. It was a dreadful battle, with constant charges and countercharges. The dead were piled in heaps, men and horses together. The blue blood of the nobles ran with the red of the common soldiers. The sun was blazing hot. Turenne's superior power had its effect; he gained strong point after strong point. Condé performed prodigies; he was everywhere, shouting, animating, killing. At one moment he stripped off his harness, rolled naked on some garden grass, and returned, a refreshed giant, to the fray. He cried in vain to the bourgeois on the walls, bidding the Paris militia come to his aid, asking at least that the gates be opened to receive his dwindling army. The leaders within Paris argued the case, but could not come to a decision.

Monsieur was the official commander of the Paris militia. The noise of battle terrified him. He took a tremendous purge and went to bed.

By two o'clock all seemed lost.

And then suddenly the cannon on the summit of the Bastille roared, laying low the King's men, burying them in the rubble of the defenses. Turenne retired out of range. The city gates swung open, and the bleeding remnants of Condé's army took refuge in the city.

It was Mademoiselle, the Grande Mademoiselle, who had saved Condé! When his extremity became clear, she had run to her father, Gaston d'Orléans, to demand that he come to the rescue with the militia. She overwhelmed his groans and made him sign an order with trembling hand. She galloped to the Bastille, showed her order, ran up the tower, and with her own hand aimed the first gun at the King's soldiers. Then she sped to the walls, cowed the guards, and by sheer force of will forced them to fling the gates wide.

She had saved Condé, but she had acted too late to save La Rochefoucauld. He had fought savagely, with all the crazy courage which came to him in moments of excitement. At last he found himself isolated on a barricade, with his son beside him, and Nemours, and Beaufort. The King's men got into the commanding houses and fired down at them from the side and rear. Nemours received thirteen wounds. A musket bullet took La Rochefoucauld in full face. The blood streamed down. He could not see.

At this moment Condé and a faithful band charged furiously from the shadow of the city walls. The Prince de Marcillac took advantage of the diversion to carry his father to the rear. Gourville ran up to give aid. Beaufort, forgetting his hatred, shouldered his wounded brother-in-law Nemours and bore him to relative safety.

When the gates were opened the Prince de Marcillac put his father on a horse to get him to his Paris lodging. Mademoiselle saw them pass. She remembers: "In the rue de la Tixeranderie I saw a most frightful spectacle; it was Monsieur de La Rochefoucauld who had received a musket shot which entered at the corner of the eye at one side and came out at the other side, between the eye and the nose, so that both eyes were affected. They seemed to be falling out of his face, he was losing so much blood. His whole face was covered with blood, and he was blowing all the time, as if he were afraid that the blood entering his mouth would choke him. His son held him by one hand and Gourville held him by the other, for he could not see at all. He was mounted, and he had on a white pourpoint, as did those who were leading him, who were all covered with blood as he was. They were weeping bitterly; for, on seeing him in such a state, I would never have believed that he could survive. I stopped to speak to him, but he did not answer; it was all he could do to hear me."

La Rochefoucauld himself says that in the ride across Paris to the Faubourg Saint-Germain he exhorted the people to come to the aid of Monsieur le Prince and to recognize how false was the story that he had made a pact with the Court. If he actually spoke the words, they must have been a mere croak, muffled with blood.

For La Rochefoucauld the war was over. And ended forever was his life of gallantry, ambition, intrigue, passion. The young La Rochefoucauld, the dreamer, was long since dead.

Now this is the end of the second La Rochefoucauld, the actor in the drama of great affairs. The third La Rochefoucauld will be only the spectator, looking at the world with dimmed, wounded eyes.

For months Gourville remained by his side. Gourville, now one of France's men of power, became again his master's valet de chambre, nurse, and secretary. Madame de La Rochefoucauld was summoned from the country and served her husband with uncomplaining humility. The physicians reported that his right eye would be saved, but a gathering film on his left eye betokened a cataract.

Gourville brought word of the world's events. The Battle of the Faubourg Saint-Antoine had caused the death of many noble gentlemen, among them Mazarin's only nephew and chief heir. But Condé had come through without a scratch. Mademoiselle thus describes him at the end of that terrible day: "He was in a pitiable state. He had two inches of dirt on his face, his hair was all matted, his neckcloth and shirt were covered with blood, although he had not been wounded; his cuirass was full of dents; he held his sword in his hand, since he had lost the scabbard."

Condé strove to reconstitute his party, but his followers looked more and more askance at him, and went over one by one to the young King. Monsieur wavered long, and finally made his abject excuses to his royal nephew, told all the guilty secrets of his allies, and was admitted to moderate favor at Court.

In September Condé left Paris to join the remnants of his faithful army. An amnesty was offered by the King to all rebels who would lay down their arms and sue for pardon.

La Rochefoucauld on his sickbed refused the offer. While almost all his old companions thankfully followed the dictates of self-interest, this disabused cynic chose to lose everything and to save fidelity and honor. His friends, his wife, Gourville, surely pled with him, alleging that Condé was deceiving him. And what of it, he replied warmly. It is more shameful to distrust one's friends than to be deceived by them.

He could not however deceive himself, nor even view his own behavior simply. He wrote to a friend on 23 October one of his revealing phrases: "I admit to you that I find myself in great embarrassment, for I assure you that I will no longer know what to do when I shall no longer do any harm."

On 12 November he was officially declared guilty of lèse-majesté, with deprivation of all his dignities, with confiscation of all his property. Tottering, he rose from his bed. To protect his eyes from the November chill he wrapped himself with "more coifs and bonnets than old women wear," as his wife wrote in a letter. Though barely able to sit his horse, he made his way east to Damvillers, near Verdun. There his sister's husband Sillery was commander, and there he could be in touch with Condé. No one bothered to pursue him.

He tried weakly to set on foot some further plots to Condé's advantage. But he was mortally tired and hopeless. He reveals his state of mind in a letter: "If I shouldn't do my duty out of honorable principle, I will assuredly always do it in order not to give them the pleasure of seeing me false to it."

Gourville hurried to his side, adjured him to have none of such noble folly, and took matters competently in hand. He arranged that La Rochefoucauld should break with Condé, who was now in Brussels under the wing of the Spanish. He then used all his credit with Mazarin to obtain a return to grace for his master, the restoration of his estates, permission for him to reside in his beloved Verteuil. Invaluable Gourville!

Thus the Fronde came dismally to its end. Condé yielded

to the strength arrayed against him, took service with Spain, and for years fought for the enemy against his fatherland.

La Rochefoucauld meditated bitterly that when great men let themselves be beaten by the length of their misfortunes, they show that they bore them only by the force of their ambition, not by the force of their souls; and, except for a great vanity, heroes are made like other men.

Condé had left France in a parlous state, with anarchy and misery everywhere. There is hardly a man so clever as to know all the evil he does. The nobles came humbly to Court to confess their misdeeds, to kiss the Cardinal's foot. Conti proposed to marry one of Mazarin's nieces. The go-between asked him which niece he would prefer. "It makes no difference," he said wearily, "since it is the Cardinal I want to marry."

The Cardinal de Retz paid the penalty of his double, triple, quadruple dealing. He was arrested by the greater Cardinal and sent off for a long stay in the castle of Vincennes.

Beaufort and Nemours, the irreconcilable brothers-in-law, came to a duel less than a month after the battle of the Faubourg Saint-Antoine. Nemours, still weak from his many wounds, could not stand against Beaufort, and was killed by the very man who had saved his life under the enemy fire.

Thus Madame de Longueville lost her last earthly lover. She fought on for a year as the queen of Bordeaux. Eventually she was forced back to the side of her hated husband in Normandy. There she sank into a sullen lethargy. When someone urged her to take part in the country sports, she roused for a moment. "I never cared for innocent pleasures," she said. She gave herself more and more to devotion, mortifying her proud mind and her beautiful body.

The Wars of the Fronde were the last effort of the nobles to assert their power against the monarchy. Confused, ill managed, indecisive, the wars proved nothing except the incapacity and venality of the nobles themselves. These had boasted much of their honor and virtue. But La Rochefoucauld was brought to conclude that what we take for virtues is often an assemblage of various actions and interests which our fortune or our industry is able to arrange. It is not always through valor and through chastity that men are valiant and women are chaste.

CHAPTER XV

The Wounds of the Soul

1653-1659

It is a kind of happiness to know how far we are bound to be wretched. La Rochefoucauld, just turned forty, recognized by his dimmed eyesight, by the gouty pains of his body, that his active life was over. Toward the end of 1653 (apparently) he received permission to retire to his estates. He made the journey across France from Damvillers by invalid's stages, his spirits rising as he descried the familiar scenes of the homeward road.

At Verteuil he found plenty of occupation. His castle had been partly razed during the wars by Mazarin's order, but evidently the demolishers had left a part of it habitable. There was a great work of rehabilitation to be done. Perhaps it was at this time that the magnificent series of Unicorn tapestries, now at the Cloisters in New York, were hung on the walls of Verteuil.[1]

---

[1] James J. Rorimer, *The Unicorn Tapestries*. They were presented by Francis I of France to the first François de La Rochefoucauld, soon after 1514. No record shows where they were kept. They were probably not at Verteuil when the raiders came in 1650, or Mazarin, a great collector, would have taken them. They were certainly in Verteuil in 1728. Doubtless they were hung in the interim in another of the La Rochefoucauld châteaux or in the Paris house.

The state of his property deeply concerned him. Since he had come to the dukedom he had been spending wildly, gallantly, and now he found his estates loaded with debts and mortgages. But Gourville was at hand. This great man labored mightily to bring order into his master's affairs, obtaining delays and compositions from creditors, lending large sums from his own capacious pockets. At the same time he speculated on La Rochefoucauld's account, engaging in some dubious and profitable deals with his Paris friends. To be sure, he was amply feathering his own nest at the same time. The sharp businessmen of the capital, especially Fouquet, Superintendent of Finance, recognized in Gourville one of their own kind. He was enabled to buy a fief conferring on its owner the rank of gentilhomme. A valet de chambre has his ambitions too.

We may hope that La Rochefoucauld was happy with his mother, his submissive wife, his four sons and three daughters. At least, he begat a fifth son, who was born in April 1655. But certainly he was never a faithful husband or a tender father. All his pride and affection were centered on his eldest son, the Prince de Marcillac, who was to be François VII, the bearer of the family name and honor. The younger sons were thrust into the Church, the daughters kept disconsolate at home, robbed of dowries to furnish forth the eldest son with proper magnificence.

In the long peace of country evenings, La Rochefoucauld found a kind of solace for his pains and disappointments. We are never so happy or so unhappy as we imagine. His friends and neighbors admired his stoic constancy, but he knew himself too well to let their admiration delude him. We often think we have constancy under affliction when we are merely exhausted. We suffer misfortunes without daring to look them

WOUNDS OF THE SOUL

in the face, as cowards let themselves be killed for fear of defending themselves.

He was occupied, if not consoled, by the day's business. He felt at the same time cravings for something that eluded him, for understanding of himself and of the world. Religion was of no use to him. He was essentially a faithless man, unmystical, unbending to God. The zeal of the pious seemed to him vulgar, even disgusting. He was like that Bautru, a courtier of Louis XIII, who doffed his hat to a crucifix, remarking: "We bow to each other, but we don't speak."

He sought and found some surcease in past wisdom. He read, or had read to him, the work of Seneca and other ancient moralists. He took a special liking for those reflective writers who generalize their observations on human behavior in lapidary phrases.

As he meditated, he realized that he must find his consolation within himself. He could do so by trying to analyze his own behavior among other men. He had watched their actions and his own in a momentous period of history, and he had come to certain conclusions about the springs of their actions. (We would often be ashamed of our finest deeds if the world could see all the motives that produced them.) He would tell his story and illustrate his convictions. He would write his Memoirs.

Narrowing his clouded eyes, writing in large but sure script, he set down the record of days past. His memories were the brighter for the dimness of the external world. He saw tenderly his young self, love's pure knight, the Queen's martyr. He saw the minuetlike ceremonial of the Louvre, he heard again the sweet confidences of his lovely monarch, he dwelt among her maids of honor, *à l'ombre des jeunes filles en fleur*. Again he galloped across France on errands of amorous and courtly intrigue. He saw the fierce-mustachioed nobles of the Fronde, beribboned and belaced, with scarves upon their corselets, white for the King, green (the color of hope) for the Cardinal, red for Spain, yellow-gray for Condé. Fiddlers' music blended with the drumming of musketry and the crash of cannon. Silvery voices sounded again in warlike councils, mettlesome amazons in wide hats with nodding plumes rode to the edge of battle.

He had a story to tell of brave adventure and of fierce loves and hates. Nor was this all. His story was the tale of nobility's downfall. He had to show how his proud caste had lost its ancient rights and had ended in immense lassitude as the submissive subjects of the King, as the mere ornaments of his splendor. His fellows had been brought low by their own defects, their inability to foresee, plan, and unite, and through the genius of Mazarin, ever yielding, ever gaining more than he had yielded.

Such was his splendid subject matter. As he meditated upon it he came to recognize the dangers that beset the historian, especially the autobiographer with a cause to defend. We do not have the courage to say in general that we have no faults and that our enemies have no good qualities, but in detail we are not far from believing it. The historian is in constant peril of letting his judgment be warped by passion. Our readiness to believe evil without sufficient examination is a result of pride and sloth; we wish to find culprits, and we do not want to take the trouble to examine the crimes.

He would do his best to be truthful and sincere. However, sincerity is not easy to attain. Our desire to talk about ourselves and to display our defects in the way we want to present them makes a large part of our sincerity. Though we admit our faults, we are not entirely frank. We admit them in order to repair by our sincerity the harm they do us in other men's minds.

And even sincerity does not assure us of finding the truth. It is as easy to deceive oneself without perceiving it as it is difficult to deceive others without their perceiving it. The fact is, we would rather say evil about ourselves than not talk of ourselves at all.

The recognition of truth demands not only freedom from passion, it demands high qualities of intellect. True, but even here there is a qualification to be made. In the study of history, as in the decisions of active life, it is dangerous to be too clever. The greatest defect of perspicacity is not that it does not reach its end, it is that it goes beyond.

These were some of La Rochefoucauld's reflections as he ordered his memories, wrote or dictated. The making of his book had the common effect of fixing his views about human behavior and human character. He had seen in men mostly futility, folly, greed, vanity, weakness. He had seen them constantly striving to outwit each other, and usually in vain. One can be cleverer than the next man, but not cleverer than all the next men.

But virtue exists. He had seen plenty of examples of courage, generosity, and fidelity. The trouble is that if one carefully examines noble deeds, one finds them somehow entangled with petty or ugly qualities. Virtue would not go far if vanity did not keep it company. The soul is a composite, perhaps, neither good nor evil. It may be pure at its beginning, but life inevitably degrades it. The defects of the soul are like the body's wounds; whatever care we may take to cure them, the scar remains forever, and they are always in danger of opening again.

Is there indeed a soul? Perhaps not. The mind at least exists, but it is a poor thing, at the mercy of circumstance. It does not even command the body; it is commanded by it. Strength and weakness of mind are ill named. They are in fact only the good or evil disposition of the body's organs.

Thus he came close to a complete materialism, alleging that the body is supreme above mind and soul. There is a kind of consolation in such a faith, for the believer in it is released from the spirit's obligations.

As La Rochefoucauld reviewed, in the light of this despairing philosophy, the behavior of men, he was forced to put valuations on his own. His Memoirs are of course a defense and justification. But one may glimpse in them a secret, barely apprehended confession. The defect of his mind was irresolution, which is the manifestation of a defect of the soul: weakness. And weakness, he says, is the only defect that cannot be corrected.

In the writing down of his memories and judgments he discovered an accessory pleasure: that of the domination of language. He had always been able to turn a phrase neatly in conversation, and in writing his *Apologie du Prince de Marcillac* he had had to consider the value and power of written words. Now with leisure to write and rewrite he took much satisfaction in erasing and superscribing, hunting the exact expression of his thought, hunting his thought.

What with his endless finicking corrections, the pains of his body, and the business of his estate, the composition of his Memoirs was the work of years.

In January 1656 we find him again in Paris. Cardinal Mazarin and King Louis were now so secure, and La Rochefoucauld so harmless, that they could permit him to dwell on the edge of the Court.

He lodged with his uncle, Marquis de Liancourt and Duc de La Roche-Guyon, who had given up his duels and his mistresses to become a ferociously pious Jansenist. He possessed a magnificent town house, the Hôtel de Liancourt, which stood on the site of the present rue des Beaux-Arts. La Rochefoucauld had business with him: to arrange the marriage of his eldest son and heir, the Prince de Marcillac, to Liancourt's granddaughter, the only heir to his vast properties. It was a most suitable match, as the La Rochefoucaulds' greater name was balanced by the Liancourts' wealth.

After his long rustication La Rochefoucauld found Paris life delightful. It was a pleasure to see the city at peace, to roll through the streets in the Liancourts' six-horse coach, upholstered in gold-threaded velours, watched over by three lackeys riding behind with folded arms. (Some poor nobles would put a stuffed lackey between two living ones.) It was a delight to drive on the Cours-la-Reine in the fashionable late afternoon, to bow and smile from carriage window to carriage window. The précieux referred to the Cours-la-Reine as "the empire of the ogle." It was enjoyable to see the more vulgar sights, such as the Samaritaine pumping station at the north end of the Pont-Neuf, where a Jack-o'-the-clock struck the hours and four lions rolled their eyes, and an organ played hymn tunes while angels and the Magi circled about it, plucking at harps and blowing trumpets. (At the same time pickpockets and cutpurses were busy in the gaping crowd.) It was agreeable to dine well with old friends at Renard's or in the magnificence of ducal mansions.

The old friends were many. There was the Grande Mademoiselle, now nearly thirty, taking ill the calms of peace and her unmarried state. There was Madame de Rambouillet, who in her old age was allowing her salon to become a home of preciosity's excesses. There was Madame du Plessis-Guénégaud, in whose parlors the more serious young literary men gathered. There was the famous courtesan Ninon de l'Enclos, ever young and witty, whose salon, half in and half out of society, was the rendezvous of freethinkers and free speakers. Like every proper gentleman, La Rochefoucauld had been her lover once. Her former lovers made a cordial club of present friends.

He was seldom to be seen at the royal Court. Still in official disfavor, he made no serious effort to gain entrance by humility to that circle where the young Sun-King cast his beneficent beams. He had served his time as a courtier, and he had no wish to resume that arduous trade. One is nearly always bored in the presence of people with whom it is not permitted to be bored.

However, we find him in 1656 assiduous in attendance upon Queen Christina of Sweden, whose visit to France caused vast excitement. She arrived attended only by menservants and a pair of bedraggled women. She was dressed in a combination of masculine and feminine garments, revealing unusual glimpses of her misshapen body. Her hands were of a noteworthy dirtiness. Received by the Queen Mother and the King, she acted with shocking unconstraint, cocking her feet on a high chair. The only lady of France she asked to see was disreputable Ninon de l'Enclos. Cardinal Mazarin refused to admit her to his art galleries for fear she would make off with some rarity. (He had every reason to be suspicious of light-fingered nobles. Cardinal Barberini himself had purloined a magnificently bound volume, which was discovered under the very cassock of Monsignor Pamphilio, who became Pope Innocent X. The misdeeds of the impoverished nobles were manifold, ranging from cheating at cards to counterfeiting and blackmail. The Comtesse de Chalais took up collections for destitute persons of quality and kept the money. . . . But we must deny ourselves such fascinating digressions.)

During his season in Paris La Rochefoucauld relapsed into his old habit of idle gallantry. There was a Madame Cornuel, a wealthy bourgeoise whose wit gave her access to aristocratic salons. (A single example of her famous *mots* will suffice. She remarked that the young men of these years were like corpses, because they said nothing and smelt bad.) La Rochefoucauld was said to be her lover, but it is hard to know how much credence to give to the eager slanderers of the Court. If the two cynics indulged in a *passade*, it was for mutual amusement only; the heart was not involved. Passion would have seemed ridiculous to the two of them. The passions, said La Rochefoucauld, they are nothing but the varying degrees of the blood's warmth or chill.

He felt certainly no sense of guilt toward his absent wife, so well trained to his infidelity. He agreed with his friend Saint-Evremond, who observed: "After all, it's very tiresome to spend one's whole life saying to one person: 'I love you!'"

More important to La Rochefoucauld than occasional nights of disillusioned amour were his afternoons in the salons of the fashionable intellectuals. He was a frequent attendant at the Saturdays of Mademoiselle de Scudéry, in her modest parlor in the bourgeois Marais.

This remarkable woman set the tone of Ridiculous Preciosity which was soon to so amuse Molière. She was nearly fifty, of an engaging ugliness; she had to her credit several interminable and intolerable novels, in which all the great of the Court could recognize themselves in pastoral trappings. She set for her guests the tone of conversation, refined and rarefied almost to a gaseous state. Poetry was much honored, but poetry of the most delicate sort, on such themes as the unhappy love of a pear tree for an apricot. Intellectual parlor games delighted the habitués, particularly a game of Mademoiselle de Scudéry's invention, the Carte de Tendre. This was a map of Tenderland, on which one could trace complicated journeys from the town of New Friendship toward Tendertown, by way of such villages as Candor and Pretty-verse, with the constant danger of stumbling into Indifference Lake or foundering on Pride's Rock in Hostile Sea.

What lured La Rochefoucauld to this haunt of affectation? Well, an intelligent man would often be embarrassed, were it not for the company of fools. Perhaps Madame Cornuel, an assiduous guest, drew him there. Perhaps he enjoyed the observation of human absurdity. He would sit withdrawn, preserving a courtly silence. (We speak little, when vanity does not make us speak.) It was a pleasure, surely, to watch and idly meditate, and occasionally to interrupt with a cynical remark which provoked twitterings of delighted horror, even the swooning of tender-spirited précieuses. "Love?" he would say. "True love is like the apparition of spirits. Everyone talks about it, but few have seen it." Or, to the tap of reproving fans, he would ruminate: "How does it happen that we have enough memory to retain the smallest details of what has happened to us, and not enough to recall how many times we have told them to the same person?"

His observation of men and ladies in social converse bore fruit in certain reflections which seem so delicate and true, and so characteristic of this era, that they deserve transcription entire.

"The reason that so few people are agreeable in conversation is that everyone thinks more of what he wants to say than of what the others are saying. If we want to be ourselves heard, we must listen to those who are speaking. We must give them freedom to speak their minds, even to say useless things. Instead of contradicting or interrupting them, we should enter into their minds, their tastes, show that we understand them, speak of what touches them close, praise what they say as much as it deserves to be praised, and make clear that we are praising them by choice rather than by complaisance. We should avoid arguing about indifferent matters, rarely ask questions, which are nearly always useless, never imply that we claim to be more right than others, and yield easily the privilege of deciding.

"We should say things that are natural, easy, and more or less serious, according to the humor and inclination of our interlocutors, not urge them to approve what we say or even to answer it. When we have thus satisfied the duties of politeness we can utter our sentiments without prejudice or obstinacy, manifesting that we are trying to support them by the opinions of our listeners.

"We should avoid talking long about ourselves or giving ourselves too often as an example. We cannot be too sedulous in recognizing the cast of mind of those we address, in grasping the thought of the most thoughtful person and in adding our thoughts to his, making him believe as far as possible that it is from him that we derive them. It takes real ability not to exhaust the subjects under discussion, and always to leave to others something to think and say.

"One should never speak with an authoritative air, using words and terms greater than the things treated. One may keep one's own opinions, if they are reasonable, but in keeping them one must never wound the feelings of others, nor appear shocked at what they have said. It is dangerous to wish to be always master of the conversation and to speak too often of one subject. One should enter indifferently into all the agreeable subjects which present themselves, and never indicate that one wants to turn the conversation toward that which one wants to say.

"It must be noted that not all sorts of conversation, however worthy or amusing, are equally proper for all sorts of gentlefolk. One must choose what is fitting for each, and even choose the time of saying it. But if there is much art in knowing how to say the right thing, there is no less in knowing how to be silent. There is an eloquent silence; it serves sometimes to approve and to condemn. There is a mocking silence; there is a respectful silence. There are finally airs, tones, and manners which cause what is agreeable or disagreeable, delicate or offensive, in conversation. The secret of using these is given to few. Even those who make rules are sometimes mistaken about them. The surest way, I think, is to have no immutable rules, and rather to permit negligences than affectations in one's words, to listen, to speak little, and never to force oneself to talk."

In the salon of Mademoiselle de Scudéry one of the best of the literary games was the writing of portraits. The guests would be set the task of describing one of their number, in person and spirit; they would proffer a bouquet of verbal roses, cunningly interspersed with thorns. Or an habitué would read to the group his self-portrait, and all would exclaim with ravished joy, and then most delicately, with infinite qualifications, would suggest retouches, rephrasings, to teach the self-portraitist to know his own faults better.

In January 1659 an enterprising publisher produced a collection of portraits, dedicated to the Grande Mademoiselle. Among them we find a Portrait of La Rochefoucauld, written by himself. This is his first published work.

"I am of medium height," he writes, "well proportioned, supple. My complexion is dark, but uniform in tone. My brow is high and reasonably wide, my eyes black, small, deeply set, the eyebrows black and thick, but well formed. I would find it hard to say what sort of nose I have, for it is neither snub, aquiline, big, nor pointed, at least as far as I can see. All I know is that it is rather large than small, and it descends a little too far. I have a big mouth, the lips ordinarily rather red, neither well nor ill formed. My teeth are white and passably well set. I have been told that I have too much chin. I have just been feeling it and looking at myself in a mirror to learn the facts, and I still don't know too well what to say of it. As for the shape of my face, it is either square or oval; it would be very hard for me to say which. My hair is black and naturally curling, and thick and long enough so that I can claim what is called 'a good head.' There is something sombre and proud in my air; that makes most people think I am contemptuous, though I am not so at all. My manners are easy, perhaps a little too easy, so that I make many gestures in speaking.

"That is frankly how I think I look; and people will agree, I imagine, that what I think of myself on this head is not very far removed from the facts. I will use the same fidelity in what remains for the making of my portrait, for I have studied myself enough to know myself well, and I lack neither assurance to say freely what good qualities I have nor sincerity to admit freely my defects.

"First, to speak of my humor, I am melancholy. I am so to the point that for three or four years I have hardly been seen to laugh three or four times. Yet it seems to me that my melancholy would be rather endurable and mild, if I had only that which comes from my temperament; but much melancholy comes to me from outside sources, and so fills my imagination and occupies my mind that I am often dreaming without saying a word, or I pay little heed to what I am saying. I am very reserved with those I don't know, and I am not even extremely open with most of those I know. This is a fault, I know well, and I shall spare no pains to correct it. But as a certain gloomy expression helps to make me appear even more reserved than I am, and as it is not in our power to banish an ugly expression which comes from the natural disposition of the features, I think that after I have corrected myself inwardly the outward blemish will still remain.

"I have wit, and I make no bones about saying so; why dissemble about it? To shift and quibble about telling your own qualities is, I think, to hide a little vanity under an apparent modesty, and to use a cunning device to make people believe more good of you than you say. As for me, I am content that one should not think me more beautiful than I picture myself, nor of a better humor than I indicate, nor more witty and sensible than I say I am. I have then wit, I repeat; but it is a wit impaired by melancholy. For although I possess my language fairly well, though I have a good memory and can think without much confusion, I am still so bound to my sulky humor that I often express fairly badly what I mean.

"The conversation of well-bred people is one of the pleasures I enjoy the most. I like this conversation to be serious and to deal chiefly with moral questions. Nevertheless I can also enjoy it when it is gay, and if I don't make many little jokes, it is not because I don't recognize the merit of a well-turned jest nor because I am not amused by this sort of trifling, in which certain quick-witted folk succeed so well. I write well in prose, I can do verse neatly, and if I were concerned with literary fame I think that with a little labor I could acquire a fair reputation in that field.

"In general, I am fond of reading. What I like best is reading which contains something which can fashion the spirit and fortify the soul. I take special pleasure in reading with an intelligent person, for in this way one reflects constantly on what one reads, and from the reflections one makes upon it arises the most agreeable and useful conversation possible. I judge fairly well of the verse and prose which people show me, but perhaps I state my feeling about it with a little too much freedom. Another fault of mine is that I have a too scrupulous delicacy in such matters and my criticism is too severe.

"I don't dislike hearing questions argued, and I often join willingly in the dispute. But ordinarily I uphold my views with too much warmth, and when someone sustains an unjust opinion against me, sometimes by becoming impassioned for the right I become rather unreasonable myself.

"My sentiments are virtuous, my inclinations upright. I have so strong a desire to be entirely the gentleman that my friends could give me no greater pleasure than by warning me sincerely of my faults. Those who know me most intimately and who have had the kindness to give me such warnings know that I have received them with all imaginable joy and all the submissiveness one could desire.

"All my passions are fairly mild and well controlled. I have almost never been seen in anger, and I have never hated anyone. Nevertheless I am not incapable of avenging myself if I have been offended and if my honor is concerned with retaliating for the injury done me. In fact I am convinced that duty would do so well in me the office of hate that I would wreak my vengeance with more vigor than the next man.

"Ambition does not bother me. I am not much afraid of anything, and not at all afraid of death.

"I am little accessible to pity; I should like to be not so at all. Still there is nothing I would not do to relieve a person in affliction. I think indeed that one should do everything for such a person, including the expression of much compassion for his troubles; for the wretched are such fools that these words do them immense good. But I also maintain that one should content himself with stating compassion and refrain carefully from feeling it. That is an emotion which is valueless in a well composed spirit. It merely weakens the heart. It should be left to the common folk, who, as they never do anything from reason, need the passions to inspire them to action.

"I am devoted to my friends, so far that I would not hesitate for a moment to sacrifice my interests to theirs. I am gracious toward them; I suffer their ill humors patiently; I easily forgive them everything. The only thing is, I do not use many endearments toward them, and I feel no great distress about them in their absence.

"I have naturally very little curiosity about most of the things which occupy other people's minds. I am very secretive, and I have no trouble at all in keeping silence about what has been told me in confidence. I keep my word rigorously; I am never false to it, no matter what may be the consequences. All my life I have made of this an indispensable obligation.

"I have a very exact and civil manner to ladies, and I don't think I have ever said anything before them which can have distressed them. When they have good understanding I like their conversation better than that of men. One finds in them a certain gentleness not encountered among us. Besides, it seems to me that they explain themselves with more acuteness, and they give a more agreeable turn to their words.

"As for being a gallant of the ladies, I was somewhat such in the past. Now I am so no longer, though I am still not old. I have given up flirtation, and I am only astonished that there are still so many respectable people who thus occupy themselves. I approve extremely of noble passions; these are a mark of greatness of soul, and although there is something contrary to severe wisdom in the disquiets they cause, they are otherwise so to be reconciled with the most austere virtue that I think they cannot justly be condemned. I who know all the delicacy and strength there is in the great sentiments of love, if ever I come to love, it will assuredly be in such a manner. But as I am today, I do not think that my knowledge of love will ever pass from my mind to my heart."

This remarkable self-analysis was written chiefly for the pleasure of the writer. La Rochefoucauld had however a secondary purpose, as Emile Magne points out. He was suggesting to Mazarin that he was now harmless, that ambition was dead. His portrait is indirectly an invitation.

It is an invitation in more ways than one. This picture of a melancholy, upright, disillusioned, lonely mind must have appealed strongly to feminine readers. Disclaiming love, he called for love. Announcing his misanthropy, he challenged some greathearted woman to prove to him that he had merely been unfortunate, that rectitude of spirit exists. In many a bosom burned the desire to heal the wounds of his soul.

CHAPTER XVI

A World of Grimaces

1659–1664

WE OFTEN console ourselves out of weakness for the ills for which reason has not strength to console us. Thus La Rochefoucauld pondered, reviewing his past life, accepting in the present the peace which comes from renunciation.

He spent long periods, entire years, in his country castles. His reasons were in part ill health, in part inclination, but chiefly poverty. Like nations, he had to pay for his wars long after they were done.

There are some items to be recorded. In November 1659 he married his eldest son, the Prince de Marcillac, to the wealthy cousin, heir of the Liancourts. Gourville was most helpful in arranging the money matters. Gourville also came to the rescue when the young Prince went to the wars, and needed, to "represent" properly, a silver dinner service worth 60,000 livres. (Veterans of our wars, remembering the Army's dinner services, may feel that democracies have their flaws.)

La Rochefoucauld made his peace with Mazarin and the Court. He received, by the intervention of all-powerful Gourville, a pension of 8000 livres, to compensate him for his losses in rebelling against his master. In 1661 the King indicated his forgiveness of past offenses, if not his favor, by making La Rochefoucauld Chevalier de l'Ordre.

In 1661 Mazarin died, fabulously wealthy, fabulously successful. By his peculiar methods he had made himself the greatest man in France, and had defeated and subjugated the whole mighty class of the aristocracy. The death of the old enemy no doubt moved La Rochefoucauld but little. He had lost hatred, and lost envy, more irreconcilable than hate.

He was constantly involved in lawsuits about land and money. Gourville kept him from financial ruin. Gourville threw good things in his way and lent him large sums without much hope of recovering them. Gourville could afford these little kindnesses. He had arrived in the world, and had gained every outward sign of success. He played cards with the King himself. He had his term as lover of Ninon de l'Enclos. He was hand in glove with the mighty Superintendent of Finance, Fouquet.

But in 1661 Fouquet fell with a resounding fall. (He sealed his fate by giving for the King a festival more splendid than the King could afford, and by attempting to buy the royal favorite, Louise de La Vallière.)

Gourville, deeply implicated, took shelter with La Rochefoucauld in the west. On his flight he was attended by his cook, his butler, who played the bass viol, his valet (a violinist), and two lackeys (second violins). Gourville, the complete parvenu, has become a patron of the arts.

He found the Duke at his imposing castle of La Rochefoucauld, which one may still admire today. He dined at the high table with the ducal family. He offered them musical evenings, dances, hunts, and paid the scot. He took great pleasure in these aristocratic diversions. Despite his fat, he led the guests in the dancing of the newly fashionable coranto. His favorite partner was his host's eldest daughter, Marie-

Catherine, now twenty-four and resentful because no marriage was arranged for her.

If the proud Duke quaked to see his former valet kissing his daughter's hand with heart-stricken sighs, he gave no sign. He had become so dependent on Gourville! Even now he was forced to sell part of his lands, and Gourville alone would give him more than the market value.

One may well see in these records the hint of an ugly transaction. And yet I think the truth is simpler. The truth is that La Rochefoucauld and Gourville were bound together by honest friendship and mutual esteem, as well as by habit and a wealth of common memories. I think that this is a case wherein human worth surmounts the prejudices and traditions of caste.

Those traditions were strong, however. The gossips say that one evening Gourville knelt before La Rochefoucauld and pulled off his boots, saying that he remembered well his old service. The gesture was a pretty one, for it symbolized not continuing servitude, but the fact that the two friends had nothing between them to conceal or forget.

A government committee made a long investigation into the details of Gourville's financial triumphs. As a result he was condemned, in 1663, to be hung. Naturally he was not on hand to hear the sentence. He escaped to England. Later he removed to Holland, and there served Louis XIV in some difficult affairs so brilliantly that he was permitted to return to France in 1668. He had left large sums of money in the care of friends, including an eminent cleric, Grand Pénitencier de France, and a light lady, Ninon de l'Enclos. The light lady returned his money intact; the cleric denied that he had ever received such a deposit.

In 1662 La Rochefoucauld suffered from a nasty bit of business. A Dutch publisher brought out what purported to be the Memoirs of La Rochefoucauld, with his full story of the Fronde, of the machinations of Condé, of the plots and deceptions of Madame de Longueville.

The appearance of the book caused a great sensation, especially among those who were mentioned in it. The Duc de Saint-Simon visited the booksellers, demanded to see all the copies in stock, and in each he wrote in the margin beside a revelation with regard to himself: "The author lies."

In fact this was not La Rochefoucauld's book, but there was much of his own in it, both in facts and phrasing. He had lent parts of his manuscript to friends, asking "corrections," but, like any author, expecting only applause. Friends lent to friends, and somewhere pieces fell into an enemy's hands, or were copied by a shrewd secretary or servant and sold to an unscrupulous Dutch literary agent. The publisher had padded these fragments out with the inventions of a hack or with other manuscripts available on the literary black market.

La Rochefoucauld was annoyed and a little frightened. He issued a general disclaimer, stating that two thirds of the book were not his own, while the other third was so garbled and falsified that he could regard it only as the work of his enemies. He sent his excuses to the principal characters mistreated in the text.

By and large, his disclaimer is justified. It remains true, however, that his genuine Memoirs were just as revelatory, as harsh in their judgments, as was the garbled version. If his authentic text had appeared it would have aroused no less resentment.

The Memoirs as we have them today are reproduced from manuscripts not published till long after La Rochefoucauld's death. They constitute one of our most precious sources of knowledge about the period of the Fronde, with keen analyses of the policies and points at issue and of the behavior of the great. They tell a pitiable story of deception, folly, and self-seeking. They breathe the author's disillusionment with statesmen and courtiers, with men and women. He had adored some few; and one by one these few had revealed to him their weakness or their baseness. He concluded bitterly that there are men of whom you can never believe evil unless you have seen it, but there are none in whom the revelation of evil should surprise us.

The Memoirs are to be recommended to the serious student, not, perhaps, to the general reader of today. They assume unduly that the reader is already acquainted with a host of characters and that he is interested in the smallest of their evolutions. They require too much annotation to be easy reading for the casually curious.

The contretemps of the Memoirs occupied La Rochefoucauld, with other incidents of no great concern to us.

These years of retirement were not unfruitful for him. He learned day by day that if one does not find one's repose within oneself it is useless to seek it elsewhere. He gained some wisdom, he learned somewhat of the nature of wisdom. The constancy of the wise is only the art of hiding their agitation in their hearts. Out of the despair that followed the Fronde a kind of peace had come to him, even a kind of hope.

Hope, deceptive as it is, at least serves to lead us to the end of our lives by an agreeable path.

He made occasional business trips to Paris, and these lengthened more and more as he found a welcome in congenial societies. The most congenial was that of Madame de Sablé.

She was an old friend; she was said even to have been on better than friendly terms with his father. She had been gay in her youth, had devotedly loved Montmorency, who died on the scaffold. "The love that this lady had for herself made her a little too receptive to that which gentlemen manifested toward her," said Madame de Motteville cattily. She became *sage,* and rebuffed the advances of Richelieu himself. She was now sixty; she had long since renounced the storms of passion in favor of literature, Jansenist religion, the care of her health, and the art of cooking. But she still kept her air of courtly gallantry. Women can less easily surmount their coquetry than their passion. She was pink, plump, and overfed, "a fat turkey," says Tallemant. Though most of her contemporaries mock her and call her insupportable, she must have possessed some compelling charm, for she received a rare group of visitors in her salon. Among them was the great Pascal, whose confidante she was. Among them also was La Rochefoucauld's early flame, Mademoiselle de Hautefort, now the imposing Duchesse de Schomberg.

It was not easy to have access to her circle, for she lived in dread of infection. She maintained that all diseases are contagious, that even the common cold is catching. The porter at her door made a summary medical examination of callers, and bravely denied entrance to any sniffling or pimply noble. When her house guest, the Comtesse de Maure, came down with a cold, the two ladies went immediately to bed, and wrote each other long letters from their adjoining rooms.

Madame de Sablé found the answer to her spiritual needs in Jansenism. This was a kind of Catholic fundamentalism, emphasizing the depravity of man's spirit, the necessity of self-examination, the rarity of grace. Its dark view of human nature appealed to such somber minds as those of Pascal and Racine. The Paris headquarters of Jansenism was the convent of Port-Royal, on the present Boulevard de Port-Royal. Madame de Sablé bought in 1656 a house adjoining the convent. She constructed a passage from her second story to the upper level of the church, and therein she built a small tribune, jutting out from the wall. Thus she might hear mass conveniently without risk of infection from the exposed bodies of Jansenist dead or from the living nuns, all too careless of hygiene.

La Rochefoucauld did not mind her little manias. We easily pardon our friends the faults which do not affect us.

She spent part of her leisure in compounding remedies, especially powdered viper, which La Rochefoucauld found excellent. But the best of her time was given to cookery. "No use her trying," said a friend, "if the devil took his stand in the kitchen she wouldn't get him out of the house." La Rochefoucauld's letters are full of lickerish praise of her marmalades and jams, particularly of her magisterial soups. He broods over a dinner where she had served a potage aux carottes, a ragoût de mouton, a chapon aux pruneaux. He asks for her recipes for eau de noix and mille-fleurs. Gouty La Rochefoucauld has become a gourmet himself. What can be sweeter than the communion of two delicate spirits bound by a common love of preciosity in food? [1]

There were other bonds between the two aging gallants, retired from the active world.

Madame de Longueville, like Madame de Sablé, had found consolation in the stern tenets of Jansenism. The two women were on the best of terms, and had many delightful conversations on grace and on the soul's nourishment. Madame de Longueville outdid her friend in austerity, practicing cruel mortifications on her still lovely body. When some new self-torture was reported to La Rochefoucauld, he sourly remarked that true mortifications are those which are never known; vanity makes the others easy.

[1] The gentle reader may wish to try her hand on Madame de Sablé's recipe for an omelette *fines herbes:* "Put into a dozen beaten eggs a pinch of green chives, one or two leaves of costmary, six leaves of marigold, three or four sprays of bloodwort, two or three leaves of borage, the same of bugloss, five or six leaves of round sorrel, one or two sprays of thyme, two or three leaves of tender lettuce, a little marjoram, hyssop, and cress."

Those who have known great passions are all their lives both happy and unhappy at their cure. La Rochefoucauld took an agonizing pleasure in hearing the news of the woman he had most truly loved. He kept Madame de Sablé to the subject, and urged her to frequent visits to Madame de Longueville; he requested full reports. He was not duped with regard to his own feelings, for he had passed beyond self-deception. Pride, like the other passions, has its peculiarities. We are ashamed to admit that we are jealous, and we honor ourselves for past jealousy, for being still capable of jealousy.

Madame de Sablé made use of her friendship with Madame de Longueville to invite to her parlors the Comte de Saint-Paul, whom Madame de Longueville had borne in the Paris Hôtel de Ville, in January 1649, during the mad first days of the glorious Fronde. Charles-Paris was a handsome boy, with his mother's curling golden hair. La Rochefoucauld caressed him as an elder stranger might, hiding his stabs of pain as he recognized the look and gesture of his lost beloved, and recognized his own dark features in his son, the creation of his love. But he could not clasp his son in a fatherly embrace, he must play the part of the kindly friend, and suffer under his courtly mask.

Such reopenings of old wounds came, however, only rarely. In general, the pleasures of Madame de Sablé's society consisted in the conversation of a small group of intelligent people with a common interest in human behavior, in moral speculation, and in literature. The tone of her salon was marked by a perfect *politesse,* by mutual compliments which modern taste would find fulsome. (Well, if we never flattered each other we would not have much pleasure.) Naturally gossip often held the floor. The doings of absent friends were amply commented upon, their flaws of character, as revealed in their actions, reviewed. But the gossipers were far too wise to assume their own superiority. They knew that if we had no faults ourselves we would not take so much pleasure in remarking them in others.

The tone of the salon was determined also by the hostess' Jansenism. The doctrine's misanthropy was congenial to La Rochefoucauld's mood, while he refused to accept its promise and its hope.

In this society he followed his own rules: to listen, speak little, abstain from the high tone of authority. Mostly he observed the behavior of his friends and took pleasant little mental notes. He remarked that in all professions everyone affects a demeanor, an exterior, to appear to be that which one wants to be considered. Thus one may say that the world is composed only of grimaces.

His observations fell naturally into the form of generalizations on human nature. "Maxims," he called them; he might as well have called them aphorisms or epigrams or proverbs, a form of expression as old as literature. The proverb game was very popular in Madame de Sablé's salon. The hostess, or Jacques Esprit, tutor to the Prince de Condé's children, or La Rochefoucauld would present a thought in epigrammatic form. The guests would discuss it at length, questioning its truth, criticizing its expression, suggesting alternative phrasings.

The *maximes* were endlessly reworked and revised, always in the direction of simplicity and concision. One may continue to play the game of the salons and try to better their expression. One will never succeed. How can one say more than this, in fewer, simpler words; "Quelque bien qu'on dise de nous, on ne nous apprend rien de nouveau?" (Whatever good one may say of us, one tells us nothing new.) Or this: "Tel homme est ingrat, qui est moins coupable de son ingratitude que celui qui lui a fait du bien." (Many an ungrateful man is less to be blamed for his ingratitude than is the man who did him the favor.)

Before long a considerable sheaf of *maximes* was assembled, and lent as a supreme privilege to admiring friends. Inevitably the enterprising Dutch pirate-publishers obtained a copy. They brought out at the end of 1663 (probably) a small unauthorized volume: *Sentences et Maximes de Morale*.[2] Though it bore no indication of authorship, it contained 189 authentic *maximes* of La Rochefoucauld. The literary world had no difficulty in ascribing them to their actual writer.

La Rochefoucauld was furious. "Well," said a friend, "if you don't marry your daughter off, someone else will marry her for you."

La Rochefoucauld determined to regularize his child's marriage. An authorized collection of his *maximes* was published early in 1665. It contains 317 entries. A few are the work of Madame de Sablé and Jacques Esprit, but these were suppressed in later editions.

La Rochefoucauld has found in the diversion of his idle years his claim to remembrance, his continuing fame.

Many of the *maximes* seem today mere commonplaces, perhaps because La Rochefoucauld has made them commonplace. Some are no more than plays on words: "Only those are despicable who fear to be despised"; "We should be astonished only at our capacity to be still astonished." Others are random observations on minor quirks of men's behavior: "Everyone complains of his memory, and no one complains of his judgment"; "We often pardon those who bore us, but we cannot pardon those we bore."

But the book as a whole is the statement of La Rochefoucauld's long conclusions about the moral qualities of man's

---

[2] The date is commonly given as 1664. But E. Magne (*Le Vrai visage de La Rochefoucauld*, 147) puts it at the end of 1663.

spirit. He takes this phrase for his epigraph: "Our virtues, most often, are only disguised vices." This is his compelling, recurring thought; he illustrates it amply. "Vices enter into the composition of virtues as poisons enter into the composition of remedies. Prudence assembles them, tempers them, and usefully employs them against life's evils." In developing this thesis, he often employs a nearly mechanical device; for it is obvious that the excess of every virtue is a vice, courage becomes foolhardiness, liberality becomes profligacy, and it is easy to condemn a virtue by identifying it with its vicious excess. All this is true, but indeed I do not argue that La Rochefoucauld is expressing ultimate truth, only that he finds in accepted valuations a regrettable simplification. Nothing is simple in the world, nothing is pure—not virtue, not vice either.

It is a dark picture that he draws, certainly, of man's baseness and especially of his folly. (If there are men whose ridiculousness has never appeared, it is because one has not seriously sought to find it.) But we should be chary of blaming man for what he is. He is not responsible; his depravity has been determined in advance. Perseverance, for instance, is worthy of neither blame nor praise, because it is only the duration of tastes and feelings, which one cannot give oneself nor take away.

Man is then helpless. He is an automaton, condemned to work evil on himself and others. Yet there is always an implicit comparison between his wicked folly and his possible wisdom and virtue. The recognition of his present state implies a conception of a better state. Pascal and the Jansenists would have heartily agreed. Pascal himself might have signed La Rochefoucauld's posthumous maxim: this is a convincing proof that man was not created as he is, that the more reasonable he becomes the more he blushes inwardly at the extravagance, baseness, and corruption of his feelings and inclinations. The cynicism of the maxims is therefore not complete. Most of his generalizations are, I think, confessions. This is the world, he implies, more wicked and stupid than any of us had realized. We had expected something better; alas that we were so befooled, alas that we have had to learn the ugly truth. La Rochefoucauld parades before us his stoic coldness, but in fact he reveals his own exasperated sensibility, the suffering of disillusion. The maxims are a cry of despair, a cry for help.

His cry was heard by a very wonderful person. This was Madame de La Fayette.

CHAPTER XVII

Few Know How to Be Old

1664–1680

MARIE-Madeleine Pioche de La Vergne was born in 1634, to a family of the minor nobility. Her mother's second marriage united her to the Sévignés and to the greater *noblesse*. She was an intellectual, fluent in Latin, a précieuse in her younger days, a writer. She was married, not brilliantly, to the Comte de La Fayette, a bumpkin of Auvergne, whose only interest was his crumbling castles on their poor mountain farms. His sister was that Mademoiselle de La Fayette who had stimulated Louis XIII to the begetting of the Sun-King. He was obliging enough to live in the south while his wife set up a small house in Paris.

Her enemies (they were many) accused her of being cold and self-seeking, of making her friends with a view to their usefulness. But she was all her life poor among the rich. She was forced to seek advantage, in order to establish her two sons in the world. She had to live by her wits—and few people have enough wits to live by them. The fact that she kept such penetrating friends as Madame de Sévigné and La Rochefoucauld is sufficient answer to the denigrators of her character.

She was evidently fascinated by La Rochefoucauld's self-portrait, published in 1659. She recognized in his brooding spirit a congenial soul, in his disillusionment an appeal to some superior woman to provide new illusions. The two had some formal acquaintance; he had sent her a *compliment* on her marriage in 1655. They met again at the salon of Madame du Plessis-Guénégaud in 1662 or 1663. Now she knew what she wanted. Deliberately she set her cap for him.

She did her best to gain access to the well-guarded cénacle of Madame de Sablé. Unfortunately she was always sickly, and Madame de Sablé allowed in her salon no illnesses but her own. Doubtless Madame de Sablé's coldness was inspired also by fear of losing her dominance over her distinguished guest.

Madame de La Fayette persisted, and succeeded occasionally in forcing the frowning doors, even in dining at the holy table, to the distress of her delicate stomach. She was not admitted, however, to the private conciliabules in which the maxims were cosily discussed. No doubt it was felt that she was not quite in key with the genial misanthropy of the little group.

When the *Maximes* were published, Madame de La Fayette read and reread them with mounting horror. She wrote to Madame de Sablé: "Ah, Madame, what corruption one must have in mind and heart to be able to imagine all that!" Though her life had been difficult, though she was incessantly tortured by illness, she was convinced that life is good, that man is impelled to action by virtue, honor, honest love. It was clearly her duty to prove to this disabused cynic that there was at least one good woman left in the naughty world.

The reading of the *Maximes* gave her three months of liver trouble. When she recovered she prepared her righteous campaign.

Madame de Longueville, meanwhile, had read the *Maximes* and had taken alarm about the lessons in misanthropy her son the Comte de Saint-Paul might be receiving at Madame de Sablé's. She forbade him to enter her old friend's house. La Rochefoucauld was bitterly wounded by the breaking of his anguished intimacy with his son.

Madame de La Fayette seized her opportunity. She used all her charm to attract the Comte de Saint-Paul, who was now sixteen, to her house on the rue de Vaugirard. The boy served as a bait to lure the father. The Duc de La Rochefoucauld soon found himself comfortably installed in an easy chair by Madame de La Fayette's fire. His son sat across the hearth from him.

Some gossip told the boy the secret of his birth. He seems not to have been much moved. Bastardy, if sufficiently illustrious, was held no shame. But the father was deeply stirred to acknowledge the child of his great love.

The Duke found himself physically and morally at ease in this welcoming house. Madame de La Fayette was a brilliant woman, stimulating his mind as he roused and challenged hers. She had read widely and well; she was a feminist in advance of her time, with radical views on the desirability of marriage for love alone. She had a deep capacity for affection, and hitherto she had found none on whom to bestow it. She needed to console and to be consoled.

The intimate and lasting friendship of La Rochefoucauld and Madame de La Fayette began in 1665. It was at the same time that Madame de Sablé forbade her door to both of them.

The nature of the famous intimacy was naturally much discussed. It was published to the social world as friendship, not love. La Rochefoucauld was persuaded that young women unwilling to appear coquettes and men of advanced years unwilling to appear ridiculous should never speak of love as something they may experience themselves. Friendship would have to do. But friendship was precious too, almost as precious as love. Men are too weak, too changeful, to bear for long the weight of friendship. However rare true love be, it is still less rare than true friendship.

With such a face on their relationship Madame de La Fayette had to be content. She learned to smile when La Rochefoucauld interpreted her effusions and his own according to his cynic rule. "We sometimes think we hate flattery," he said, "but we only hate the manner of flattering." He was not willing to disavow for her sake the moral system which made him celebrated in the lettered world. Rather, he would surprise her own inconsequences and little absurdities to make observations to serve for his picture of human folly. She did not convert him; he even converted her to his aphoristic habit. One of her remarks is preserved among his *Maximes*. She said: "We give advice, we do not inspire conduct." Very good; very good indeed.

Shall we classify their relation as friendship or love? As for the work of flesh, as the French put it, we must remember that both were valetudinarians, on the way to becoming chronic invalids. But perhaps the work of flesh has not much to do with the question. The contemporaries themselves were puzzled. A lady wrote to Bussy-Rabutin, a few years later: "Monsieur de La Rochefoucauld lives very honestly with Madame de La Fayette; only friendship is evident. Fear of God on both their parts, perhaps policy too, have clipped the wings of love. She is his favorite, his first friend." Bussy replied: "Even though one now sees only honest commerce between Monsieur de La Rochefoucauld and Madame de La Fayette, that doesn't mean that there is nothing but friendship there. As for me, I maintain that there is still love, and even if it were possible that it has disappeared, there is still something which according to religion is as much condemned as love itself."

In this unsatisfactory uncertainty we must leave the question. We know only the externals of their life, and that is all they intended us to know. We know also, for La Rochefoucauld tells us, that when the vices leave us we flatter ourselves with the belief that it is we who are leaving them.

It was time for him to prepare for the winter of his life, to find what serenity and ease he might.

And then all of a sudden, in the summer of 1667, he went as a noble volunteer to war.

He was nearly fifty-four, and in those days a man of fifty-four was physically older than in our hygienic civilization. His eyesight was very bad; he was constantly assailed by furious attacks of gout. He had no business in the army, and surely he was an intolerable nuisance there. Nevertheless he followed the campaign against the Spaniard in Flanders, and if he performed no feats of prowess, at least he seems not to have disgraced himself.

What inspired him to this quixotic adventure? Perhaps he wished to distinguish himself in the eyes of King Louis, who had never received him into full favor. But this explanation is not, I think, sufficient. The old restless ardor burned in him unquenched. He was still in imagination the knight-errant out of *Astrée*, terrible in war, submissive and faithful in love. Yes, he was a disillusioned cynic, of course, but when the trumpet sounded he was also Roland, he was Amadis de Gaule. The fact is that in his secret heart he was not a disillusioned cynic at all. He was a romantic dreamer who had adopted cynicism to hide the ruin of his dreams.

His martial excursion did not last long. He returned to Paris, to the humdrum life he had tried to escape. Old fools, he decided, are worse fools than young ones. Folly, indeed, follows us at all stages of life. If a man appears wise, it is only because his follies are proper to his age and fortune.

He must accept the follies proper to the decline of life. He must say farewell to adventure and to the storms of love. Few know how to be old; he knew no better than the next man. After a brief reconciliation with Madame de Sablé he was again won away by the compelling kindness of Madame de La Fayette. He formed an old-gentlemanly routine. Every day he had himself carried in a sedan chair from the Hôtel de Liancourt to Madame de La Fayette's house, a matter of a half mile. (No doubt he tipped the porters well, to avoid the joggling they gave the stingy.) He settled down in his easy chair, his gouty foot swaddled and cushioned. Or in fine weather he would sit with Madame de La Fayette in a pleasant arbor in her garden, beside a little spurting fountain, of which she was mightily proud. She did her best to attract interesting guests to brighten her companion's melancholy. Madame de Sévigné was always in and out, pouring forth the gossip of the Court with her quizzical comment, her incessant ripple of laughter. Old friends dropped in, Gourville, Jacques Esprit, many others. The Prince de Condé, pardoned for his treasons on his promise to stay quiet, came to review with his lieutenant their past adventures. Cardinal de Retz once found himself sitting opposite La Rochefoucauld. The two laughed together as they recalled how one had once tried to assassinate the other; they revealed to each other some of the profoundest secrets of their dead parties in the dead wars. La Fontaine stopped in, with a Fable in pocket which he burned to read aloud. The simpering Abbé de Choisy called, wearing earrings and beauty patches. "My dear, you should wear nothing but women's clothes," said Madame de La Fayette. Choisy took her at her word, and returned in the richest of female finery, laden with jewels. "Ah, the lovely creature!" she cried, and La Rochefoucauld turned the young Abbé round and round, applauding the transformation.

There were other diversions: literary readings, little dinner parties. La Rochefoucauld, Madame de La Fayette, Madame de Sévigné, and others dined every Friday with the Bishop of Le Mans, whose fast-day fare was famous. A group would visit a country house for a few days; or they would go to the Foire Saint-Germain and see the wild animals and the savage women in cages.

And on quiet afternoons when there were no guests or only one or two sympathetic spirits, someone would read aloud. The favorite book, the breviary, was still *Astrée*. Though La Rochefoucauld knew it almost by heart, he loved to listen to a sympathetic voice reciting again the interminable adventures of the sighing swains and the timorous, unforgiving nymphs. He was transported to the magic world of his own young imagination. He saw himself reading by a brook in his Poitou, dreaming again in a world of purity, chastity, honor, and heartbreaking beauty. Remembered tears welled once more in the eyes of the old cynic, notorious for his contempt for living men and women. Madame de La Fayette's fitful fountain babbled of other days and the shadowy dead.

Thus Madame de La Fayette sought to divert and occupy her darling. He seemed to have lost the power of entertaining himself. To his old vigor had succeeded an habitual idleness, rotting sloth. It seems that the devil has deliberately placed sloth on the frontier of various virtues. The repose of sloth is a secret charm in the soul which suddenly suspends its most ardent pursuits and most stubborn resolutions. It is a kind of beatitude of the soul which consoles it for all its losses and takes the place of all its boons.

On the heels of sloth came boredom. Ennui was the curse of the idle nobles, robbed of their normal duties and occupations, tended by swarms of solicitous servants. As La Rochefoucauld slipped into old age his boredom gnawed like a parasitic worm. Madame de Sévigné engaged with him one day in a conversation so sad that, she told her daughter, there seemed to be nothing left but to get buried. He found curious diversions, going so far as to raise white mice in cages. He remarked to Retz that one of the greatest secrets of life is to know how to be bored. For boredom, if pushed to a certain point, serves to distract us. Or, as his modern disciple Logan Pearsall Smith put it: "One can be bored until boredom becomes a mystical experience."

Madame de La Fayette recognized the menace of his boredom and sought distractions of compelling interest. She urged him to try for the Academy, but he refused. He was strangely timid in groups of strangers; he could not bear the thought of making a formal discourse to the captious literary body. He made a limp effort to obtain the post of tutor to the Dauphin. He was unsuccessful; doubtless the King feared the effects of the cynic's maxims on the tender prince.

Madame de La Fayette's best device was literature. She had already published a novelette, anonymously, of course; fiction was hardly respectable for a noble. She had an idea for a romantic story in a Spanish setting. La Rochefoucauld should help her with the background, structure, and style.

He found the distraction very agreeable. When *Zayde* appeared in 1669, he took much pride in it. The noble authors would not acknowledge their authorship; an obliging literary man, Segrais, lent his name. Madame de La Fayette and La Rochefoucauld devoted themselves to publicity and promotion, writing letters to the press in defense of the book against its critics.

Madame de La Fayette now proposed to write a more serious novel, the study of an honorable wife who loved a gallant in spite of herself, but who respected her husband, honored her vows, and prized her own self-respect. Drawn by an overpowering love, she would confess all to her husband

and appeal to him for support against her temptation. The husband, brokenhearted, should die of the revelation, the lady should seek protection in a convent, and the gallant, sobered and abashed, should learn the greatness of spirit of a truly honorable woman.

The novel is *La Princesse de Clèves,* which is now prescribed reading for every French schoolboy and for every American collegian aspiring to honors in French. (Nancy Mitford has recently published a new English translation.) It is the first realistic psychological novel in French, and the ancestor of surely a half million others in every tongue.

The share of La Rochefoucauld in the book is hard to determine. The critics disagree whether he should be termed coauthor or active, participating critic. Certainly he took an important part in the composition, reading and noting books on the historical background, discussing the characters and their behavior, criticizing and rewriting Madame de La Fayette's text. He had every reason to be proud of the novel, and proud of his collaborator.

La Princesse de Clèves appeared in 1678, and scored a great success. Its authorship was an open secret. A lady wrote to Bussy-Rabutin: "Monsieur de La Rochefoucauld and Madame de La Fayette have done a novel on the gallantries of the court of Henri II, which is said to be admirably well written. They are no longer of an age to do anything else together."

Many items of fact might be set down concerning La Rochefoucauld's dull declining years. The reader will certainly pardon me for abridging the record. La Rochefoucauld was waiting for death. Most of the incidents of which we are still informed were of small concern to him and of less to us.

He had frightful spells of gout, when he would bound on his easy chair and scream. He told Madame de Sévigné that the racked do not know such pain as he had suffered half his life. He wished for death as a *coup de grâce*.

His financial troubles were cruel and constant. At one time he saw his entire estates put up to auction, but he succeeded by various devices in buying them in. Madame de La Fayette, a most practical person, aided him efficiently against his creditors.

His wife died in 1670. This devoted woman, mother of eight, valiant defender of the family name and property, patient supporter of her husband's manifold infidelities, deserves a word of sympathy and admiration, if not our tears. La Rochefoucauld tells us no more of her death than of her life. He reflected, perhaps with her in mind, that we sometimes lose persons whose passing causes us more regret than affliction, and others who leave us in affliction, but whom we hardly regret.

Two years later his mother died, and he wept her bitterly. He said to Madame de Sévigné: "She is the only woman who never ceased to love me." And she reports: "I saw him weep for her with a tenderness which made me adore him. Monsieur de La Rochefoucauld's feeling for his family is something incomparable."

Others have been less admiring on this score. La Rochefoucauld did everything for his eldest son, turning over his dukedom in 1671, carefully safeguarding the young man's future as a favorite of Louis XIV. The younger sons were thrust into the Church or the army to shift for themselves. The three daughters were denied dowries. Saint-Simon pictures them as aging sibyls, confined to a corner of the town house, hardly getting enough to eat.

The son for whom he had the greatest natural affection was the Comte de Saint-Paul, the fruit of his love for Madame de Longueville.

One day in June 1672, Madame de Sévigné was calling on Madame de La Fayette and Monsieur de La Rochefoucauld. A messenger arrived with the news that the Duke's eldest son and heir, the Prince de Marcillac, was wounded in the crossing of the Rhine, and the Comte de Saint-Paul was killed. A few days later word came that his fourth son, the Chevalier de Marcillac, had died of wounds. "This hail fell upon him in my presence," Madame de Sévigné wrote to her daughter. "His tears flowed from the very depth of his heart; his firmness prevented his heart from bursting." And a few days later: "Don't forget to write to Monsieur de La Rochefoucauld about the death of his Chevalier and the wound of Monsieur de Marcillac; that is what afflicts him so. Alas, I am lying! Between us two, my dear daughter, he did not much feel the loss of the Chevalier and he is inconsolable for the loss of the one whom everyone regrets." This of course was the gallant, the handsome, the adored Comte de Saint-Paul.

But the record is not all one of woe and despair. There were happy hours. Corneille came to his house and read his tragedy *Pulchérie* aloud, and again Molière read *Les Femmes savantes*. La Fontaine, the charming Madame Deshoulières, and others dedicated poems to him in token of friendship. He and Boileau spent some pleasant afternoons at a country house guessing rebuses composed by the Prince de Condé, composing others for the great warrior to divine.

A rather curious episode is worth recording. Madame de Thianges, who is noteworthy for having inspired the love of Louis XIV, Racine, and the Prince de Marcillac, had a doll's house constructed for the four-year-old Duc du Maine, son of King Louis and Madame de Thianges' sister, Madame de Montespan. It was a sumptuous gilded bedroom, completely furnished. The little Duke was represented by a wax figure seated in a chair, holding out a poem to La Rochefoucauld.

His governess, Madame Scarron, destined to be Madame de Maintenon and wife of Louis XIV, stood behind her charge. Bossuet in his bishop's robes conversed with the Prince de Marcillac. Madame de La Fayette and Madame de Thianges read poetry together. In the foreground Boileau, with Racine by his side, made a welcoming gesture to La Fontaine, while with a pitchfork in his other hand he kept at bay a group of bad poets. A banner identified the room as the *Chambre du Sublime*.

The magnificent doll's house caused a sensation at Court, though probably it brought little pleasure to the four-year-old recipient. The *Chambre du Sublime* is still soberly discussed in literary studies as an indication of the courtly taste of 1674, and of the esteem in which La Rochefoucauld's work was then held.

During these years La Rochefoucauld was very close to Gourville. The former valet was now business manager for the Prince de Condé, and occupied as master the Condé château of Saint-Maur. We find La Rochefoucauld, Madame de La Fayette, Madame de Sévigné, and the Prince de Condé dining there with him in 1673. Boileau came out from Paris to read his *Art poétique*. The château was redolent with memories for at least two of the party. Condé had held high court there in September 1651, when he had defied briefly the greater Court of Anne of Austria, Mazarin, and the boy King of France. And there La Rochefoucauld had blissfully loved Madame de Longueville.

Gourville did not like Madame de La Fayette; he gives a sharp description of her in his memoirs. Perhaps he was jealous of her influence on his old master. Her imperious manner was certainly irritating. She calmly appropriated to her own use the summer house at his château, assuming that La Rochefoucauld had only to give an order to have it obeyed by his retainer. Gourville forced her out, of course, but she bore him constant ill will, and no doubt had some hard words to say about upstarts who forget their proper place.

No one could beat Gourville. According to Saint-Simon and other contemporaries, he took the final step of the valet's progress, and married Marie-Catherine, eldest daughter of the Duc de La Rochefoucauld. Modern students are inclined to credit the story, but the alliance, if it took place, was never publicly acknowledged, and its date, whether before or after La Rochefoucauld's death, is far from certain. But it presents a fascinating theme for the observer of men's behavior as it is determined by social ideas and habits. For Gourville the marriage was the utmost achievement of his ambition. For La Rochefoucauld it must have been the capsheaf of his cynical structure of human valuations, the ultimate proof that self-interest, his own as well as others', rules the world. At the same time, if it gave honest Gourville pleasure . . . And for poor Marie-Catherine, marriage with fat, baseborn, elderly Gourville was the end of any hope for a proper life in the world. Still, Gourville was very amusing, very clever. Perhaps it was better than no marriage at all.

During these later days, La Rochefoucauld made at least two journeys to his estates in Poitou. He saw his old friends and retainers, fished in the Charente, was assailed by sudden sweet or melancholy memories. But his gout tortured him and he could barely walk; and his heart was otherwhere. As soon as might be, he hurried back to Paris.

He was old, bending under the weight of mortality. His friends were dying. Madame de Sablé passed in 1678, Madame de Longueville in the following year. His wits were slowing down. The mind's defects increase as one grows older, as do those of the face.

He occupied himself with the composition of new maxims, and with the incessant revision of those already published, and with the composition of a series of *Réflexions morales*. The public demanded four new editions of the *Maximes* during his lifetime, and he was pleased to provide them. He was amused by his own pretensions as a moralist. Old men like to give good precepts, to console themselves for no longer being in a position to give bad examples.

He wrote a little essay on his state. Old men, he said, withdraw from the frequentation of their kind, just as other animals do. "Pride, which is inseparable from self-esteem, takes the place of reason. They can no longer be flattered by some of the things that flatter others. Experience has taught them the true worth of what all men desire in their youth, and the impossibility of enjoying it afterwards. . . .

"Every day takes from them a parcel of themselves. They have no longer enough life to enjoy that which is left them, and even less to attain what they desire. They see before them only sorrows, illnesses, degradation. Everything has been seen, nothing can have for them the charm of novelty. Time removes them insensibly from the point of view from which they would fain regard things, from which things should be seen. Those who have been fortunate are still endured, the others are despised; the only course still open to them is to hide from the world what they have perhaps revealed only too much. . . .

"The wiser ones use their remaining time in the interests of their salvation; having so small a share in this life, they render themselves more worthy of a better one. The others at least have only themselves as witnesses of their wretchedness. Their own infirmities occupy them; the slightest relaxation in them takes the place of happiness. Nature, growing weaker, and wiser than they are, often takes from them the trouble of desiring. In short, they forget the world, which is quite inclined to forget them. Their very vanity is consoled by their retreat; and with many annoyances, incertitudes and weaknesses, they bear, out of piety, out of reason, and most commonly out of habit, the weight of an insipid and languishing life."

It was death that was drawing near, though he dares not use the word. The sun and death cannot be looked in the face.

He fell into a fever, which the doctors diagnosed as "mounting gout." Bishop Bossuet was summoned to give him the last rites. La Rochefoucauld had never shown the slightest concern with religion, but in death as in life he wished to do the correct thing.

He died on 17 March 1680, at the age of 66.

Madame de La Fayette was inconsolable. "She no longer knows what to do with herself," wrote Madame de Sévigné to her daughter. "She is no longer the same person. I don't think she can ever remove from her heart the impress of such a loss. Her health is upset; she is completely changed. She thinks only of stupefying herself and removing all thought from her mind. Time, which is so kind to others, only increases, as it will continue to increase, her sadness." Madame de Grignan replied coldly: "They'll just close ranks; the gap won't be noticed."

Madame de Grignan was right. Men closed ranks, as they always do. The gap left by La Rochefoucauld was not long noticed.

His words have lived on, to serve the mockers of three centuries. His name has become a symbol of disillusioned cynicism, exhaling itself in cruel, bitter phrases revealing the worst of man. Young T. S. Eliot said:

> I mount the steps and ring the bell, turning
> Wearily, as one would turn to nod good-bye to La
>   Rochefoucauld,
> If the street were time and he at the end of the street.[1]

The man La Rochefoucauld is nearly forgotten: that shy, self-conscious dreamer, who went out in the service of honor and beauty to conquer the wicked monsters of the world, and who was conquered by them. He took their pay and their livery, and gave them words to say. But the words are infinitely sad, for they reveal how honor is corrupted and beauty befouled. The man La Rochefoucauld may be a symbol of the human spirit undone by life.

The end of good is an evil, the end of evil, a good.

---

[1] T. S. Eliot, *Collected Poems, 1909–1935*. Quoted by permission of the publishers, Harcourt, Brace and Co., New York.

Bibliographical Note

To know things well, we must know the details. As these are almost infinite, our knowledge is always superficial and imperfect.—LA ROCHEFOUCAULD

THE standard edition of the works of La Rochefoucauld is that of D. L. Gilbert and J. Gourdault (Paris, 1868–1883.) Strangely enough, there is no definitive biography. The best general study is that of J. Bourdeau (Paris, 1895), but it is very brief. To this Emile Magne has added a wealth of *inédit*, in *Le Vrai visage de La Rochefoucauld* (Paris, 1923). Considerable material, unnoticed by biographers, exists in the published memoirs and letters of the period. I have noted a few such items in my text, but I have not taken it as my task to record everything extant on La Rochefoucauld's life.

The *Maximes* are commonly said to be the cynical observations of a detached spectator of Court life. I have tried to suggest that they are rather personal confessions. My only predecessor, to my knowledge, is M.-A.-L. Ehrhard, in *Les Sources historiques des Maximes de La Rochefoucauld* (Heidelberg, 1891.)

Index

Académie Française, 68
Agen, 214
Amiens, 40
Angoulême, 1, 2
Angoumois, 219
Anne of Austria, vii, viii, ix, 6-9, 14-58, 66-106, 114, 120, 126-228 *passim*, 231, 236, 269
Apologie de M. le Prince de Marcillac (La Rochefoucauld), 168-170, 234
Art poétique (Boileau), 269
Astrée (D'Urfé), 9-11, 22, 26, 33, 38, 98, 108, 146, 262, 264
Austria, 19, 21, 77, 92
Auvergne, 258
Auvergne Regiment, 19
Avein, 38

Bagnères-de-Bigorre, 60-61
Balzac, Guez de, 63, 69
Barberini, Cardinal, 236
Baschet, A., 28n.
Bassompierre, Maréchal de, 25, 63, 173n.
Bastille, 25, 45, 47-52, 62, 100, 147, 222, 223
Bautru, 231

Beaufort, François de Vendôme, Duc de, vii, ix, 86, 88, 91, 97-98, 100-101, 104, 134, 136, 148, 159, 160, 162-164, 170, 184, 190-191, 208, 213, 218, 223-224, 227
Beaux-Arts, rue des, 235
Belgium, 40, 42, 88
Bellegarde, 183
Bercenay, Monsieur de, 116
Berquigny, Monsieur de, 144
Bléneau, 219
Blois, 25
Boileau, 268, 269
Bois-d'Arcy, 50-52
Bordeaux, 36, 50, 182, 208, 209, 212, 213, 214, 220, 227
Bossuet, Bishop, 269, 272
Bouillon, Duchesse de, 145, 150
Bouillon, Frédéric-Maurice, Duc de, vii, ix, 72-74, 142, 146, 177, 181-184, 195, 198, 206-210, 213, 219
Bourbon, César de, *see* Vendôme, Duc de
Bourbon family, vii
Bourges, 199, 206, 209
Bray, René, 107

Bretagne, Marie de, *see* Montbazon, Duchesse de
Brie-Comte-Robert, 153, 154
Brienne, 80
Broussel, 136-137, 139
Brussels, 46, 89, 160, 226
Buckingham, George Villiers, Duke of, 16, 18, 43, 61, 80
Burgundy, 79
Bussy-Rabutin, 117, 261, 266

Cahuzac, 60, 215
Canillac, Marquis de, 201
Carignan, 21
Casale, 21, 80
Chalais, Comtesse de, 236
Chalais, Henri de Talleyrand, Comte de, 8-9, 28, 34, 43, 61
Chambre du Sublime, 269
Chantilly, 55
Chapelain, 72n.
Charente River, 1
Charles I of England, 92, 130, 150-151
Charles, Duke of Lorraine, 18, 27, 34, 36-37, 41, 43, 85, 221
Charonne, 222
Châteauneuf, Charles de L'Aubespine, Marquis de, vii, 29, 35-36, 43, 91, 185
Châtellerault, 58
Châtillon, Isabelle-Angélique de Montmorency Bouteville, Duchesse de, vii, ix, 195, 197, 208, 210, 220
Châtillon, Maréchal de, vii
Chaumont, Comte de, 116
Chavaignac, Monsieur de, 216
Chavigny, Monsieur de, 56
Chevreuse, Charlotte de, 105, 161, 186, 191, 193-195, 200
Chevreuse, Duc de, vii

Chevreuse, Marie de Rohan-Montbazon, Duchesse de, vii, viii, 8-9, 16, 18, 27, 32, 34-38, 42-46, 48, 55-65, 67-68, 71, 82, 88-105, 122, 126, 160, 170, 171, 184, 186, 191, 193-194, 213
Choisy, Abbé de, 263
Christina of Sweden, 236
Cid, Le (Corneille), 60, 69
Cinq-Mars, 73-76
Cognac, 1
Coligny, Maurice de, vii, 97-103, 110, 120
Collardeau, Julien, 4
Cologne, 194, 199
Comminges, 173-175
Condé, Henri II, Prince de, vii, viii, 8-9, 16, 18, 34, 44, 60, 73, 76, 82, 92, 98, 104, 119
Condé, Louis II, Prince de, vii, viii, 26, 60, 85, 98, 110, 114-117, 119-120, 123, 124, 133, 139-151, 160-176, 182-227, 249, 263, 268, 269
Condé, Princesse de (wife of Henri II, Prince de Condé), 85, 98-100, 124, 172, 183
Condé, Princesse de (wife of Louis II, Prince de Condé), 124, 193, 199
Condé family, 100, 112, 126, 133, 159, 164-167
Conti, Armand, Prince de, viii, 26, 85, 121, 133-134, 139, 141-147, 155-156, 162-163, 165, 171-176, 185-193, 206, 208, 209, 212-214, 227
Corbie, 40
Corneille, Pierre, 60, 69, 167, 268
Cornuel, Madame, 237-238

INDEX

Couhé, 58
Cours-la-Reine, 235
Courtrai, 117
Cousin, Victor, 123, 125
Couzières, Château of, 37, 38
Craft, Count William, 37, 56, 57
Cramail, Comte de, 63

Dampierre, 37, 160
Damvillers, 226, 229
Descartes, René, 68
Deshoulières, Madame, 268
Des Noyers, Monsieur, 55
Dictionnaire de Citations, 184
Dieppe, 178, 180
Discours de la Méthode (Descartes), 68
du Maine, Duc, 268
Dunkerque, 117
du Plessis-Guénégaud, Madame, 235, 259
du Plessis-Liancourt, Gabrielle, *see* La Rochefoucauld, Gabrielle du Plessis-Liancourt, Duchesse de

Elbeuf, Duc d', 28n., 146
Eliot, T. S., 272-273
Enghien, Duc d', *see* Condé, Louis II, Prince de
Enghien, Duc d' (son of Louis II, Prince de Condé), 199
England, 8, 18, 42, 61-62, 67-68, 76, 84, 92, 105, 150-151, 159
Esprit, Jacques, 254, 255, 263
Estrées, Gabrielle d', ix, 86
Estrées, Maréchal d', 33
Etampes, 221

Faubourg Saint-Antoine, 222-225
Femmes savantes, Les (Molière), 268

Ferdinand II of Spain, 19, 41, 61
Flamarens, 155-156
Flanders, 38, 70, 89, 105, 115, 117, 196, 262
Foire Saint-Germain, 264
Fontainebleau, 117, 120
Fontenay-le-Comte, 2, 4
Fontrailles, 74
Foucauld I, seigneur de La Roche, 5
Fouquerolles, Madame de, 98n.
Fouquet, 230, 247
Francis I, 229n.
Fronde, vii, ix, 124, 132-228, 248, 249
Fronde, First War of, 132-158
Fronde, Second War of, 175-189
Fronde, Third War of, 206-228

Germany, 43
Gien, 218
Gonzague, Anne de, *see* Palatine, Princesse
Gourdault, J., 170n.
Gourville, Jean de, viii, 115-117, 139-140, 142, 151, 177-179, 189, 190, 209, 215-220, 224-226, 230, 246-248, 263
Graf, Monsieur (name assumed by François VI de La Rochefoucauld), 67
Grancey, Comte de, 151
Grande Mademoiselle, La, *see* Montpensier, Anne-Marie-Louise d'Orléans, Duchesse de
Grappe, G., 170n.
Grève, Place de la, 145
Grignan, Madame de, 272
Grosménil, 189
Guéméné, Duc de, 219
Guercheville, Marquise de, 2
Guise, Duc de, vii, 33, 103

278 INDEX

Guitaut, 172-173

Hautefort, Marie de, viii, 29-33, 38, 41, 44, 46-53, 57-58, 73, 87-88, 104-105, 251
Hautefort, Marquis de, 38
Henri II, 266
Henri IV, vii, viii, ix, 2, 6, 39, 83, 85, 86
Henrietta of England, 105
Hilaire, 58-59
Hollac, Comte d', 152
Holland, 8, 19, 248
Hôtel de Ville, 145, 150, 253

Importants, 91-92, 95-105, 136
Infante of Spain, Cardinal, 40, 42
Italy, 20-22, 74, 80, 81, 120

Jansenism, 235, 251-257
Jars, Commandeur de, 49-52, 63, 78
Jesuits, 2
Joan of Arc, 218

La Charité, 217
La Fayette, Comte de, 258
La Fayette, Mademoiselle de, 54, 258
La Fayette, Marie-Madeleine Pioche de La Vergne, Comtesse de, viii, 257-272
La Fontaine, 263, 268, 269
Lagny, 153
La Meilleraie, Maréchal de, 63, 70
Languedoc, 35
Laporte, Pierre de, viii, 41, 45, 47-52, 78
La Rivière, Abbé, 104, 163-164
La Rochefoucauld, Andrée de Vivonne, Duchesse de, 12-13, 14- 15, 19, 33, 39, 55, 66, 112, 125-129, 137-138, 161, 166, 184, 208, 225-226, 230, 237, 267
La Rochefoucauld, Cardinal de, 2
La Rochefoucauld, François III, Duc de, 5
La Rochefoucauld, François IV, Duc de, 5
La Rochefoucauld, François V, Duc de, viii, 1-13, 18, 25, 39, 44, 55-56, 62, 65, 66, 71-72, 76, 83, 104, 119, 139, 180, 250
La Rochefoucauld, François VI, Duc de, *passim*
La Rochefoucauld, François VII, Duc de, 39, 214-219, 224, 230, 246, 267, 268
La Rochefoucauld, Gabrielle du Plessis-Liancourt, Duchesse de, 2, 4, 62, 184, 230, 267
La Rochefoucauld, Marie-Catherine, 247-248, 270
La Rocheguyon, Comte de, 17
La Roche-Guyon, Duc de, *see* Liancourt, Marquis de
La Rochelle, 16, 77
La Tour d'Auvergne, Henri de, *see* Turenne, Vicomte de
La Trémoille family, 126
La Trousse, Marquis de, 120
L'Aubespine, Charles de, *see* Châteauneuf, Marquis de
La Vallière, Louise de, 247
La Vergne, Marie-Madeleine Pioche de, *see* La Fayette, Comtesse de
Le Coudray-Montpensier, 63
Le Fargis, 63
Le Havre, 46, 91, 177-180, 189
Le Mans, Bishop of, 264

INDEX

L'Enclos, Ninon de, 235-236, 247, 248
Lenet, 87, 183
Lens, battle of, 136, 176
Lérida, 119
Lévis, Marquis de, 214-218
Liancourt, Marquis de, Duc de La Roche-Guyon, 234-235
Liancourt family, 246
Loire River, 212, 217
Longueville, Anne-Geneviève, Duchesse de, viii, ix, 26, 85-86, 96-103, 113, 119-128, 133-150, 156-157, 160-169, 177-180, 184, 192-200, 207-214, 220, 227, 249, 252-253, 259, 267, 269, 270
Longueville, Charles-Paris de, see Saint-Paul, Comte de
Longueville, Henri II d'Orléans, Duc de, viii, 20, 96, 115, 119, 139, 141-143, 147, 150, 161, 164-166, 171-176, 189, 190, 195, 197, 198, 206, 211, 227
Longueville, Mademoiselle de, 177, 192
L'Orme, Marion de, 73
Lorraine, 34, 41, 85
Lorraine family, vii, 179; see also Charles, Duke of Lorraine
Louis XIII, vii, viii, ix, 2, 3, 6-9, 11, 14-50, 62-65, 67-84, 87, 88, 91, 94, 126, 167, 231, 258
Louis XIV, vii, viii, 54, 67, 80, 83-85, 120, 131, 132, 137, 140-145, 151, 172, 206, 209, 212-214, 217, 219, 222, 225, 232, 234, 236, 246-247, 262, 265, 267-269
Louvre, 6, 14, 46, 54, 91, 100, 125-126, 166
Low Countries, 19, 25

Luxembourg Palace, 24
Luynes, Duc de, vii, 28n.
Luynes, Duchesse de, see Chevreuse, Duchesse de
Lyon, 29, 75

Madrid, 61
Magne, Emile, 245, 255n.
Maine, state of, 2
Maintenon, Madame de, 269
Malbâti, 60-62
Mancini, Laure, 164
Marais, 237
Marcillac, Chevalier de, 268
Marcillac, Prince de, viii; see also La Rochefoucauld, François VI, Duc de and La Rochefoucauld, François VII, Duc de
Mardijk, 117
Marguerite de Lorraine, 34
Marguerite de Valois, 2
Marillac, Maréchal de, 51
Marlou, 220
Matha, Comte de, 153
Maulevrier, Marquis de, 98n.
Mauny, Marquis de, 116
Maure, Comtesse de, 251
Maximes (La Rochefoucauld), see *Sentences et Maximes de Morale*
Mazarin, Jules, viii, 21-22, 80-82, 87-105, 114-115, 119, 120, 127-228 *passim*, 229, 232, 234, 236, 245-247, 269
Médicis, Marie de, viii, 2, 23-25, 39
Mercoeur, Duc de, ix, 164
Milan, 21
Miossens, 110-111, 174
Miradoux, 213
Mitford, Nancy, 266
Molière, 107, 237, 268

Monsieur, *see* Orléans, Gaston d'
Montagu, Baron Walter, 37, 43, 89-90
Montausier, Duc de, 127
Montbazon, Hercule de Rohan, Duc de, 96
Montbazon, Marie de Bretagne, Duchesse de, viii, 96-103, 167
Montégut, E., 11n.
Montespan, Madame de, 268
Montferrat, 21
Mont-Genèvre, 20
Montglat, 159, 188
Montmorency, Henri II, Duc de, viii, 34-36, 250
Montmorency Bouteville, Isabelle-Angélique, *see* Châtillon, Duchesse de
Montmorency family, vii
Montpensier, Anne-Marie-Louise d'Orléans, Duchesse de (La Grande Mademoiselle), viii, 30, 112, 124, 132, 218-219, 221, 223-224, 235, 240
Montpensier, Mademoiselle de (wife of Gaston d'Orléans), 8-9, 34
Montrond, 199, 206-209
Motteville, Françoise Bertaut de, ix, 16, 106, 107, 120, 123, 124, 125, 144, 148-149, 163, 164, 167, 170, 171, 174, 181, 186, 191, 195, 207, 214, 219, 250
Münster, 115, 119-120

Naples, 120
Nemours, Charles-Amédée, Duc de, vii, ix, 195, 208, 209, 212-214, 218, 220, 223-224, 227
Nemours, Duchesse de, 170
Netherlands, Spanish, 179
New France, 35n.

Noirmoutiers, Monsieur de, 143-144, 146, 151-154
Nordlingen, 176
Normandy, 86, 141, 177, 195, 198, 206, 227
Notre-Dame, 124

Orléans, 212, 218
Orléans, Anne-Marie-Louise d', *see* Montpensier, Duchesse de
Orléans, Forest of, 218
Orléans, Gaston, Duc d', viii, ix, 7-9, 16, 18, 30, 33-35, 37, 40-41, 44-45, 74-76, 78, 82, 85, 92, 96, 104, 112, 114-117, 124, 132, 140, 155, 159, 160, 163, 165, 170, 175, 184, 187, 190-191, 196, 199, 200, 212, 213, 214, 218, 223, 225
Orléans, Henri II d', *see* Longueville, Duc de

Palais de Justice, 201
Palais-Royal, 140, 171, 177, 186, 190
Palatine, Anne de Gonzague, Princesse, 177, 185, 187
Pamphilio, Monsignor, 236
Parabère, Comte de, 119
Paris, 3, 14, 23, 40, 45, 68, 90, 141, 145, 148-150, 159, 160, 190, 200, 208, 213, 219, 222-225, 234-235, 262
Parlement de Paris, 3, 44, 72, 83-84, 129, 131, 136, 141, 146, 154, 156-157, 159, 165, 187, 200-204, 212, 213, 221
Pascal, Blaise, 251, 256
Périni, Hardy de, 20n.
Philip III of Spain, vii
Philippe (brother of Louis XIV), 80, 85, 132, 140
Piedmont, Prince of, 18

INDEX

Pignerol, 21
Poitiers, 58, 212, 213
Poitou, province of, 3, 25, 38, 71, 104, 105, 119, 127-129, 137, 148, 155, 157, 161, 178, 179, 181, 184, 188, 264, 270
Pont-Neuf, 235
Port-Royal, convent of, 251
Précieuses ridicules, Les (Molière), 107
Princesse de Clèves, La (De La Fayette), viii, 266
Pulchérie (Corneille), 268
Pyrenees, 61

Quebec, 35n.

Racine, Jean Baptiste, 251, 268, 269
Rambouillet, Catherine de Vivonne, Marquise de, ix, 72, 98, 101, 107-108, 235
Rancé, Abbé de, 96
Réflexions morales (La Rochefoucauld), 271
Renard's, 99-100
Renault, 58
Retz, Jean-François-Paul de Gondi, Cardinal de, ix, 26, 44, 72, 79, 81, 101, 134-135, 139, 142, 146-150, 153, 156, 159, 170, 171, 184, 190-191, 193-195, 198-204, 206, 209, 212, 213, 220, 227, 263, 265
Réveillon, 51
Rhône River, 75
Richelieu, Armand-Jean du Plessis, Cardinal de, vii, ix, 3, 7-9, 16-27, 35-37, 40-58, 62-65, 67-77, 78, 80-81, 84, 90, 92, 131, 251
Rocroy, 176
Roederer, P. L., 26n.

Rohan, Hercule de, *see* Montbazon, Duc de
Rohan family, vii, 126
Rohan-Montbazon, Marie de, *see* Chevreuse, Duchesse de
Rorimer, James J., 229n.
Rotterdam, 179
Rouen, 177, 180, 197
Rouillac, Marquis de, 201
Rouvroy, Louis de, *see* Saint-Simon, Duc de
Royal Council, 171
Royaumont, 55
Roye, 89
Rozan, Comte de, 152
Rueil, 63
Rueil, Peace of, 157-158, 159
Ruffec, 59

Sablé, Magdeleine de Souvré, Marquise de, ix, 26, 71-72, 98, 250-255, 259, 260, 263, 270
St. Evremond, 87, 237
Saint-Germain, 73, 83, 141-145, 157
St. Malo, 105
Saint-Maur, Château de, 197, 198, 269
Saint-Michel, 197
Saint-Paul, Charles-Paris de Longueville, Comte de, 150, 253, 260, 267-268
Saint-Simon, Louis de Rouvroy, Duc de, 44, 70, 72, 249, 267, 270
Sainte Chapelle, 206
Saintonge, 219
Saumur, 181
Savoy, 8, 20, 43
Savoy, Duke of, 20
Scarron, Madame, 269
Schomberg, Duchesse de, *see* Hautefort, Marie de

INDEX

Schomberg, Marshal, 35
Scudéry, Magdeleine de, 237, 238, 240
Segrais, 109, 265
Séguier, Chancellor, 45-48
Senecé, Madame de, 46, 55
Sentences et Maximes de Morale (La Rochefoucauld), 255, 259, 261, 271
Sérizay, Jacques de, 68-69
Sévigné, Marie de Rabutin-Chantal, Marquise de, 258, 263-266, 268, 269, 272
Sillery (brother-in-law of La Rochefoucauld), 182, 199, 226
Smith, Logan Pearsall, 265
Soissons, Comte de, viii, 8-9, 40, 72-73
Sorbonne, 120
Souvré, Magdeleine de, *see* Sablé, Marquise de
Spain, 8, 19, 21, 38, 40, 41, 43, 58, 61, 70, 74, 80, 89, 92, 105, 117, 119, 136, 154, 160, 182, 184, 196, 208, 209, 226, 262
States-General, 167
Stenay, 179, 184, 192, 208, 211
Susa Pass, 20, 22

Tallemant des Réaux, 96-97, 251
Talleyrand, Henri de, *see* Chalais, Comte de
Tarascon, 75
Tenance, Baron de, 51
Thianges, Madame de, 268
Thou, François de, 75
Toulouse, 36
Touraine, 37, 42, 101, 105
Tours, 56, 61
Turenne, Henri de La Tour d'Auvergne, Vicomte de, vii, ix, 177, 179, 181, 184, 195, 198, 209, 211, 219, 221-223
Turin, 21

Unicorn tapestries, 229
Urfé, Honoré d', 10

Val-de-Grâce, convent of, 37, 45
Vaugirard, rue de, 260
Vautier, 63
Vendôme, César de Bourbon, Duc de, vii, ix, 8-9, 18, 78, 86, 101-102, 164
Vendôme, François de, *see* Beaufort, Duc de
Vendôme, Grand Prieur de, 8-9, 18, 78, 101-102
Vendôme, Mademoiselle de, 28n.
Vendôme family, 136, 164
Venice, 159
Verdun, 226
Versailles, 24, 54
Verteuil, 1-2, 44, 57, 59, 62, 63, 66, 69, 70, 76, 118, 180, 184, 185, 208, 226, 229
Villars, Madame de, 173n.
Villefore, 150
Villiers, George, *see* Buckingham, Duke of
Vincennes, Castle of, 101, 136, 148, 171, 173, 175, 189, 227
Vitry, Maréchal de, 63
Vivonne, André de, 12
Vivonne, Andrée de, *see* La Rochefoucauld, Andrée de Vivonne, Duchesse de
Vivonne, Catherine de, *see* Rambouillet, Marquise de

Zayde (De La Fayette and La Rochefoucauld), 265